HerStory

HerStory

The Alpha Literary and Improvement Club

Mary Lou Parks

Mary Lou Parks

A General Federated Women's Club

ISBN: 978-1-466-47693-6

Printed in the United States of America

www.marylouparks.com

Cover and book design by Greg Parks
Cover photo composite by Kam Jacoby

This book is dedicated to the Alpha Literary and Improvement Club.
To the charter members who saw the need for women to gain equality
through improvement so they could have a say in the world around them.
To all the Alpha members who have come after those brave women,
for 113 years now, learning, growing and doing what needs to be done.
Here's to a bright future, for Alpha and all General Federated Women's
Clubs. May we keep the spirit alive and keep on doing what we do best!

TABLE OF CONTENTS

Acknowledgments

Thank you to the book committee from the 1980s for their research and work. To Myra Manfria at the Lompoc Historical Society, who at age 90 can remember most of what her numerous files contain, for helping us get started. To long time Alpha member, Alyce Martin for assisting us negotiate through the years with her many memories. To Alpha members Maxine Scanlon and Ann Ruhge, as well as friend Ella Gail, who edited this book. A special thanks to Alpha President Anna Dinter who helped dig through every cupboard and file to find club minutes and scrapbooks and then read the story offering suggestions. Also thank you to past President Susan Lindman for reading the story and offering her insights. To photographer, Kam Jacoby, who worked his magic bringing the past and present together with his pictures. To Greg Parks who prepared the book for printing, and used his wonderful graphic skills on the cover.

Last but not least, to Alpha members Martha Galisky, Norma Harrison, Louisa Van Ausdal, Marjorie White, Nannie Wilkins, Marge Scott and Mary Lou Parks for sharing stories.

A big thank you to Alpha relatives James Sloan, Rennie Adam, Cathy Rudolph and Dwayne Holmdahl, who happily shared memories whenever we called on you. A special thanks to Art and Edith Hicks for sharing their clippings and story about the Lompoc Elks Club in 1989.

This story has been an amazing journey. We have learned so much about the history of women's clubs and the part they played in the evolution of women. We have learned wonderful stories about ourselves and our club. We have also discovered important stories of Lompoc's past that seem more complete now that our perspective is included. HerStory may never have been written if not for the determination of Marge Scott. We thank her for never giving up!

Part of the reason we agreed to write HerStory was that we want all people, especially younger women to understand their past. What women have been through in their quest to gain equality, what we still need to do to be fully recognized as equal. Here's to our wish that the world will become as aware of HerStory as it is of History.

Introduction

In the year 2010, the National Woman's History Project celebrated the 30th anniversary of National Women's History Week. The project includes numerous venues which focus on writing "her"-story back into history. They include young people who are learning and writing about the one hundred and one women's history sites—accounted for so far—that honor women's place in the development and organization of this country. Equally important, 2010 marked the 90th anniversary of American women winning the right to vote.

All over the country there were celebrations and marches to honor these milestones and the strong, brave women who struggled and even went to prison to gain the right to vote. In many communities today, there are still a few women living who were children in 1920 who most likely watched their mothers and grandmothers organize and fight for this right. Most of us nowadays are busy going about our own business and haven't paid much attention to these celebrations of past victories. Many younger women have no idea that most of this took place.

Until recently, there was not much written about women in the history books used in schools, but that is changing. Thanks to groups like the Woman's History Project, there is an awakening starting in our country to get women's stories into writing while we still can. We have decided to take the opportunity to write a piece of history about a small women's club on the central coast of California—one of many that organized in the later part of the nineteenth century. There are old records and archives still available, and most importantly, there are still some of these older women who can help tell the stories. We hope our story will serve as a microcosm of the much bigger story of the evolution of women and their accomplishments during the last two centuries.

We're overdue in asking these older women what it was like and what they might remember about those days. When we do, we are surprised—shocked even—at the courage and grit it took to gain the rights we now all take for granted. In 1920, the national suffrage movement finally, after many failed attempts, succeeded in getting Congress to form a constitutional amendment (the 19th Amendment) that granted women the right to vote. For the sake of our daughters and granddaughters and those who come after them, we need to visit these women before they leave us, write their stories, and honor our foremothers' work and diligence in making our country a better place for home and family. For it is only by understanding our story as women that we can protect the place we have earned in society and not slip backwards.

Women in the American West were known for their tenacity and activism. Most were tougher than their eastern sisters. They came with their families across the country in covered wagons and learned how to work alongside their men. The land in the west was harsh, unforgiving and wild and they made it their mission to try and tame it, at least civilize it to the extent they could feel it was safe enough to raise their children. They needed to extend their concerns to the public arena and to control the crime and liquor. They were seen as "purifiers and protectors of the home and family."[1]

By the 1840s our country was industrializing and then came the Civil War. After it was over, the entire nation took on a sense of renewal. The country was changing; people were leaving their farms for factory jobs. Until the war the country had suffered inequality but, after fighting for change, people wanted a more democratic society, especially women who had always been marginalized.

In the eastern part of the country, women of some means realized they needed to educate themselves in order to keep up with their changing world. They felt the need to become more involved in social issues. They lived boring lives centered on afternoon tea parties and fancy social events and felt the need for self-improvement. At first they formed "Literary and Improvement" clubs and would meet at each other's homes to discuss literature and periodicals. But, as industrialization grew, it became obvious that many social issues grew along with it. Some people, men as well as women, felt that after the war, there had been a trade off of one kind of inequality for others and so, after a few years, many of these women's groups became interested in these "causes" outside the home. Many women grew to understand that if they had the vote and equal representation, they could be much more effective in making changes and improving these social problems. So they became active in the suffrage movement.

In the West, women had been up against an uncivilized society from the day they arrived, so they developed a sense of their own strength as they organized during the abolition movement to fight the evils of liquor in the "Wild West." California women especially learned how to conduct campaigns and began to evolve a place in society and realize their entitlement to basic rights. It only followed, then, that when the women's suffrage movement was achieving its greatest strength, California women's propensity to move forward in a more politically responsible way granted them the vote with a franchise through popular referendum in 1911. California State Amendment 8 gave California women "their right to representation" and "the sovereignty of full citizenship." Many felt that woman's suffrage was granted in the West for one underlying reason. It provided a stable nucleus of voting strength, which could assist and protect the process of civilizing the frontier. Some also agree that the development of women's clubs helped focus that strength and moved suffrage forward.

The General Federation of Women's Clubs was first organized in 1890. Jane Croly, founder of Sorosis, extended an invitation to women's clubs throughout the United States to attend a ratification convention in New York City. Sixty-three clubs attended on April 23–25 and took action to form the General Federation of Women's Clubs (GFWC).

By 1904, the number of women's clubs had grown throughout the country and it became obvious that as a united or federated group they would hold some power and authority. California women were anxious to move forward and had organized a federation of women's clubs for the state in 1900. In the years before suffrage passed in California, the women participated in politics indirectly, or as one woman said it, they (the clubs) didn't always think of themselves as political, they just became interested in community issues. After 1911 they took more active roles.

The power of clubwomen was best expressed by Mrs. J. C. Orr, president of the California federation during the 1913 legislative session:

> "We are, in effect, a public body, with representation in each community, town, and city in the state. Each unit, or club, has the power of immediate influence and action in its own community and if it works in accord with other departments in the California Federation of Woman's Clubs, it has the weight of the state organization behind it."

The federation, as the umbrella for clubs around the country and state, provided a natural place for women to become active, working to effect positive changes in their communities. The federation's involvement in statewide politics was extensive and resulted in passage of many laws to protect women, children and family. Federated women's clubs provided even more than a political forum, however. They provided enrichment of communities, education, and friendships that lasted many lifetimes. This is the story of one such club.

Part 1

The Early Days

CHAPTER ONE

The Settlers

The Alpha Literary and Improvement Club turned 113 this spring of 2011. It is uniquely a small town women's club, even today. We would venture to say that Alpha Club has retained much of the flavor of older times, while at the same time the club has moved forward in time, keeping up with society's needs in the 21st century. But we can't get ahead of ourselves; we want to tell the story from the beginning.

Lompoc has a very interesting history, as many California central coast towns do. To help the reader get to know Lompoc and the women of the Alpha Club, we need to go back and visit those long-ago times so we may be better able to capture the feel, the culture, the very soul of the town and the people who founded and lived in it. Fortunately, a great number of artifacts were saved: club minutes, articles, pictures, club books and booklets prepared for various celebrations over the years. There have also been a number of interviews from several of those women who have lived in Lompoc for 90-plus years and who remember enough to help bring parts of the past alive.

Lompoc, California, is a small town on the central coast of California in Northern Santa Barbara County. The first known settlers were the Chumash Indians who were central California coast dwellers in the 1700s and early 1800s. They lived on the Channel Islands off the coast, but later settled on shore; which enabled them to use a greater hunting area. The Lompoc Chumash lived for many years surrounded in the peace and serenity of a pristine area. There were mountains, filled with canyons and crevices, covered with manzanita, scrub oaks and chaparral where bears, wild boar, and deer roamed. A large untamed river twisted and wandered through the valley as it flowed to the ocean, serving as a watershed for the Santa Ynez mountains lying to the east. A smaller range, now called the Lompoc or Santa Rita Hills, bordered the valley on the north and the south. The valley floor was full of growth, small streams and very marshy. As the river met the ocean it spread out into a large lagoon.

The Indians called the lagoon Lum-poc, which meant, Little Lake or lakes. When the Spanish came up the virgin coast in 1759 to explore and acquire land along the way, they found the Chumash living around the lagoon. Hearing the Indian name for it, the Spanish pronounced it "Lumpoco." Several attempts to change this name were made over the years but the Settlers always refused. Lum-poc eventually became Americanized to Lompoc (pronounced Lom-poke).

A priest who was the diarist on the Spanish quest became determined that this beautiful area would be a grand place to build a mission and so the work started.

The cross was raised on the first location of La Purisima Mission along El Camino Real in 1787. The mission was the eleventh of the chain of twenty-one missions established by the Franciscan Padres. Its maximum population of 1,520 Indians was reached by 1804. Its main purpose was to control and convert the coastal Indians in order to strengthen the Spanish outposts with their forced labor and protect newcomers as they traveled up and down the narrow strip of land between mountains and the sea. The hope that one day the Chumash would be able to enter Spanish society was a secondary purpose.

The plan worked for only about 25 years due to sickness (catching the white man's diseases, mostly syphilis) and by 1812 the Indian population had been reduced to 999. On December 21, 1812 a great earthquake struck the area, destroying the mission. After heavy rainfalls in early 1813 it was decided to move the site and build a new mission farther east at the mouth of the little canyon known to them as Los Berros. "In 1824 there was a spectacular uprising caused by real or fancied unjust treatment on the part of the soldiers that broke out in open rebellion and created great consternation at La Purisima Mission."[1] By 1846 there were only 160 Indians left at the mission. The Chumash did mix with the Spanish however, and their descendants remain in the Lompoc and Santa Ynez Valleys to this day.

Next came the white man from the east, starting in 1851 to acquire land from Mexican land grants in which to develop wealth using the divided land called "Ranchos" to feed their cattle and sheep. One of them was called the Lompoc Rancho. After about 25 years of making large sums of money from the Ranchos, the owners felt they needed to sell the land as settlement plots in order to continue making profits. At the same time there was a movement in the aftermath of the Civil War to develop temperance colonies so the excessive use of liquor, started during the gold rush, could be controlled. Many California businessmen were interested in this possibility.

One gentleman, W. W. Broughton, who ran a newspaper in Santa Cruz, California, came to the central coast eager to set up such a colony along with Colonel W. W. Hollister from Ohio, the first Anglo-American land owner, and other businessmen from San Francisco, Santa Barbara and Santa Cruz. William Rennie, a wealthy landowner from Santa Cruz, was included in the group. They formed the Lompoc Valley Land Company in 1871. The Lompoc Rancho was sold to the Lompoc Valley Land Company the same year and became one of the spots where hungry land seekers were encouraged to come after the Civil War. After several delays over the next three years, The Lompoc Valley Land Company began their efforts to sell to eager buyers. A big drawing card was the fact that Lompoc was a temperance colony and it was the first subdivision in California to sell small acre parcels. "Imagine the excitement in late 1874, when an advertisement appeared in the Santa Cruz newspaper, owned by W. W. Broughton, announcing there was a "Great Land Sale in the Lompoc Temperance Colony where one could find a rare opportunity to secure a home in the most delightful and healthful climate on the Pacific Coast."[2] Sales began on November 9, 1874 and went at fever pitch for three days as prices soared. Caravans of folks in a variety of vehicles including four horse stages, two horse stages, ditto wagons, buggies and other "go-carts." A total of 250 men and only 20 women arrived from Ohio, Indiana, Kentucky, Missouri, Iowa and Michigan, and two-thirds of the settlers came from other parts of California. At week's end, the Land Company had realized $700,000 from the sale of about 13,000 acres.

Among these early settlers was Robert Rennie, William's son, who had purchased 4,000 acres of ranch property on the Honda south of Surf Beach with his father. Other settlers were John Dwight and Margaret McLean McCabe. Dwight McCabe bought a ranch in 1876 from the Lompoc Valley Land Co. He and his wife Margaret lived in Santa Cruz, where he was employed for about a year cutting lumber in the woods. The couple had come from Michigan right after their wedding in May of 1874.

When the opportunity to pioneer new land came up, it was appealing to them. Margaret's brother David and his wife Ehroza were eager to go with them so they could buy land together.

Margaret was only twenty-two, but was adventurous and willing to travel with her husband hoping they could buy land they could afford so the family could farm. By this time the word was that the Lompoc Valley soil was fertile and good for growing vegetables. Driving 4-horse wagons for the eight-day trip to Lompoc, the two couples started off, Margaret and Dwight, Margaret's brother, David McLean and wife Ehroza.

They didn't have much, some articles of clothing, some cooking utensils, a few personal items and pieces of furniture. We would like to think they had enough money to spend the nights in shelter, but even if they had some money, there was very little civilization between Santa Cruz and San Luis Obispo. Maybe a few ranches along the way, but the chances are they spent the nights in their wagons and cooked over campfires. They had to travel over some pretty challenging mountain passes along the way. There were certainly no paved roads or freeways.

The couples traveled as far as San Luis Obispo, where they were met by Judge Heacock and William Cantlay. Judge Heacock was president of the Lompoc Valley Land Co. at that time, and it was common for someone of the group to ride to a larger town to meet the new settlers and guide them to Lompoc. The Judge brought the party over the old Barker grade (now Hwy 1 past Vandenberg Air Force Base) and "they forded the Santa Ynez River (north of town) which was entirely innocent of bridges."[3]

We must realize that the country was also entirely innocent of dams at that time and imagine that the river, unlike today's little stream or trickle, was mostly always full except during droughts.

On her 80th birthday celebration, Margaret recalled that as they drove their wagons into town, she saw only one general store, a drug store and the "Lompoc Record" office, owned by newspaper man, W. W. Broughton. The streets were unpaved and had board walks in front of shops.

Margaret realized then what being a pioneer really meant. She told her sister-in-law, "We've gotten ourselves into a lot of work here; looks like we'll have to help settle the town as well as ourselves."

The McCabes and McLeans had purchased 68 acres of land, but soon traded for 450 acres in the Honda, three miles west and two-and-a-half miles south of Lompoc. They settled on that land in fall of 1876 but, although the view was spectacular, it was much too windy to be comfortable. So, after three years of farming there, they decided to move a little closer to town. They traded again for a 57-acre ranch on the northwest corner of Douglass and Ocean Avenues, on Highway 246, in the lower valley. They stayed there for 30 years, adding to the land until they had 213 acres.

Margaret had two daughters, Mary born in 1876 and Olivia in 1882. Margaret was kept busy every waking moment as a rancher's wife. She took care of the animals, a few goats and cows for milk and cheese, some chickens and hogs. The cattle were her husband's job. Everything inside the house was her responsibility—cooking, cleaning, sewing most of the clothes the family wore, washing those clothes on a washboard, and tending to the garden in back of the house. She also preserved most of what she grew, although in the Lompoc climate you could grow crops year round. Beans did well in the fertile soil as did carrots, beets and lettuce. Truth be told, she enjoyed the gardening most of all. It was a joyful sight watching things grow in the Lompoc Valley soil.

Margaret's duties didn't stop with her house and garden. She felt a need to improve the fledgling town, so she was willing to help with socials, parades and other celebrations being put together in town and at the park in Miguelito Canyon. Like some of the other women in town, Margaret was unhappy about the flow of liquor in Lompoc. She and Dwight thought they had moved to a temperance colony. According to an editorial in the Lompoc Record, "word got in the San Luis Obispo paper that liquor was abundant in Lompoc. This enraged the local women and on August 2, 1875 about 60 women, Margaret among them, led by Mrs. J. B. Pierce, carrying an axe, marched into Green's Drug Store and chopped open the apothecary's barrels of whiskey letting it flow across the floor and down the street." That stopped the flow of the forbidden nectar, at least for a while.

After several extremely difficult years of illness and drought, the Lompoc Valley Land Company became defunct by 1879. However, people continued to arrive in the new "temperance colony" and the battle between the "wets" and the "drys" continued for some time.

At another time, even though the owners of another liquor store had threatened to shoot them, a group of women headed again by Mrs. Pierce, fastened a rope securely around the building with the proprietors inside and with a mighty tug, the women pulled the building from its foundations and dragged it a half block down the street, spilling its contents. The proprietors learned never to underestimate the power of a woman. We believe the women also learned just how forceful they could be when they tried.

Soon businesses were undertaken, calling upon the talents of the new residents. Many lovely large homes were built copying lifestyles of more established communities, which they had left. Churches and schools were founded. By 1875, there were 225 children attending Lompoc's first school. There was a town celebration in late 1875 where five hundred people gathered in San Miguelito Park (in a canyon south of town) to celebrate the founding of the community. It's not hard to imagine, even today, how proud the newcomers were, having come to settle such a beautiful place.

"The first postal and express office was opened on South I Street. The first church services were held in a grove of Box Elder trees three blocks east of the center of town. Stages traveled three times a week between Lompoc and Santa Maria and daily between Lompoc and Santa Barbara."[4]

The water systems were primitive. At first, each home had its own well or cistern. Later they used a spring up Miguelito Canyon that had also been used for the Mission. But by early 1900, that became inadequate and a reservoir was constructed.[5]

The first store in Lompoc was operated by a B. F. Tucker and the second larger store was built by the Rudolph family and then a third by the Moore family.[6]

Lompoc's first grammar school was constructed in 1875 with three rooms. The town developed a love of festivals, parades and group picnics. By 1881 Lompoc had a brass band that played at these events. Lompoc was incorporated in 1888 and the temperance provision was nullified, but the town continued to grow. Fraternal groups were organized such as the Independent Order of Odd Fellows (IOOF) and the Grange. A Forrester's Hall and an Opera House were soon established.

The women in the Valley formed friendships as they worked together to organize cultural programs, entertainment for the town and to benefit their own families. Some of the women came together in 1876 for literature readings and musical programs. An article in the January 1876 Lompoc Record reported, "a full house is predicted at the Literary Meeting tonight to listen to the various exercises of reading and oratories and a debate on Women's Suffrage." It appears that even in towns as remote as Lompoc; women were on the move to gain their right to vote!

The 1890s brought drought and with it some hard times. Lompoc had always been an important livestock center and without rain there was no feed (grass) for the cattle. On January 2, 1892 an editorial in the Lompoc Record noted; "We wonder if there is a land under the sun where three inches of rain makes the people as happy as in Southern California." Fortunately, no great losses occurred due to the drought in 1892–94 and again in '98 when only three inches of rain fell with no relief coming until late 1899.[7] It was during these hard times that a few women of Lompoc banded together to improve themselves and the town.

As in other parts of the country, women's groups were organizing in every town. There was a women's book club that formed around 1899 and eventually became the Civic Club, but in 1898 a small group of Lompoc women banded together to fulfill the need for study of the arts, literature and civic improvement by forming a small literary club.

Who were these women? Margaret McCabe was one. We have chosen to get to know as much as we can about six of them and to follow them and their family's involvement in Alpha Club down toward the present as far as possible. We will also insert several new women as they join the club and we begin to lose descendents during the middle part of the twentieth century. Only in a small town like Lompoc is this even possible, where everyone knew everybody and kept some records. Even so, it is hard to find anything much about any of them in the public records. In those days the only reliable information available about a woman (even if she was in a prominent family) was her birth date, who her father was, who she married, who her children were and when she died. In very few cases was anything she accomplished considered important enough to record.

We intend to research all material available: Alpha Club books, club minutes, newspaper articles, information from the Lompoc Historical Society, and last but not least, interviews with family and some older club members. We hope to capture the profile and essence of the members of Alpha Club. One thing we do know about these women is that they were intelligent, tough, and hard working professionals, wives and mothers who cared deeply about their families and the town in which they had come to settle.

CHAPTER TWO

The Harmony Club 1898

According to the early club records there were twelve women who were founding members. Among them were:

*Mrs. Idella Rudolph Webb
*Mrs. Nina Morehead Rudolph, her sister-in-law.
*Mrs. Margaret McLean McCabe
*Mrs. Emily Wright Bissinger
*Anna Williams Moore
Mrs. Bertha Dean
Mrs. Martha McFee Farnum
Mrs. Alice Hall
*Mrs. Cevilla Sloan
Mrs. Hortense Lehmann Levy
Mrs. Mary Nevis
Mrs. Orland Poland

* *Indicates one of the six women profiled in this book.*

We have a picture that was probably taken around 1899 which includes all of the founding members, as well as others who had joined by that time. Another identification problem we encountered is that folks years back didn't make a habit of putting dates on their pictures, but our estimates are close.

Margaret McLean McCabe was forty-six in 1898 and in the pictures she looks strong and tall with sharp features. Margaret seems to have been a "no nonsense" type of person who took charge and got things done. She made many friends, among them Elizabeth Rudolph, wife of Harvey Sampson Rudolph (H.S.), Lompoc's first mayor. Like Margaret and her husband Dwight, the Rudolphs had traveled with their six children and H.S.'s father, John Casper II, and his wife and family from Petrolina California in 1876 to be pioneers in Lompoc and set up their mercantile business.

Margaret remained close to her sister-in-law, but sadly Ehroza died around 1883–84. Margaret's brother David McLean was despondent at first but after some time he recovered. He met Elizabeth and H.S.'s oldest daughter, Malvina, through his sister Margaret's friendship with her mother and in November of 1887 "Mellie," and David were married, later moving to Pasadena to start a new life. Margaret was relieved and happy that her brother had found a lovely new wife. In 1890, David and Mellie had a daughter, Marie, Elizabeth and H.S.'s grandchild. Another daughter is said to have been born to them first, and grew up in Pasadena, but there is only one mention of her existence that we could trace.

Idella Rudolph Webb was born in July 1870 in Ferndale, California and was only six when her father, John Casper Rudolph II and her oldest brother, Harvey Sampson, (H.S.) Rudolph decided to move to Lompoc. They had been working together in the mercantile business in the Santa Cruz and then Petrolina, California areas. When they heard about the new

Temperance Colony selling small land grants and the pleasing Lompoc climate, they packed up their families and came. Idella was the fifth child of John Casper, but his second wife Emeline was her mother. Harvey Sampson was 26 years older than his little sister.

Idella was considered a tomboy. She was short with dark curly hair and her eyes twinkled with interest in life. It is hard to tell looking at her pictures with all the bustles and waist cinchers, but she doesn't look undernourished. There are pictures of her as a child visiting various cousins around the area. She seemed a very happy child.

Idella attended Lompoc Grammar School and graduated at age 14. The principal was Holton Webb. There wasn't a high school yet, so Idella studied hard, took the teacher's examination and passed it, the only thing that was required in those days. She got a job at the La Salle School off Ocean Ave. (Hwy 246) in La Salle Canyon. She rode horseback everyday from her home in town. She was said to be a fine horsewoman.

In 1890 at age 20, Idella married Holton Webb, her grammar school principal. He was thirty-seven at the time. They were married in the Methodist Church that her father had founded in Lompoc. Professor Webb ran the Lompoc Grammar School and was a highly respected man in the area being asked to give lectures at times in surrounding towns

Idella always thought of her sister-in-law, Elizabeth as a second mother and confided in her often when she had her three children, two sons and a daughter. The youngest was born in 1897. Elizabeth and H.S had seven children and Idella felt they could answer all her questions. Idella quit teaching, as was expected, when her children were born. She did not give up her interest in literature and music as she continued playing in the Mandolin Club, a group of young women who put on entertainment for the community. When Idella heard Margaret McCabe talking to Elizabeth one day about forming a women's literary club she was eager to join. She and Margaret tried to talk Elizabeth into joining too, but she did not feel up to it at that point in her life.

It seems that soon after Idella and Holton's marriage, around 1891, Elizabeth and H.S. realized that three of their grown children were suffering from a serious lung infection, probably tuberculosis. Just a year after Elizabeth's daughter, Mellie, (Melvina) had baby Marie, she and her husband David and the baby became ill with this dreadful disease. Of course Margaret was upset. It seemed that fate was especially unkind to her poor brother. Now that he had a beautiful young bride and a sweet baby girl their very lives were in danger.

Margaret and Idella visited Elizabeth often and they worried together. Then, as if things weren't bad enough, two more of Elizabeth and H.S.'s children, still living at home, came down with the same illness. The distraught parents tried everything; different local doctors, sending the two younger children up to San Francisco to see special physicians, to the San Gabriel Valley to stay with their sister, Mellie, off to Arizona, all kinds of medicinal remedies, but *nothing* had stopped the course of the deadly disease. Idella spent her days praying for her brother's children. Life seemed so unfair. A cloud of despair fell over all of them as they tried to keep up their spirits for the sake of those who were ill.

By May of 1892 word came that baby Marie was very ill and several days later they received a wire that she had died. Autumn of 1892 was very rainy and in Millie's sister Belle's diary she writes of the dismal continuous cold rain while she was spending time with the McLeans in Pasadena. The weather couldn't have helped any of them as they were forced to go out in it frequently for supplies and errands. At that time Margaret's brother David began to fail and he died in November of 1892.

Belle and her younger brother, Harvey Ulysses, came back to Lompoc from Arizona at the end of 1892, both of them feverish and coughing blood. They struggled on for many more months and it was heart breaking for Idella to watch. Belle married just seven months before her death, hoping for some kind of miracle so she could go on living. She is buried in the family plot in the Lompoc Evergreen Cemetery, under her maiden name. All three of H. S. and Elizabeth Rudolph's children died in 1893. Mellie had moved to Nordhoff, (Ojai) California where she was the first to die in October, Ulysses in November, and Belle in December. Elizabeth was 49 and although she had four sons who remained, she never completely recovered the loss of the others. She was grateful for friends like Margaret and her sister-in-law, Idella.

Idella felt very strongly about starting a women's club that would focus on intellectual endeavors and especially women's suffrage. She immediately became involved and helped Margaret recruit other prominent women in the community. Idella also persuaded her sister-in-law, Nina to join. Idella was 28 in 1898 and very active in the first years of the Harmony/Alpha Club. She served as president of the club in 1899. She served on the library committee from the beginning and helped get the store-front library on H Street for the club. Idella and Margaret and several other members were responsible for getting the Harmony Club signed up as a charter member of the California Federation of Women's Clubs and changing the name of the club.

Nina Morehead Rudolph was born November, 1874 to Olivia and Franklin Morehead and they came to Lompoc in 1877 to farm on the mesa in Pine Canyon (Mesa Oaks area) Nina grew up in Lompoc, attending the same Lompoc Grammar School as Idella who was four years older.

In pictures Nina was thin and gracious looking. She wore her hair piled up on her head with curled bangs when she was young but after marriage she pulled it back into a twist. Nina married H. S. Rudolph and Idella Rudolph Webb's brother, John Casper III, in April 1893. It was his second marriage.

At the time of Nina's marriage, the Lompoc Valley looked especially lovely and was said to have "waving fields of grain and mustard, sweeping fine orchards, and pretty farm houses. The town was a revelation of architectural beauty and cleanliness. The streets were clean.... Nothing more adequately expresses it than to say it is a great town surrounded by a great wealth-producing country, guaranteeing for it a brilliant future."[1]

Nina and John Casper III had four children, a daughter and three sons. Nina was also a music lover and played the mandolin with Idella and others. Idella naturally invited her sister-in-law to consider joining the small group of women who were talking about starting the literary club. Nina had been newly married and pregnant with her first child when her husband's brother H.S. and his wife Elizabeth had suffered the loss of part of their family. They had all suffered. It had been a very difficult time and she was happy to look forward to something that sounded worthwhile and enjoyable. Nina joined with Idella and the others to become founding members of the Harmony Club. She was only 24 when she served as vice president during the first year and president in 1899. Nina worked tirelessly those first few years on the various causes of the club, while at the same time bearing her children and taking care of her home.

Idella and Nina weren't the only talented women who helped start a literary club. In fact it may have been Cevilla Sloan's idea to name the new club, the Harmony Club, as she loved music and had helped start the Mandolin Club.

Cevilla Harris Sloan was born in Cedar County Iowa on May 20, 1860. Her father was a carpenter and farmer who enlisted in the Thirty-fifth Regiment of Iowa Volunteers on August 12, 1862 and fought at Vicksburg. He was honorably discharged and later moved his family to Lompoc in 1878. Cevilla at eighteen was unmarried, so came with her family.

Cevilla was tall and amply built. She had a round kind face that displayed her character. She grew to have many friends and was always willing to be of help. She soon met a shy young man with a soft Scottish brogue, James Sloan from Kirkcudbright, Scotland. Three years after her arrival in Lompoc, Cevilla and James were married. She was twenty-one and he was thirty-six.

James was a pioneer who came to Lompoc in 1874 with very little. He started out as a sheepherder then took a job as a "Wharfer" at the Lompoc Wharf for a very short time, because the wharf washed out during a big storm in November 1876. He then acquired some cattle and land and had a ranch on south A Street where the Hapgood School is now. He began butchering his own meat in a small structure on his property and acquired a "Butcher Wagon," selling his fresh meat around the town. All this was before Cevilla arrived in Lompoc.

Around the time of their marriage in May of 1881, James began taking partners into his business and it grew. His became the only butcher shop in town with a meat packing plant.

In 1882 Cevilla and James had their only child, Harry. In 1892 they built their grand home on the northwest corner of H Street and Hickory Ave. James quickly made a name for himself and became the vice president and then president of the Bank of Lompoc for 25 years. In 1890 he was appointed president (mayor) of Lompoc, and served until 1896, then remained on the board (city council) for 20 more years. Cevilla had many talents, according to her grandson Jim, who still lives in the Lompoc area. She made and re-finished furniture, could paint well and of course loved music. As the wife of one of Lompoc's movers and shakers, Cevilla became very active in the town's affairs, assisting with literary and musical presentations for the community. She enjoyed playing the mandolin with Idella, Nina Rudolph and several other friends.

There's a picture of a large group of Lompoc folks, many of whom were pioneers, gathered for a picnic in "Sloan's Grove," down San Pasqual Canyon. All of the Sloan's friends are there; the Rennies, the Bissingers, the Moores, and many young children including Harry Sloan and Marguerite Rennie who look very young. They are having a "Head Bake," a very popular feast for a large Sunday gathering. They would actually take the heads of freshly killed beef along with a leg of pork, a leg of lamb and a crock of beans, wrap it all in very wet gunny sacks and cook it in a pit over hot coals. It was said to be very savory, including the brains and tongue. Everyone looks like they're having a good time. There are probably at least 40 people, counting the children, in the picture.

Other pictures show Cevilla, James and Harry and friends camping by Surf or having picnics in Miguelito Canyon. You get the sense that people were a lot more grounded in those days, maybe because life was physically so much harder. They shared more of their lives with each other, the hard times and good times. There were no movies, certainly no TVs or computers. Nothing was "virtual" like today, so they had to get out and about and mix with each other to have fun. People became more attached to each other and their communities. They seemed to be one big family in these pictures.

Cevilla was also acquainted with Margaret McCabe and heard about the plan to form a literary club. It was said that the club also planned to promote music and work on some things that needed attention in town. The idea of such a group appealed to Cevilla whose husband was very involved with the city. She felt some things needed a boost from women to get the right results. In her opinion the men were so focused on the economic issues of the community, they seemed to set aside problems that she felt were equally important, like education, more social opportunities and making aesthetic improvements to the town such as planting trees and cleaning up the streets.

Cevilla joined with her friends to become a founding member of the Harmony Club. She served as president for part of the first year, 1898. She was 38 years old. At first the members served only three months at a time, but they met weekly, so each president actually chaired twelve meetings, the same number as they do today with a yearly term and monthly meetings. Their work must have been much more intense as they had to move forward every week.

Cevilla enjoyed the challenge of starting a literary club, as she was very active those first years, being instrumental in getting the Harmony Club to join the California Federation of Women's Clubs as charter members so the club would be more effective. Cevilla was the club's Librarian at first, keeping track of who borrowed what from their small lending library. She led many presentations, which included the classics and studies of other countries. According to the club's first programs, she took part in many of the musical presentations, singing and playing with the members of the Mandolin Club who were her best friends, especially Emily Bissinger.

Emily Wright Bissinger was born October 16, 1861 in Michigan and came by wagon with her parents to San Jose, California where she spent her childhood. We could find very little about her except that her family was of German descent. There is a picture of her father, Edward Lee Wright, when he was in his old age. Her parents may have moved to Lompoc after Emily's marriage because they both died here, he at age 83. Emily married John George Bissinger in San Jose, California in 1885, but George had come to Lompoc in 1882 and purchased land. He brought his bride here to live on his farmland 3 miles from town west on Ocean Ave. (Hwy 246) where they farmed and raised 3 sons. Emily became friends with Cevilla Sloan and Appie Rennie. George formed a life long friendship with Robert Rennie, a fellow farmer.

There's a picture of the "Victorian era Musical Group," at the Historical Society taken sometime in the 1890s and Emily is there with a group of friends. Emily is playing a guitar, Cevilla is playing a banjo and Idella is possibly playing a mandolin. Cevilla's husband James is sitting on the floor beside her. Emily's husband George is standing behind her on her right. In this and all the pictures available of Emily, she has a distant mellow look with sleepy eyes but Emily was very active and motivated. Her looks were deceiving.

Cevilla wanted her friend Emily to help organize the Harmony Club with her, as she knew Emily's love of music would be of great value to the club. Emily was eager to be a part of the group and so she became involved in organizing it from the beginning and was also a charter member. She was 37 at the time. Emily served as Harmony Club president in 1899. She often played and sang music after the roll call at the beginning of a meeting. Emily and Margaret McCabe were listed in the program on December 15, 1899 as giving a presentation about "What Club Life is doing for Women in the Home." Maybe women back then were as conflicted as some modern women.

Emily seemed to have many talents and often led discussions. One was "Current Events in South Africa," including providing the music, "Paradise Lost." A number of classic plays were presented in part. One was Othello; Act II Scene III, acted by Emily. She served on the library committee and helped get funding from Carnegie for Lompoc's first library.

Anna Fatima Williams Moore was born on November 14, 1868 in Santa Barbara, (Goleta) California to Margaret McDonald and James Orlando Williams, who were pioneers from New England. Anna grew up in Santa Barbara and received her grammar and high school education there. After graduating high school, Anna attended the Los Angeles Normal School (now UCLA). During the time she was in Los Angeles her family moved to Lompoc, where her father became a cattle rancher.

After graduation from college, Anna came to Lompoc and taught for only a year at Miguelito School before she married Frank Moore in Santa Barbara, her former hometown, on October 25, 1893.

Anna and Frank had two sons, Harold and Ernest, who grew up in Lompoc and eventually went to work with their father in his mercantile business. Anna was a very bright and ambitious young woman and was noted as a book reviewer. She was very concerned that Lompoc didn't have a library. In her pictures she looks about average height for that era. She had a pleasant smile, straight brown hair in a soft bun around her face, fastened in a French knot in back. In later life she curled her shorter hair and wore glasses.

Anna became good friends with Idella Webb who had also been a schoolteacher and of course was married to one. When Idella told Anna about the idea to start a women's club that would sponsor the interests of literature and work toward setting up a lending library, she too was eager to join.

Anna was a founding member of Harmony/Alpha Club. She was 30 at the time. Anna also became a member of the American Legion Auxiliary, the Pythian Sisters, the Women of Woodcraft, and the Order of the Eastern Star. In addition she helped her husband manage their mercantile business, after his father, George, died in 1912.

These women were remarkable. They worked like farm hands. They studied the classics and the arts, music and famous musicians. They put on plays and organized events for the town. Some were college educated when that was very rare for women. Several were schoolteachers. Most were married to the leaders of the town who we like to think encouraged them to become involved to step forward and improve their community and the lives of all women.

They joined together because they knew they would accomplish so much more as a large group. Friendship was a part of their motivation, as it always is, but the idea of being part of a group that had such impressive goals, for most of these women, was very enticing.

Emily Wright Bissenger playing a guitar in musical group. Taken in the 1890s.

Idella Rudolph Webb in late 1890s.

Nina Moorhead Rudolph taken in late 1890s

Anna Williams Moore in late 1890s

CHAPTER THREE

Club Meetings: Getting Started

We sometimes think that in the distant past folks were very isolated and worked alone, or at least were limited to working with people in their own towns. After all, there was no information highway. People had no radios, television, nor telephones, let alone the Internet with its e-mail, Facebook, Twitters and tweets. Cell phones, of course, hadn't even been imagined, so we might assume that people did things on their own, that they didn't know what was going on in other parts of the world.

But, there were newspapers, which most people read. Wire services were available in almost every town, no matter how small, for emergencies and more importantly; everyone wrote letters to everyone they knew all the time. Of course everything took longer to get passed around. Snail mail couldn't compete with e-mail time-wise, but people used it far more often and in greater depth to keep in touch with friends and loved ones. How often do we get lengthy messages from people now? Maybe a chatty phone call on occasion, but e-mails and texts are very short and Facebook, well, that's certainly no way to have a real conversation. Our worry now is that future generations won't even know how to have interactive discourse.

Back in the 19th and early 20th Centuries, neighbors became real friends; no one was self-sufficient during hard times or bad weather. Everyone knew everyone else in small towns and big city neighborhoods. Today, many folks are too busy to notice or care what's going on with their neighbors. We may feel independent of others in our world now because we don't interact with as many people. We have no personal contact with most of the people who make our lives possible. Our lives seem confined to commuting back and forth to work, school and home alone, except for those cell phones, e-mails, texting, Facebook and Twitters.

In 1898 the world was different. People depended on each other for friendship, assistance in a crisis and entertainment. You couldn't just come home from work, heat up a meal in the microwave, turn on the TV and be entertained. Most women couldn't work outside their home and farms. They provided the constant labor it took to keep things going. Most households had more than one grown woman, usually a grandmother or aunt and hopefully a daughter or daughter-in-law or two to help with the housework. It took more than one cook in their kitchens to feed those large families and farm workers. A few had hired help but many, even the wealthy of the town, did a lot of their own washing, cleaning, cooking and baking. Even so they found the time to organize clubs that would make significant changes for women, their communities and society as a whole.

In spring of 1898, twelve women met in Martha McFee Farnum's home for the first time and elected her to be the first president of the new club. The twelve claimed themselves the founding members and determined to elect officers every three months so as not to over-burden any one woman, at least until they became more established. There was no proper meeting place, so it was logical that they would meet at each other's homes.

They set their meetings from 2:30 to 4:30 p.m. every Saturday afternoon, as they wanted to accommodate those who lived out on the Honda (the mountain area to the south, by the coast, stretching from Surf Beach south to Point Honda, that belongs to Vandenberg Air Force Base now). Others also lived west of town on ranches in the area known as the lower valley and some lived south of town in canyons with fresh water creeks nearby. Most of these families needed to come into the town on Saturday afternoon to shop and gather supplies, so it was convenient for the women to meet then. You couldn't just jump in your wagon and head to town for an errand or meeting any old time. It probably took several hours to get there and back, for one thing.

Club colors were chosen to be purple and gold. A floral emblem for the club, the pansy, was selected on September 17, 1898 and has never been changed. This verse was taken from a book of old poetry and expresses Alpha's opinion of the pansy:

The flowers of life are many,
And all of them are sweet,
From roses in the garden
To lilies at my feet.
The sweetest lily withers,
The roses soon depart,
But oh, the dainty pansies—
They live within my heart!

—author unknown

A piece of stitchery depicting brightly colored pansies hangs on the clubhouse wall to this day (2011). Notes from early meetings indicate that members studied poets, such as Shakespeare and Tennyson. Biographies were read to the group. Members were assigned to do these presentations. The women held roll call and it was required that each one respond by reciting a piece from Shakespeare or another famous poet. That first autumn of 1898 much attention was given King Arthur's round table and the history of the Holy Grail and its myths. They also studied manners and customs in King Arthur's day. Current literature was studied at the end of every meeting as a comparison to the classics. A critic was appointed for each meeting and did a critique after presentations. The women also introduced a scrap basket idea for quilting.

The members weren't just interested in learning. They also wanted to provide social activities for the community. At their October 22, 1898 meeting, the club decided to meet on the last Friday evening of each month to play six-handed euchre. Only books were to be given as prizes. That first year, the club sponsored a New Year's Eve party on December 31, 1898. During it's first year the Harmony Club had four presidents, Mrs. Martha Farnum, Mrs. Anna Moore, Mrs. Cevilla Sloan, and Mrs. Emily Bissinger, the last of the year.

The meetings were highly organized. Members provided solos and quartets, studied world events and foreign countries. They held a successful Japanese evening complete with a Japanese wedding, when studying Japan. These women were very intelligent and eager to learn.

The following excerpts were taken from the first year's minutes of the Harmony Club with a few changes to suit a later play about the club that members put on in May 1959.

According to the Alpha minutes membership into the Harmony Club was by invitation and open to "only those who will endeavor faithfully to further the aims for which this society was organized, and who have been residents of the town for three months." Any member of the club could propose the name of such lady or ladies, who would, in her estimation, make a desirable member. The names proposed at one meeting shall be voted on by ballot at the next regular meeting of the society. Three opposing ballots shall prevent a person becoming a member. No record was to be kept in the society's journal and no ballot could be taken when visitors were present. "Membership shall be terminated whenever a member shall have failed twice within a quarter to perform any literary work assigned or shall have absented herself from four consecutive meetings, without a reasonable excuse."

In the beginning each new member was required to take an oath, "I solemnly and sincerely promise that I will not speak evil of any member of the club, under penalty of expulsion." [1]

There were from the beginning, several women's names listed as Honorary Members of the club. These names remained on the Honorary Members list until they died. Appolona Rennie was on that list. No one is alive now who can tell us why, but we know that Appie was a good friend of Cevilla Sloan, Emily Bissinger and Anna Moore, and that she contributed to the club from time to time by working with her friends on fund raising events and social occasions. Maybe she was invited to attend club meetings as a guest at times. For whatever reason, her name was listed in the club books as an Honorary Member until the year she died.

Today we have set up a group of women called "Friends of Alpha." These women would like to be Alpha members, but work full time, have too many other obligations, or for whatever reason just can't join at this time, but want to be a part of the club in some way. They apply and if approved they must assist with at least one large event each year. They can come to a meeting if possible and they are covered by our insurance for their club activities. Appie would certainly have qualified as a "Friend of Alpha."

Appalona (Appie) Davis Rennie was born September 2, 1862 in Mount Vernon Iowa, which is close to Iowa City. She came with her parents, Mr. and Mrs. Joseph Davis, across the plains when she was only three or four years old. They came first to Virginia City, California, and later to Dixon, California where she and her sister, Mary, and her brother, Will, grew up in a rather well-to-do home.

According to the local newspaper of Binghampton California, Appalona was married to Robert Dawson Rennie, at her parent's residence on September 30, 1883, and it was quite an important social event. The attendants were Will Davis, the bride's brother, and Minnie Rennie, sister of the groom. Appie wore white nun's veiling, Basque and train, trimmed with lace and profusely ornamented with orange blossoms. The gown was cream-colored nun's veiling, cut princess style. In the picture, Appie has a sweet, round face. Her hair is curled in the front with a French bun in back, as was the style. Both Appie and Robert were small, but her parents were big people, tall and ample. Robert's father William was also a small man. According to the same article, Appie and Robert left on a train for Sacramento for a honeymoon and a few days later they traveled to Lompoc where Robert owned ranch property on the Honda; the property he and his father had bought during the Lompoc Land Sale in 1875, called Espada Ranch.

Appie and Robert had two daughters while living at the Espada Ranch. Marguerite was born in 1887 and Hattie in 1890. A younger daughter, Minnie, was born years later in 1899 at their Lompoc ranch.

Appie and Robert lived at Espada Ranch until 1893 when they bought 85 acres of land north of town and Robert's brother, Allen, who was a carpenter in Santa Cruz, built a lovely home for them, virtually all out of redwood which Allen had brought in by steamship and horse drawn wagon. Robert experimented with several kinds of plantings at his new place, and in 1908 he attempted to grow the first crop of sweet peas in the Valley. From which point the flower seed industry developed in Lompoc.

Appie and Robert were well liked in the Lompoc community and had many friends, James and Cevila Sloan, George and Emily Bissinger and Anna and Frank Moore to name a few. In a picture taken around 1899 in the Rennie home, Cevilla and James Sloan are sitting at the table with Appie and Robert, playing cards. The Sloan's son Harry, who must have been seventeen, is playing with the adults while the Rennie's young daughters; Marguerite and Hattie are standing around the table watching them. Appie had her third daughter, Minnie, around that time.

Appie and her family were always in the group pictures at picnics and camping at Surf. They took part in all the outings and celebrations at Miguelito Park. Her girls grew up around their parents' friends and were included in most events.

In spite of the fact that Appie didn't seem interested in joining the club, the Harmony Club members wasted no time in recruiting new members. They arranged for dinners at each other's homes in which guests were invited and they would always provide literary and musical programs. By the end of the first year, there were twenty-three members of the new club.

One of the members recruited was Gertrude Reed Rudolph. Gertrude was a niece of Idella and Nina. She had married H. S. and Elizabeth Rudolph's son, Charles, in 1897.

Gertrude Margaret Read Rudolph was born in Suffolk England, February 12, 1878 and came with her parents to the United States, when she was very young. They came to Southern California settling in Azusa, where there were vineyards and flourmills.

It's possible that Charles Rudolph met Gertrude's family while he was visiting his older sister Millie and her husband David McCabe when they lived in Pasadena. We aren't sure, but the two met somehow and then married in Azusa in 1897 when Gertrude was only 19.

Although Idella and Nina were her aunts by marriage, Gertrude was only slightly younger and had a lot in common with them. She was a horsewoman like Idella, prim and idealistic like Nina. They barely gave her a chance to get settled as a new bride, they were so eager to have her join Alpha. So, although she wasn't a founding member, Gertrude joined the club after the first few months, at age 21, and was a member from 1899 to 1902. By that time she and Charles had established a home on Salsipuedes Ranch, which was south of town off Highway 1, and down the hill on Santa Rosa Road.

Charles worked with his father in the mercantile business. He ran the grocery store and Gertrude helped run the ranch. There's a picture of Gertrude standing in front of the new library in about 1914 or 1915. Her daughter Lucille is on horseback and looks about 12. Nephew, Kenneth, is standing next to Gertrude and her son Harvey is on horseback to her left.

There's another picture of Gertrude and Charles and their children, Harvey and Lucille, standing with H. S. and Elizabeth in front of the mansion.

At the January 14, 1899 meeting it was the consensus of the club members that their first priority toward improving their community would be to organize a club library committee. The committee consisted of four members, Idella Webb, Margaret McCabe, Nina Rudolph and Anna Moore. They were to investigate the possibility of a lending library for members only. Lompoc had no library building so the women had to start from scratch.

Meetings continued every Saturday at club member's homes and the hostess served refreshments. These treats were duly recorded in the minutes. In addition to working on their lending library, and planning how to raise money to build a real library for the town, club member Nina Rudolph discussed the idea of the club doing something to improve the course of study for the high school. Idella Webb agreed that improvements needed to be made and encouraged her husband Holton, who was the Principal of the grammar school, to help in this effort.

One thing, as a result of this concern was that Luceum (language) courses were started in Lompoc and the club began sponsoring concerts. The club members tried not to miss any opportunity to improve their town. The Mandolin Club, which was very popular at that time, performed fairly often for the club.

Club members were anxious to join the California Federation of Women's Clubs for many of the same reasons other small clubs were joining. It was an exciting time. Things were changing for women and they looked forward to gaining the right to vote and the momentum that such a membership would give them to improve their communities and country. On April 7, 1900, a motion was duly made and carried to consider changing the name of the club and a committee was appointed to select a new name and to consider joining the state federation of women's clubs. As a result, The Harmony Club became the Alpha Literary Club of Lompoc and is a charter member of the California federation. At the time, there were thirty-six members in the Alpha Club.

After joining the California Federation of Women's Clubs, the newly named Alpha Literary Club wrote the by-laws stating that the object of the club "shall be the mutual improvement of its members in literature and the vital interests of the day." The "vital interests" of the day could be almost anything the club members considered worthy.

Of particular interest was Article II, Duties of Members, Section 1: "Every member has an equal right with every other member to offer in a proper way any motion or resolution, but should abstain from all personalities or the discussion of anything of an unpleasant nature, and should labor for the peace and harmony of the club."[2] As we look back it seems that people had better manners and tried to live in a more dignified way. Certainly, a lot of effort was put into self-improvement!

Being true to their mission, club members began organizing discussions of current topics of interest, which were placed at the end of the agenda for each meeting. At the Aug 17, 1900 meeting, for example, a discussion was held about the "Waste of Time and Strength in Housekeeping." It seems this was not a feeling that Betty Freidan first discovered in the 1960s. Many women have probably felt like this for centuries.

Anna Moore somehow managed to keep all her projects going, as well as her household. True, she may have had some help, but ultimately, she was responsible. She was very active in Alpha Club, even though she helped her husband run their store. She was club president in 1899, served on the executive committee several times, the literature committee, played music at meetings, did her share of presentations and poetic readings in the early days and served as hostess a number of times, as well as being active in her other clubs and raising her two sons. She was an early example of a "Super Mom."

At the August 15, 1900 meeting, efforts were made to start a public library with assistance of the secret orders (the Masons?) of the town, but the members didn't meet with much success. So a motion was made and carried that each member be assessed 50 cents as a nucleus for a library fund and that any books the members would care to donate would make a very nice start. The books were circulated regularly for members only and kept in the small storefront library that was available on H Street.

An example of interests on a higher plane would be a meeting on January 4, 1901 with a discussion about "The Native, the Missionary, the English Trader and the Boers' policy toward them." This discussion continued for several meetings with the question still open for debate.

The press committee held a very important function in the club. It was the job of these members to get as much information as possible about the activities of the club into the Lompoc Record, and that they did. Margaret McCabe served on this committee for some time and she could be very persuasive.

By December 1901, the club was attending Federation meetings and Margaret McCabe gave a concise report of the meeting, which was enjoyed by all. She reported, "We were pleased to learn that Alpha Club is doing as good a work as any club in the federation. We also learned that the chair should be addressed as 'Madam President'."

By the year 1900, it became obvious to Idella, Nina and other members who visited the local Lompoc cemetery that the conditions were in a sorry state. The original cemetery had been located down by the Santa Ynez River, but for obvious reasons it was moved in 1875 to higher ground. When folks were asked to move the remains of family to the new cemetery, not everyone carried out the chore satisfactorily. There still wasn't a grounds keeper, nor had any trees been planted in the area and the roads were in bad repair. The women of Alpha Club invited their husbands to come along with their rakes and shovels and a sizeable group of them cleaned up the cemetery.

The club members also kept watch on unruly cows and dogs in town, provided a drinking fountain on H Street and closed establishments that seemed out of keeping with the temperance philosophy on which the town had been founded.

At the end of 1901, Idella Webb announced to her sister club members that unfortunately, she, Holton and their children were going to move to Riverside, California. It was an opportunity for Holton to improve his standing. She regretted leaving the town where she grew up and was so much a part of. She would miss her family and her friends in Alpha terribly. As it turned out, she had only been a member of the club for the first three years.

It's possible that Gertrude Rudolph was disappointed in the fact that her aunt moved away, but more likely that her duties on the ranch along with raising her children took too much of her time. Gertrude resigned from the club at the same time Idella moved away. Everyone missed Idella. She had been one of the motivators of the club, a hard worker and good friend. She left a huge gap in the Mandolin Club.

At the January 4, 1902 meeting the members led a discussion about "Famous Women of the Netherlands, Alva, The Reign of Terror and Queen Wilhelmina."

At the February 22, 1902 meeting an interesting discussion took place; "How to inspire our delinquent or indifferent members to take more interest in the club." Perhaps the members were feeling the loss of such an active member after Idella left. On motion it was decided to give a social evening in the near future, inviting the gentlemen related to the members of the club. Members had been working hard and needed some fun.

In 1902, people generally had a life span of less than 60 years. That's not to say, of course, that some didn't live way beyond that age, but it seems that many were taken while in their prime and it must have been terribly difficult knowing that any serious infection or illness could take you or a loved one. There were no miracle drugs or treatments. Not many surgeries performed successfully to "save" people. Life was even more uncertain than it is now. A serious case of the "grippe" and that could be it.

Cevilla Sloan continued to enjoy her involvement with the club. In a picture taken about this time with her son, Harry, her mother and grandmother, Cevilla looks well and hardy. Her last presentation in a program at an Alpha Club meeting seems to have been on February 8, 1902. After that, it became apparent that Cevilla was ill. She began having "stomach" problems and losing weight. There's a picture of Cevilla in a nightgown, resting on a chaise lounge, with a book. There's a tea set on a small table (that she made) next to her. She appears to be ill. By summer, it was apparent that something grave was wrong and a good friend, Ida Simpson, who was living and teaching in Gilroy, invited her to come stay with her so that she might be able to get the best medical advice and treatment in near-by San Jose. But it was too late.

Cevilla did not live to see the Alpha Literary Club join the General Federation of Women's Clubs. It was discovered she had a cancerous tumor in her abdomen and she died during surgery on September 21, 1902. Cevilla was only 42 years and four months old. Her son Harry was twenty. She was buried from her house in Lompoc on September twenty-third, 1902 with most of the town attending. In the Alpha Club Yearbook for 1903, this memoriam appears alone on one page;

Cevilla Harris Sloan

"From a sweet and noble life there springs an influence which can never die; It is the fragrance of an immortal soul."

Her death came as a great shock, especially to her closest friends Emily Bissinger and Appolonia Rennie. It was hard to carry on with the Mandolin Club with Idella gone and now Cevilla's loss, but those who remained, did.

After Idella moved away, Nina finally convinced Elizabeth to join the club. "Lizzie" as she was called, joined in 1902 and by 1903 served on the reception committee and took her part in several presentations. At the February 20, 1904 meeting she discussed "How presidents are elected."

At the Jan 10, 1902 meeting the members again had a discussion about "Cooperative Housekeeping as Portrayed by Bellamy- Are we Likely to Accept it?" Women seemed to want more than the right to vote. The idea of liberation from housework had always appealed to women, especially as they became involved as volunteer librarians, animal control officers, cemetery custodians and assistants to the sheriff.

In 1903, the club met with cemetery trustees to discuss upkeep of the graves and maintenance of the area, of which there was very little. It was decided that the Alpha Club women would be responsible for tending the graves for a fee of $3 a year per plot, which would also help with keeping the Alpha coffers filled. In addition, "the Alpha Club would also see to the planting of pepper trees on the road leading into the cemetery." The members decided it would be easier to get the women to work if the club got paid. This was probably a new concept for many of them.

In April at a meeting following one cancelled due to heavy rain, Margaret McCabe reported on the cemetery work done by Mr. McCabe. Posts had been painted and one palm tree purchased and planted in spite of the rain. (Imagine, with no graveled or paved streets, the mud, the soiled clothing with only washboards to clean it all. What a mess it must have been when it rained) “Mesdames, McCabe, Poland and Cameron were reappointed as the cemetery committee.” We think that means they were the custodians.

Life wasn’t all hard work. Even in our little town of Lompoc, exciting things sometimes happened. In 1903 the club minutes reported that the May 9 meeting would recess so members could go to Surf to see President Teddy Roosevelt make a brief stop at the railroad station. Those who went reported later that it was a very interesting experience and that the President gave a four-minute talk.

Some of the older members were still concerned about the temperance issue in Lompoc in 1903 and Margaret McCabe asked that responses to roll call be given on that subject. In September 1903, they put on a production of “An Old Maid’s Convention.” At one point, they arranged to hire an actor from San Francisco to play “Hamlet” in their production. They had to pay him $45.

The members of Alpha continued to offer readings of verse and studies of different countries around the world. Their roll call responses still focused on famous poets. At one meeting the responses were given from memory of *Evangeline*. At another meeting, they responded with pieces from *Hiawatha*, from memory.

Alpha Club members were interested in psychological issues, such as how to combat anxiety and how to develop strength of character in spite of bad genes and disturbing environments. At the Feb 7, 1903 meeting, a discussion was held about the “Waste of Nervous Energy.” Nina Rudolph was on that committee. That same meeting, the women tackled another tough issue. They “Resolved that Heredity has a Greater Influence upon Character than Environment,” Emily Bissinger was on that committee. We still haven’t resolved that issue.

The Alpha women were much braver back then and took on spiritual issues that we wouldn’t touch with a ten-foot pole today.

At a meeting on June 13, 1903, a discussion was held entitled "Is it possible to live up to the Golden Rule?"

Some of the women must have expressed concern about Women's Suffrage. Maybe they read about some of the brave women in other parts of the country, who were marching and being thrown in jail, and the whole movement began to seem uninviting to them. They questioned if it would all be worth it. So, at the meeting on Sept 5, 1903, according to the minutes of the meeting, they held quite a discussion on the issue "Would the Ballot for Woman Prove a Gain or Loss?"

By this time, the club had 158 books in their library collection, including a collection of Shakespeare's works they added at the cost of $16. The library committee purchased new books from time to time using money made at socials, dinners, plays and musicals. At times, the committee would ask members to offer book suggestions for their library, a small storefront Alpha had secured for the club's use. Club members took their reading seriously and ordered books that they needed for their presentations.

After the first several years the club was growing too large to meet in private homes and there were discussions held about meeting in the Independent Order of Odd Fellows (IOOF) Hall. In January of 1904, a discussion was held to consider the Forrester's Hall for a meeting place instead, but the club chose to move meetings to the IOOF Hall.

At the January 16, 1904 meeting a discussion was held as to "whether a woman's character is strengthened, as well as her mind, by the wise choice of many pursuits and the more branches she takes hold of and performs thoroughly the more she will be capable of. " It still holds true today that "if you want something done ask a busy person."

In March of 1904, Margaret McCabe started a discussion on whether the club could do something to help worthy high school students gain a higher education. She won hearty approval and a motion was made that the Alpha Club of Lompoc establish a scholarship for the most worthy student graduating from high school in June. It passed unanimously. "The decision of who the student would be was left to a committee of Mrs. McCabe's choice." Alpha Club was the only California Federated Woman's Club with a scholarship fund at that time. We still give out scholarships every spring, awarding three now, one for each high school and one for a re-entry student at the local junior college.

At the March 26 meeting, Lizzie Rudolph was appointed to take Mrs. Badgley's place on the press committee.

The April 4, 1904 minutes stated "several hundred trees were planted and more to arrive for next week's work." Can we just imagine women of all ages and some husbands out along the cemetery road planting trees, in addition to keeping the grounds maintained? It's not like they had nothing else to do.

Alpha Club always found time for big entertainment events. They planned for an entertainment and social dance for the spring of 1904 with various committees including refreshment, coffee, and lemonade. The doorkeepers and ticket agents were Anna Moore and her husband Fred. Nina Rudolph held a meeting of her committee at her home to make children's costumes for their part in the production, which was given Saturday evening, April 9.

Nina Rudolph felt like she had stepped onto a carousel that wouldn't stop. Soon after the big event was over, she and her husband would be leaving on a two-month trip. She was excited, as they would be attending the World's Fair in St. Louis, but she had so much to do. Nina could barely hold back her tears when a surprise tea was given for her and another member who had announced they would be leaving the community for a time. Alpha's secretary wrote in the minutes "a sadness overcame the usual gaiety of our teas, for we always feel sad losing any of our members, and especially two, who have been so much to the club.

We adjourned bidding good-buy to Mrs. Rontrus. Nina Rudolph remains with us another week."

Nina would be back for a few months after the Fair, but then she and her family were moving away. It seemed that no matter how important a woman's work was to her community, she was expected to pick up and follow anytime her husband decided to move on. Lately, Nina felt, everything was changing. Life was so difficult. Just when you adjust to one thing, something else comes along to disturb your plans. She did not want to move away from family and friends, but what could she do? Her husband, J. C., had a business opportunity he didn't want to pass up, so they were all going to move to Alameda, California. She would have to start all over again with a new life, when she didn't want to leave the old one. Nina and her family were gone by autumn.

Alpha Club had been eager to join the California Federation of Women's Clubs in 1900 but had not yet joined the general federation by 1904. Then in April, the club was told that since they were not members of the general federation, they could not send a delegate to the biannual convention in St. Louis. Only if one of the appointed state delegates did not plan to go could someone from Alpha Club attend.

At the May 7, 1904 meeting a motion was made by Mrs. McCabe and Mrs. Dimock that:

> "The club secretary take steps immediately to ascertain how the club may become affiliated with GFWC." Later that month it was reported that the club would have a delegate sent to GFWC's biannual meeting in St. Louis.

At that same meeting, Emily Bissinger made a motion that the club consider holding meetings every other week, instead of weekly, by the next club year, but "the matter met with some discussion and was laid over for further consideration."[3]

In June 1904 the club members were happy to hear that James Sloan had married Ida Simpson up north in Gilroy, and that the newlyweds were back in Lompoc after a brief honeymoon.

Emily and Appie had been in touch with Cevilla's friend Ida, since Cevilla's death and had been kept informed of the romance that had developed between Ida and James. Cevilla had been a good friend of Ida's and spoke very kindly of her. Ida had come to visit the Sloans, in Lompoc, several times after she left her teaching job here and went back to Gilroy. She appears in a group picture with them and their friends taken around 1900. By 1905, Ida's name is listed as a member of Alpha Club. Cevilla's old friends felt that James' new wife would fit right in, and they were right. Ida proved to be a great asset to the club, a wonderful club member.

Ida Luella Simpson Sloan was born, May 24, 1859 in Paris, Illinois and came to California with her parents, Henry and Laura Bruner Simpson, when she was two years old. She grew up in Gilroy where she became a schoolteacher. Ida became acquainted with Cevilla when she came to Lompoc to teach for a time. Ida was concerned when Cevilla became ill, and invited her to come stay with her because Lompoc did not have a hospital and it became obvious that Cevilla needed good medical attention. She was shocked and saddened by Cevilla's untimely death and traveled with James and her friend's remains back to Lompoc for the funeral.

Ida had a sweet face, appears to be slighter then Cevilla but wore her hair the same way. She was a gentle woman with a strong spirit. She returned to Lompoc the summer after Cevilla's death, to visit old friends and found to her surprise, that a romance was developing with James. They were married at Ida's home in Gilroy June 6, 1904. Ida was 45 years old. After the wedding, she came to Lompoc with James and took over as the lady of the house, stepping into the void Cevilla had left, filling it well. She became known as a "kind and fastidious lady" by James' employees.[4] Ida was asked to join Alpha by Cevilla's friends, Emily and Anna and did so on February 4, 1905 after being duly elected. She knew she had big shoes to fill and she certainly did so. She served on the executive committee with Emily Bissinger, the library committee, took part in a study about Russia, and gave a paper on Voltaire along with other presentations in her first year as a member.

At the same meeting that Ida became a member of Alpha Club, the members discussed a lower rental fee at the Odd Fellows Hall, if they only held meetings every other week. The first meeting at the Odd Fellows Hall took place on February 11, 1905. Emily was disappointed that she had failed in getting members to listen to the benefits of reducing the number of meetings and the club continued to meet every week.

The group went back to concerns about housekeeping again at the July 16, 1904 meeting with a discussion; "What constitutes good housekeeping?" There just didn't seem to be a solution to this concern. There still isn't! Our only solution these days is whoever does it whenever it gets done!

During that summer of 1904 attendance at meetings was low with only 9 to 12 members attending. At the August meeting Emily Bissinger brought up the idea of the club taking a summer vacation, but again no action was taken. We think Emily was trying to tell the club she was getting tired!

In early October, the women returned to an earlier discussion about members who were in poor health wanting to remain as members, but not able to do the work. It was decided that each committee would use their own judgment and divide the work as they thought best. We still do things this way, although we allow for those who really can't do work to be Inactive Members. We now have members up in their nineties.

Later at the October 15, 1904 meeting, communication was read regarding an amendment to the State Constitution, being proposed in Sacramento that would give women equal political rights with men. This news must have been a great relief for the members, to think that getting the vote in California might be less difficult than it was in many other places.

At the October 22 meeting, it was announced that two women in town offered to fry doughnuts on election evening, to help get the men in town out to vote, if someone would furnish two pails of lard. The offer was accepted that the club would furnish the lard. Margaret was disgusted to think they had to work to get the men to vote when women wanted to vote so badly. It only made her resolve to push harder for the new law.

Club minutes show that on October 29, 1904 the club voted to make additions to their name, "Alpha Literary Club" adding "and Improvement." The new name, Alpha Literary and Improvement Club became effective at the time the club was officially accepted as part of the general federation. Thereafter, the club was listed in the official Directory and Register of 1904–05 Federated Clubs.

At the November 11, 1904 meeting, there was a debate that the club should "resolve that the child's belief in Santa Claus be encouraged" and with great relief the motion passed.

At the January 7, 1905 meeting the discussion was "Are Women as Loyal to Their Own Sex as Men?"

As life in the slow Lompoc lane accelerated in the early Twentieth Century, the members of the Alpha Club began introducing new ideas and themes at their meetings. One was "Personal Magnetism," another caused the members to rush through the dinner dishes (noontime meal) so that they could attend when speakers discussed, "The Effect of Funny Papers on Children."[5] That seems such a mild concern, after we have since worried about the influence of TV on our children, and now even more worrying, the effects of Facebook and texting on our grandchildren.

The members were not without their practical side; always intent on "improvement" as other discussion topics included "Insurance Policies," "Community Property Laws" and "International Relations and the World Court."

At the June 10, 1905 meeting the women discussed "Does the Wage-Earning Woman Surpass the Wealthy Woman in Character Building?" It's as though when we look back to that time we see an awakening of a "sleeping giant." We witness the hunger of these women to learn and explore the world around them and the options they might have for their own lives in it. They never lost sight of the practical side of life and the part they needed to play in it, however.

Emily Bissinger again suggested that in her study of other women's clubs around the state, responses had indicated, "all other clubs finished their year's work in May and we should do the same." She told the members there was even an Alpha Literary Club of Bakersfield and was to find out if it was a namesake or not. The members appointed a committee to look into the matter of summer vacations. (Emily was making progress!)

After Nina moved away, Lizzie remained until the end of 1905 and then resigned. There were no Rudolphs in the Alpha Club until Gertrude came back in 1914. Elizabeth lived only five more years and died in 1910 at the age of 66, which was considered to be a long life. In 1905 a meeting discussion was held to determine "things to be done in our district."

In October 1906 the members spent the first half of the year studying everything they could about Russia, and in the first half of 1907 they studied Japan.

In 1906, Margaret McCabe and her husband Dwight moved into Lompoc from the Lower Valley and rebuilt the Orson Peck (a relative of Dwight's) home at Walnut and N Street. Margaret enjoyed living in town and was happy to show off their rebuilt home to club members. She was also very proud that Olivia had joined Alpha Club.

Olivia Rebekah McCabe was born to Margaret and Dwight McCabe on December 8, 1882 at their lower valley ranch. She grew up on the ranch and graduated from Lompoc Union High School. Olivia joined Alpha Club in 1902, when she was 20 years old. Margaret was so happy to share her beloved club life with her daughter. Olivia had one sister, Mary, who was older but never an Alpha member.

In club year 1906–07, Ida Sloan's stepson Harry's lovely young bride Stella, joined Alpha and immediately became a member of the library committee, while Ida remained on the executive committee. That year Ida led the October 5 meeting about England. On October 19, Stella spoke on "The Elizabethan Age." At the January 18 meeting she gave a synopsis of "English Literature."

The club declared February 29, 1907 to be "Library Day," with a quotation in the club book; "What is a great love of books? It is something like a personal introduction to the great and good of all times." Alpha members appreciated books and couldn't understand the resistance they received when they began to push forward to get a library for the town.

Early gathering of Alpha Club: Taken about 1902. All but three women in picture are Alpha members and include: Nina Rudolph on the left end of the second row, Margaret McCabe next to her in second row, Anna Moore second from left end of the third row, Appie Rennie standing sixth from left end of third row(in middle,) Idella Rudolph second from right end of the third row with face partially hidden, Emily Bissinger second from left end of top row and Margaret's daughter, Olivia McCabe is at the right end of the top row.

Appalonia Davis Rennie's wedding picture in 1883.

Cevilla Harris Sloan (left) and her friend Ida Simpson on Cevilla's side porch. Taken around 1900 when Ida was visiting.

CHAPTER 4

The Library and the Vote

"The club believed in the importance of books and so took up the cause of starting a formal movement to get a public library, circulating a petition requiring a number of signatures obtained, to assure success."[1] It seems not everyone thought a free public library was a good idea. "Some feared the cost and others were sure that there would be a contagion of radical new ideas that they thought spread in books—ideas like women wanting the vote."[2]

It has been difficult to put this part of the story together. Over a period of several months we have discovered at least three different versions of how the Lompoc Carnegie Library came to be. We thought of writing each version but it became obvious that would be very repetitious and so we have combined the stories in a way we think it may have taken place. We do know for sure that Alpha Club was involved every step of the way, petitioning the city to take over their small storefront library including all the books, serving on the Library Board of Trustees, initiating the idea of the Carnegie grant, raising money to buy the property and helping to pick out the land itself.

The women of Alpha Club had persevered since 1900 in getting a public library and on June 24, 1907 an ordinance was passed and the trustees of the town of Lompoc voted to establish it. Six months later December 9, 1907 the one story frame building on North H Street opened its doors as the Lompoc Public Library. It was no longer just for Alpha members.

An article written in the Santa Barbara News Press about the 100th birthday in 2011 of the Carnegie building states that "in 1906, the secretary of the Lompoc Women's Temperance Union (Mrs. J. Loynachan) wrote a letter to Andrew Carnegie." The letter stated "We are a progressive, go-ahead and up-to-times little community and we feel assured that every effort would be made to meet your requirements, for the establishment of a library in our town, should you consider the project at all practical or possible." She was not a member of Alpha Club and her plea went unheeded until the request from the trustees of the library board in 1908.

According to a recent article in the Lompoc Historical Society Newsletter written by Carolyn Huyck Strobel, for the celebration of the 100th birthday (2011) of the Carnegie building, "in 1908 the trustees of the Lompoc *free* library initiated the idea of obtaining a Carnegie Library building. The trustees were Richard A. Lazier, Mrs. James Sloan (Ida), Mrs. Frank Moore (Anna), J. D. Black and F. S. Lewis." We believe the idea may have come from the General Federation of Women's Clubs, as two of the trustees were members of Alpha and the federation. In any case the trustees turned over the project to the Alpha Club, according to this article.

In the meantime Alpha continued with other business as well. In 1908, the club members wrote the Governor, endorsing a bill allowing schools to be used for social events and began helping the school with art exhibits. During club year 1908–09, Ida Sloan served as vice president of Alpha Club, remaining on the executive committee, while her step daughter-in-law, Stella, served on the music committee with Emily Bissinger. By November Stella Sloan knew she was expecting her first child. Although she remained a member, she did not take part in any more programs and tragically, on June 29, 1909 she died in childbirth. The baby was named Stella Cevilla, after her mother and grandmother.

Ida Sloan had never had children but at age 50, quickly took on the role of surrogate mother for Harry's baby daughter, while she continued her dedication to Alpha. Club members would certainly have excused Ida from her obligation to take on the leadership of the club, but she insisted that she could do the job. So, in 1909–10 she served as president of the club. As it turned out however, Ida did have some problems getting to meetings and at times her vice president was obliged to "chair" them. She was also unable to attend as a delegate to the ninth convention of the Los Angeles District. She had her hands full.

At a number of meetings over those few years, the club's "Constitution and Bylaws" continued to be modified by a committee and read aloud by Emily Bissinger, before final approval.

At the January 16, 1909 meeting Mrs. Poland reported for a committee that had been appointed to agitate for the naming of streets. Her husband had said to her "the streets needed gravel more than names."[3]

At the January 23, 1909 meeting, Emily Bissinger reported that, "the club's library committee appointed to speak about a site for a public library building, had met and arranged that Mr. Servis should get the prices of several desirable locations and report same to the Lompoc Board of Trustees." It was thought advisable to have the building either on H Street or Ocean Avenue.[4] The Historical Society article of 2011 says, "In January of 1909 the town committed some money to the purchase of a site."

At that same meeting the subject of poor attendance took up considerable time, but no action was taken on any suggestions. We notice the club meetings were attended mostly by the Mmes. McCabe, Bissinger, Poland, Moore, (founding members) and the Mmes. Ida Sloan, McClure, Rios, Dimock and Harris, at that time.

In March 1909, the library committee selected the corner of Cypress and H Streets and "by July, $400 of the estimated $650 purchase price had been raised." In December 1909 the committee received Mr. Carnegie's secretary's letter: 'if the town will provide a site and maintain the building and a library therein to the turn of $1,000 per year, Mr. Carnegie will give $10,000 to erect a building.' A resolution was adopted by the town board of trustees."[5]

In the spring of 1909, there was much discussion about sanitary drinking fountains and a decision to hold another entertainment event at the Opera House, in order to afford putting up a sanitary drinking fountain in town. By this time, the state federation was asking for reports by each club on work done toward civic improvement.

In 1909, Appie Rennie became seriously ill, when her youngest daughter, Minnie, was only around ten years old. Marguerite had graduated and was back home teaching, so was able to help care for Minnie and her mother. Hattie was still away in Nursing School. The family did all they could, finally taking their mother to specialists in Los Angeles, where she was hospitalized. But Appie did not improve. Lompoc still didn't have a real medical facility.

At the Alpha Club's February 26, 1910 meeting, the issue was addressed; "matter of the Ladies of Lompoc taking charge of the sanitarium (a small institution to treat chronic diseases, that had been started in 1908) and assuming control of same, was introduced by Anna Moore, who gave a concise account of the affairs of the sanitarium, financial and otherwise. An interesting discussion followed with members present giving suggestions and views on the subject that were interesting and instructive. As it was not expected that any decisive action would be taken, it was moved, and carried that, as a preliminary step, a committee should be appointed to interview physicians to see if they would give patronage to a hospital if Alpha ladies take it up. Anna Moore and two others were appointed."

A sanitarium? Take charge of the sanitarium? In addition to the business of getting a suitable public library built for the town? Apparently, the club did not pursue the sanitarium idea, but several physicians went forward, naming the facility the Buena Vista Sanitarium. It was located at the northwest corner of Maple and K St. The Lompoc District Hospital was not built until 1943.

Alpha women were incredible. In today's world very little gets done in a timely way by businesses or city government. People just expect there to be big problems with getting anything accomplished. We could all use a few lessons from those remarkable women of the past!

In March 1910, the club members were told by Margaret McCabe that Nina Rudolph's husband had died and they sent her a sympathy card, to which she replied her thank you.

Alpha Club held their second to the last meeting for the year on May 21, 1910 and the sad news was announced that Appie Rennie had died earlier that day. Members arranged for flowers from the Alpha Club to be delivered for her funeral. According to her obituary, Appie died in a Los Angeles hospital. She "had suffered a long and painful illness." It's possible she may have died of cancer. She was 46. Her obituary also stated that "She was a woman greatly loved and respected by all who knew her, a kind mother and loving wife, and her untimely demise was a matter of much regret." "A long and mournful cortege followed the remains to the grave and many beautiful floral offerings were in evidence as tokens of sympathy and respect"[6]

Appie's daughters were devastated, Marguerite had just turned 23, Hattie was 20 and Minnie was eleven and dependent on her older sisters to help their father finish raising her. Hattie finished Nursing School just a month after her mother's death.

Robert never remarried and lived to be a month short of 87. He became known as the Father of the Flower Seed Industry, after he started planting the sweet pea in the Lompoc Valley in 1908. Appie may never have realized this honor, but her daughters certainly did. Both of Appie's older daughters, Marguerite and Hattie, joined Alpha Club the very next year, in 1911.

That same year, 1910, the McCabe's beautiful home burned to the ground. Friends and neighbors were very helpful and put the couple up while they rebuilt the house (now known as the "Marks House") as quickly as possible, but Margaret was weary. She, too, had been saddened by Appie Rennie's death. There had been far too many of her friends who suffered an "untimely demise." She herself was 58 years old, which was considered "getting up there," in the early 1900s.

By autumn of 1910, the library committee, consisting of mostly Alpha Club members, had raised all the money necessary to pay for the lot purchased for the Carnegie Library. By October 2010 the construction bid of $9,170 from A. D. Burke was accepted. The Library was one of 1,679 built in 1,412 communities between the years 1886–1919.[7]

It felt like a happy victory for Margaret McCabe. In spite of her sadness over the loss of so many of her old friends, she was proud that they had all worked so hard to accomplish this goal. Getting a library for the town had been a priority from the beginning of the Harmony Club, and it felt good to know it was happening.

The beautiful Lompoc Carnegie Library opened in August 1911 supplied by Alpha Club's 1,230 books that were donated and purchased by members over the years while operating their storefront library. The new library's architectural style, which had been objected to, turned out to be pleasing to everyone. It entailed a one-story building with classical colonnades supporting triangular pediments and surmounted by domes. The interior was an open space without partitions, so that the librarian could be seated and have a view of the whole room. Therefore a single librarian could operate the facility. Carnegie did allow for substantial basements, but these housed only subsidiary functions: a public meeting room, a staff room, restrooms and a furnace room.

The building served as the town library for almost 60 years. It now houses the Lompoc Museum and has been designated as a Lompoc Historical Landmark, registered in 1990 on the National Register.

At the club's first meeting of the new club year, September 11, 1911, a committee was appointed, including Ida Sloan, "to ascertain particulars regarding the completion of the library basement and the probability of it being a permanent home for the club, if finished." The main floor of the library had been opened so the women were hopeful the basement wouldn't take too long to complete. But the basement clubroom took more time getting finished than hoped. Since it was not part of the Carnegie grant, the town had to fund it. When the meeting room was finally ready in 1915, the club moved their meetings to that location.

Olivia McCabe married Dr. Charles Joseph Beers, a physician and dental surgeon, when she was 29 and he was 41. Olivia had been very active in Alpha Club but after her marriage in 1911 she regretfully resigned and moved away. Margaret was happy for her daughter's marriage but disappointed that the newlyweds moved to the Bay area.

An even bigger victory for women in 1911, that was not highly publicized then, or ever, was that California State Amendment 8 was passed to give California women "their right to representation" and "the sovereignty of full citizenship" The women of California had gained the right to vote!

After her death, many of Appie Rennie's friends were sorrowful, Emily Bissinger and Anna Moore particularly. Emily introduced her daughter-in-law, Idella, to Alpha Club shortly after she married Emily's oldest son, Wright, in 1910 in Los

Angeles. Emily was happy and proud that the young woman wanted to join the club and was anxious to work with her on different projects. Emily served as vice president in the club year 1911–12 and was very involved with the new library project. She was as thrilled as Margaret to see the opening of the new library and saw it as a great accomplishment for the club.

CHAPTER 5

The Next Generation, Moving Forward

Two of the three older friends might have passed on, but their daughters and daughters-in-law were involved with Alpha. Marguerite and her sister Hattie joined the same year as Idella Bissinger. These families remained close over the years with pictures showing the Bissingers at the Rennie/Hall home for get-togethers and holidays. Cevilla's daughters-in-law also seemed devoted to Alpha Club. Possibly Ida had something to do with that.

Marguerite Rennie Hall was Appie and Robert Rennie's first child, born on May 10, 1887. She was born at the home of the late Mr. and Mrs. John Forbes in Lompoc, as the Lompoc Sanitarium wasn't built until 1908.

Marguerite lived on the Espada Ranch, part of the coastal Hollister Ranch, with her parents and younger sister, Hattie, who was born March 9, 1890, until 1895 when her father built a ranch on North H St. near Central Ave. in Lompoc. (where the Embassy

Suites are today) Marguerite and Hattie's younger sister, Minnie, was born November 26, 1899 at the new family ranch in town.

Marguerite grew up in this small friendly town where her parents and their friends spent most of their free time together. There are pictures of Marguerite and her little sister, Hattie, with their parents at gatherings in various homes with other adults, the Sloans, Bissingers and Moores and their children. In one picture, Marguerite is holding a doll and looks about eight or nine. There were pictures taken of outdoor camping at the Lagoon at Surf and at picnics with other Lompoc families. A number of pictures show family reunions with Marguerite's grandparents, the Davis's and Rennies. Often there were aunts and uncles visiting back and forth.

Marguerite was impressed by her mother's friends, especially those in the Mandolin Club. She was also curious about their involvement in the Alpha Club and couldn't wait to grow up and join them. She and Hattie would listen to the women talk about women's suffrage, and all the things they were doing, especially their plans to get a library built in town. They sounded important and she wanted to be like them. She was twelve when her baby sister was born, and she grew up quickly, needing to help her mother with the baby.

Marguerite always wanted to be a teacher. She attended Lompoc Union High School, graduating in 1907, going immediately up to San Jose Normal that fall. She enjoyed college and graduated with her teaching certificate in 1909. She returned to Lompoc to teach, first at Maple School and then Lompoc Grammar School. Unfortunately, by this time, her mother was ill.

Hattie attended Santa Barbara High School. She graduated from the Stanford Nursing program in 1910, and then returned to Lompoc, working at the Lompoc Sanitarium for about ten years until her marriage. Marguerite and Hattie were the career women of their day. Working as nurses or teachers were some of the few professional options open to women. They had just come of age when women got the vote in California. There was some question at that time whether women should work outside the home at all. But, when given the opportunity, many were happy to become clubwomen. Marguerite and Hattie joined Alpha Club in 1911, even though they were both working in their professions at that time. Maybe they wanted to set up an interesting club life, so that they would still feel part of something important after they married.

In 1911, Ida Sloan's stepson Harry married a second wife:

Irene (Mae) Turner

Mae was born in Wall Lake, Iowa where she grew up. She came to Los Angeles, with her family, when she was 20 years old. Mae met Harry when he visited mutual friends with his father in Claremont, California. She and Harry were married on April 8, 1911 in Los Angeles. As was the case of Ida stepping into Cevilla's shoes, Mae took on the roles of wife to Harry and mother to his not quite three-year-old little girl. Ida would not have said, but she was deeply relieved for Harry's sake as well as her own. She and her husband James had worried often about Harry being a single father, trying to raise a daughter alone if something would happen to either of them. Ida felt Mae was a kind person and would make a good mother for Stella Cevilla.

By 1911, the club had been meeting in the I00F Hall for some time. They paid 25 cents to the Rebekah Lodge to use their piano. They continued to put on plays, but the programs seem focused mostly on reviews of contemporary literature and plays. The "roll calls" had disappeared. The club continued their interest in civic affairs and voted in favor of the "Anti-Alien Bill."

The club program of 1911–12 shows that Marguerite Hall had joined the music committee and Hattie served as part of the presentation of "A Doll's House." By 1912, Marguerite was serving on the library committee and Hattie on the flower committee.

Marguerite was delighted to meet Harry Sloan's new wife. She and Hattie had been friends with Harry since they were small children. Their parents had been very close, doing everything together. Harry's first wife had died so tragically leaving him to care for his infant daughter, Marguerite felt happy that he had found someone who seemed able to fit right in and take over. Marguerite and Hattie befriended Mae and although they knew Ida would ask her to join Alpha, they also invited her, wanting her to feel welcome.

It was about this time that Marguerite, Hattie and two of their friends took a trip together, driving to Salt Lake City. This was really adventurous for young single women in those days. Women usually didn't travel without a male escort. It was just the beginning of the traveling adventures these women would have over the years. They toured the Mormon Temple and heard the choir sing, something they had wanted to do since they were children.

The next club year, 1912–13, Idella Bissinger served as the club Librarian and enjoyed work in the club with her mother-in-law. Emily was first vice president, but took over the job of president when Olivia McCabe, who had been elected to serve as president, announced that after her marriage she would be moving away. At the October 12, 1912 meeting Emily and Idella took part in a presentation on plays together. Emily served on the press committee for club year 1913–14 and continued to be very active, giving papers, playing music through autumn of 1913, as dependable as ever.

In 1913, a point of discussion was that the club would favor the schools teaching children the bad effects of alcohol and tobacco. Children never have listened it seems. There were 42 members at that time. The club was still providing custodial services for the cemetery, cleaning up areas of town and also agreed to clean up brush and trash around the cross on the hill.

As early as 1913, the club began to discuss building their own clubhouse and how to fund this tremendous undertaking.

Nominations for new officers for the year, 1913–14 were taken at the May 10, 1913 meeting. Mrs. Harry Sloan, (Harry's second wife, Mae) was to be second vice president, and Idella Bissinger would remain Librarian for the next club year. These women just stepped in and took the place of those who went before them carrying on the duties of the club. At the same meeting, club members voted not to contribute Alpha funds toward finishing the basement of the library. They felt that library funds should be used. The club year was now extended until the first week in June before the summer break.

That same year, word came from Gertrude Rudolph that she was going with her father-in-law, H.S., to attend the funeral of Holton Webb. Idella's husband, Holton, had become a judge, but was killed in 1913 by a man he had sentenced. There is a picture of Idella, her brother H.S. and her niece, Gertrude Rudolph, standing by one of the enormous rocks near Azusa where Gertrude grew up. They appear to be up the west fork of the San Gabriel Canyon looking at the Indian markings on the rocks. The picture was taken at the time of Holton's death. Idella was 43 and Gertrude was 35.

In the fall of 1913, Gertrude came back into Alpha Club. Her children were older and she had more time. She reported to the club members that her Aunt Idella was doing better, and in fact, had met a gentleman she was interested in.

In January 1914, Emily Bissinger suddenly became ill, so ill in fact that she could no longer attend club meetings. On February 7, 1914, the minutes of the club read, "No meeting on account of sad news received that Mrs. Emily Bissinger was at point of death."[1] She died suddenly at age 53, on February 8, 1914. The members of Alpha were shocked. Emily "was a very dear member of our club,"[2] always active and helpful over the years. Another founding member was gone. Marguerite felt especially bad. Emily had been her mother's good friend and was always kind and caring to Marguerite and Hattie, but especially to Minnie. Why did these three wonderful women have to die at such young ages? Marguerite tried to comfort Emily's family but it was so hard to lose the people one cared for. It was the end of an era. The Mandolin Club was no more. The three dear friends had all passed on.

Delegates were sent to both district and state conventions by 1914, which may be part of the reason that club meetings were becoming very sophisticated. By this time, there were many committees—the executive committee, reception committee, music committee, press committee and a flower committee. We're not sure what the flower committee did but we're pretty sure it came about due to the Rennie sisters' influence. Flowers were to become very important, as time went along.

In addition to those committees, there were multiple department representatives; such as: art, civics, civil service reform, club extension, conservation (forestry and waterways), country life, education, health, history and landmarks, home economics, industrial and social conditions, legislation, literature, peace, philanthropy, redistricting, reciprocity and information for a state university clubhouse loan. These are all listed in the front of the 1914–15 clubbook. At this time the club still met every Saturday from 2:30 to 4:30 p.m. We don't know how they got all this into a meeting but it looks like they had taken on more than the city government or even a university curriculum could handle.

Some yearly programs were more interesting than others and 1914's has a quote that we think is still very appropriate:

"If you cannot at the meeting
Speak with grace to move the heart,
You can come with cheer and greeting,
Helping in the social part.
Though you're timid in the forum
Or command no power rare,
You can help to make a quorum,
You can occupy a chair."

In spite of the fact that Emily Bissinger died earlier that year, Margaret McCabe got her energy back and was president again in 1914–15 at the age of 62, an encore for her. Mae Sloan served as second vice president. That year you could find a listing of the weekly programs in the yearbook. The federation dues were 10 cents per member and 5 cents for district dues. The women repaired the town fountain they had finally purchased in 1911 after much research and discussion, and then turned it over to the city council.

The big social event in September 1914, as the new club year started, was the wedding of Miss Marguerite Rennie to Frank William Hall. The bride's father gave her away at a beautiful ceremony in the Presbyterian Church and many Alpha Club members were there. Hattie was bridesmaid and Minnie served as junior bridesmaid. Old friends, Anna Moore and Ida Sloan, shed a few tears as they wished Appie could have been there, but everyone was thrilled about the marriage. They all needed something to celebrate after the loss of Emily.

Marguerite joined Will at his family ranch in the Honda district where they lived for the first several years before they moved into her father's home on North H Street.

There are pictures of Marguerite and Will, at the time of their marriage, visiting her Rennie Grandparents in Santa Cruz on their honeymoon. Marguerite is tall and thin with a round face. She has a smile that lights up her entire face and made others smile too. Will is quite handsome and looks the same height, could have been taller though as Marguerite wore fashionable shoes with a heel.

After her wedding, Marguerite began giving garden parties in her father's beautiful garden, surrounded by all of his sweet peas. There were, also, flower arranging classes held for club members. This interest in flowers seemed to develop after Marguerite and Hattie joined the club, probably because the two young women had grown up surrounded by the flowers their father grew and had learned to love them so. The Alpha Club was still very interested in literature and music, but it seems this third interest was growing due to the care and nurturing it was receiving.

In 1914, there are many interesting quotations, one at the top of every page of the club's yearbook such as: "*A club is worth to a member as much as she puts into it, and no more.*" Other quotes at the top of these pages are parts of the Clubwomen Collect; that we still recite today. On the last pages the current membership is listed, including phone numbers for the very first time. They consist of only two or three digits depending on if you lived in town or on the surrounding ranch land. There is also a quote that still applies:

> *"To be alive in every part of our being,*
> *To realize the possibilities that are in us,*
> *To become all that we are capable of becoming;*
> *This is the aim of life."*

At the January 23, 1915 meeting Gertrude "favored the club with a vocal solo and kindly responded with hearty encore. She was accompanied by her daughter, Lucile."[3]

The club finally moved into the new library for their first meeting of club year, 1915–16. The meeting room in the basement had finally been finished and furnished. At the same time they finally, after much discussion over several years, changed the meetings from weekly to twice a month.

About this same time, in 1915, after visiting the World's Fair in San Francisco, a number of Lompoc Valley residents, including Alpha members Margaret McCabe and Ida Sloan, began growing dahlias. The flowers became a delight for fall gardens. Lloyd Callis, an established florist, exhibited a great interest in dahlias and "planted 2,000 tubers for his trade."[4]

We know from the club minutes that Marguerite was also enthusiastic about growing dahlias. Her father, William Rennie, who had great success growing sweet peas by then, may have been interested in dahlias as well. Before long you couldn't go for a walk, or a ride in one of those automobiles that were showing up all over town, without seeing beds of delightful multicolored dahlias popping up in everyone's yards come late summer and early fall.

Emily's daughter-in-law, Idella, remained in the club for one more club year after Emily died, but wasn't very active. In spite of their friendship, Marguerite could not convince her friend to stay in Alpha Club any longer. Idella asked the club to accept her resignation at the end of club year 1915–16. Things were just not the same with her mother-in-law gone.

In 1916, Marguerite Hall served as president, even though she and her husband Will traveled to Hawaii, possibly for a second honeymoon. Upon return she gave an interesting account of their trip to the club, with the accompaniment of "Aloha" on the Victrola.

Even though Nina Rudolph had been gone from Lompoc for over ten years, she was still missed by club members who were saddened to hear that she had died that year, 1916, in Alameda at the age of only 42. Her youngest son was just 12. Sadly, it was another early demise of a founding member of the club, another name to be added to the memorandum page of the club book.

In 1917, Margaret and Dwight McCabe took a vacation to Hawaii after hearing how lovely it was from Marguerite. When they returned they bought a 480-acre ranch in Fresno County. Margaret was 64 years old by then and Dwight was 66. People didn't retire back then, unless they were ill. Alpha members couldn't understand why the McCabes wanted to move away from Lompoc. They missed Margaret and her tenacity terribly.

Mrs. Ronald Adam, (Linda) joined Alpha in Club year 1917–18. Her husband had taken over as publisher for the Lompoc Record in 1912 and she was interested in joining an active club, especially when she was invited by several members, one of who was Marguerite Hall. Linda and Marguerite became good friends.

On the cover of the 1918 club book is an American flag. The country was fighting "the war to end all wars!" Mae Sloan was president and Gertrude Rudolph was second vice president, her name appearing in the minutes frequently. Anna Moore served on the press committee, an easy job for her as a prominent merchant in town. The paper was always anxious to please one of their best customers. Marguerite had her first child, Harriet that year, while she continued to take part in presentations at Alpha Club during her pregnancy.

During the First World War in 1918–19, the clubwomen sent Christmas gifts to European children. The club was asked to help with a fund to benefit Belgians. The club bank balance held $35.38. Relatively speaking, that's about what we have now in our account.

The club also gave books of hymns and prayers, to be put in Christmas boxes for the soldiers. They contributed towards establishing and maintaining furlough homes for soldiers in France. Knitting bees were held to make afghans for soldiers. Doing good deeds while visiting (perhaps a little gossip while they worked) was always fun!

Lack of funds never stops the Alpha Club and, around the same time, they sent $10 to the National Consumers' League in New York for use in defending women's labor laws. The club was still very much involved with cultural affairs and paid $35 to rent film for use at the Opera House. Seats were priced at 50 cents, 35 cents, and 25 cents.

On June 13, 1919, Alpha held a committee meeting and decided to "ask the chamber of commerce, churches and all other organizations to consider a project intended to call the attention of the people of Lompoc to take up the matter of building a new grammar school .... They did not intend to make the building of a new grammar school a question to be voted upon but the aim was to arouse interest in the question." It seems after visiting the school, parts of which were built in 1876, they found it to be a "fire trap" and an unsafe place for children. "Floors were worn almost through in places, lighting was very bad, boards were rotting, lavatories ancient and very unsanitary." Those on the committee were: Mmes. Mark Rucker, James Sloan, R. M. Adam, W. S. Wright and J. E. Burton. Leave it to retired schoolteachers to get things done!

In 1920, the club joined the Santa Barbara Federation, a division of the state federation. It was about this time when Mae Sloan discovered a lump in her breast. She told Marguerite first, as they had become good friends. Mae was terrified and when Marguerite suggested they talk to Hattie, who worked as a nurse at the Lompoc Sanitarium, Mae agreed.

Hattie felt that Mae should see a trusted physician in town and when she did, he sent her to Santa Barbara for treatment. Treatment for breast cancer in those days and until the mid-70s was to have a radical mastectomy. Mae survived the surgery, but the cancer had spread. She came home for a while but was so sick by December of 1920 that Harry took her back to Santa Barbara and she was hospitalized again. In those days a person who was that sick would be allowed to stay in the hospital and receive palliative care, (comfort measures and pain control).

In 1921, Gertrude Rudolph was president of the club, but needed to resign the office to go to her Aunt Idella's second husband's funeral. Gertrude informed her sister Alpha members that, Idella, who was still living in Riverside had remarried Mr. Theodore Crossley soon after Holton's death, but had again been struck by an unkind fate when Theodore, a deputy sheriff, was killed by Mexican bandits. Gertrude left for the funeral and stayed with her aunt for a while. Idella Rudolph Webb Crossley was 51 at the time of her second husband's death. She never married again, or returned to Lompoc. Idella died in Riverside in 1933 at the age of 63.

On January 13, 1921 Irene "Mae" Sloan died of breast cancer at the age of 35. She never left the Santa Barbara hospital. Sadly, she left her husband Harry, his 12 year old daughter, his step mother Ida to help with Stella Cevilla, and her sister Alpha Club members who had been hopeful that Mae would spend many years as their friend in the service of the club. It was again a very sad time for the Sloan family.

In September, 1921, Margaret Heiges, club president took on as her club project for the year, "the beginning of an Alpha clubhouse fund."[4] By this time the club meetings were opened with the singing of a patriotic song, such as "America" or "The Star Spangled Banner."

In October 1921 Ida Sloan, always eager to support the club with hard work and good ideas, in spite of all the tragedy at home, suggested to the members that since the town had grown so fond of dahlias, the Alpha Club could stage a dahlia show the next year. Marguerite agreed and the decision was unanimous.

CHAPTER 6

The Flower Show

Alpha clubwomen were never afraid of hard work and so, in addition to taking on a clubhouse fund, the members officially started plans for a dahlia show for late summer of 1922. President Margaret Heiges suggested a show enabling residents to enjoy each other's blooms, with a small admission fee charged to benefit the building fund.

Margaret and Dwight McCabe returned to Lompoc due to Margaret's health. By this time she was 69 and had lost weight, looking quite thin. Plus, she couldn't take the heat in Fresno. Everyone was happy to have them back and they moved back into their house at Walnut and N Street (called the Marks House in modern times) where their daughter, Mary and her husband, William Edwards, a teacher at the high school had been living.

Even though Margaret had been gone, her name remained on Alpha's membership list all three years, so she must have believed she would come back. When she did, her niece, Hazel, joined the club in 1922, just in time to help start up the flower show.

Hazel Gladys Bean McCabe

Hazel was born January 24, 1896 in Santa Barbara, California, the daughter of Frank and Mary Bean. Frank appears to have been born in Santa Barbara while Hazel's mother came from Ohio. Hazel grew up in Santa Barbara, becoming a teacher and a journalist. She was the society editor for the Santa Barbara News Press, the only job women could hold in the newspaper business at that time.

Hazel married Carl McCabe, Dwight's McCabe's brother Henry's son, on July 27, 1921 in Santa Barbara and came to Lompoc as a new bride. Carl McCabe had been born and grew up in the lower valley near Surf. His father, Henry, like Dwight and Margaret, was a pioneer coming to Lompoc with his family around the same time that they had, in 1875.

Hazel joined Alpha at the invitation of her aunt Margaret in 1922. Hazel was of small stature, but she was a spirited woman, who held herself erect with dignity. She later won numerous prizes at many flower shows. Everyone envied her talent over the years. She had a great deal of worldly knowledge and newspaper savvy. She was always curious to learn and loved to teach others.

Marguerite missed her friend Mae, but she felt very sad for Harry. He was a good man and she couldn't begin to comfort him. She prayed that he would get through his grief and somehow go on to a better life. "It's a good thing we don't know our futures or we might give up too soon," she told Hattie.

At least Marguerite had a distraction for which she was grateful. Hattie was getting married to James M. Smith on June 15, 1921. Marguerite had been watching, for the past year, while James courted Hattie. He was a widower and quite a bit older, but was a very nice gentleman and made her sister happy.

It would have been exciting to help plan for another Rennie family wedding, but Hattie and James wanted to have a small ceremony at a relative's home in Riverside. They felt it was more fitting as he was a widower and they were both older. Hattie Rennie was 31 and James was 52. He was an old friend of the Sloan family. In fact his first wife had been a cousin of Cevilla's. He, himself, had been a partner with James Sloan in the meat business, but as a hobby he loved growing flowers. Hattie was thrilled to be marrying someone who loved flowers as much as she did. Later, a reception was held at the Rennie/Hall home, to help the couple celebrate their union with their friends in Lompoc.

Club members had many issues to deal with in 1922, in addition to the dahlia show and raising money for a clubhouse. They were getting heavily involved in community affairs and at the January meeting, members were asked to speak on civic improvements, such as building restrictions, cruelty to animals, curfew and garbage disposal. Margaret McCabe suggested they take these matters to the city fathers and all but the issue of garbage disposal were answered satisfactorily for them.

They never lost their sense of humor and love of performing, however, and at one meeting they put on a program where some of them dressed as comedians and one woman turned the handle of a clothes wringer, pretending to be operating a motion picture machine.

The main issue for the year remained a dahlia show, however, and minutes of the Alpha Club dated February 4, 1922 state, "Mrs. Marguerite Hall spoke very interestingly on a dahlia show to be held later in the year, and she was asked to send to the local papers an article on the subject, so all might have a chance to know the plans and where to get bulbs."[1]

Things went well for a beginning project, which was a good omen for the many years to come. Members were reminded, at the end of March, to plant dahlia bulbs immediately for prime bloom, in time for the fall show. The members were excited about their plans for a clubhouse and entered a float in the Fourth of July Lompoc parade depicting the replica of their contemplated facility, decked with colorful blooms and accompanied by a large American flag made of brilliant red, white and blue sweet peas, and it won first prize.

An emergency meeting was held on July 8, 1922 to transact any business concerning the upcoming dahlia show. The question of what should constitute prizes was discussed at some length and finally a motion was made and passed to have the committee decide, and do as they pleased. Various suggestions were made as to how the show should be financed and a decision to take $20 out of the treasury was made.

The first flower show was originally to have taken place on August 24, 1922, at the clubrooms in the Lompoc Library basement. But for some reason (space maybe) the plans were changed and the first dahlia show took place on August 16 in the American Legion Hall. Marguerite and Margaret Heiges were the co-chairs of the dahlia show, which offered prizes for 12 categories, with a silver vase offered as prize for the "Best General Collection." Dahlia tubers were first prizes for other entries, with ribbons given for second prizes. A 10-cent tea was served. Alpha's flower show teas are still held in the tea room of the Veterans Building. They have been a delightful success, offering homemade cookies, tea, coffee, and punch, all for just a donation.

At the first meeting of the club year, September 3, 1922–23, Marguerite told members that the dahlia show was a decided success, with much interest shown. She said she felt sure $20 would cover expenses, but could not know exactly for some time. We now budget just over $5,000 for the flower show, which is a bargain by today's standards.

The club began holding suppers and social evenings for members and escorts and various members would be responsible. These events were held at the Knights of Pythias Hall. This grew into "Escort Night" and was held every fall for many years. It was a fun way for members to meet each other's husbands or friends.

In September, the club announced that the Midland Lyceum Bureau was scheduled to give a series of five very worthwhile entertainments. They would include; a Stewart Long lecture, a Colonial play, the Chicago Orchestral Club, the Theresa Sheenan Concert Company with Irish Readings and the Little Players, with vocal and instrumental music.

In January 1923, when Harriet was five, Marguerite Hall had her second daughter; Margaret, while she was the federation's secretary and involved in many other civic, political and social affairs in town. At that time she was a member of Civic Club, past Worthy Matron of the Miguelito Chapter order of the Eastern Star, member of the Rebekahs and the White Shrine. Unlike her mother, Appie, Marguerite's motto seems to have been, if it seems like a worthwhile organization, then it's worth joining.

Hazel McCabe's son was born in 1923, the year after she joined Alpha and a daughter was born the next year in 1924. Her husband Carl became Lompoc city treasurer and served for 40 years. He was also deputy county assessor.

On July 10, 1923 Harry Sloan married Mae's sister in Claremont California.

Clara ("Toots") Pauline Turner

The Sloans had friends there who offered to host the wedding. The couple didn't want to have a big wedding, under the circumstances. They were attended by the bride's parents and just a few friends. Clara was 31 and Harry was 41 years old. Clara's nickname was "Toots" according to her son Jim. Everyone called her that but he was never sure why. She must have picked up the name as a young girl, either in Wall Lake, Iowa where she was born in 1892 and lived until she was 14, or in Los Angeles where she went to high school graduating in 1911. Clara went on to

Normal School for her teaching certificate. Clara was more than welcomed into the family and by everyone who knew them and soon had many friends.

Ida was cautiously optimistic for the family and especially Stella Cevilla who was now 14 years old and surely needed a mother. By the beginning of club year 1923–24, you guessed it, Clara, "Toots" had joined Alpha and in May 1924, she was elected to be president for the coming club year starting in September.

Marguerite, being the open, friendly and helpful person she was, made it her business to welcome "Toots," and make her feel at home in Lompoc. Clara was herself a friendly, fun loving person who good-naturedly stepped right in to fill her sister's place as best she could.

Alpha Club members took their voting rights seriously, and in January 1924, Margaret McCabe suggested that the women give non-partisan talks on presidential possibilities for the coming election. They conducted the talks for two meetings, covering many candidates including, C. E. Hughes, Henry Ford, Herbert Hoover, William McAdoo. The second talk included Hiram Johnson, Calvin Coolidge, R. M. LaFollette, O. W. Underwood and Gifford Pinchot. Margaret spoke on Hiram Johnson and Gertrude Rudolph on Gifford Pinchot.

At the February 20, 1924 meeting, Hattie Smith announced that the Girl Scouts were prepared to take care of children in the afternoons of club meetings. One could apply to, Stella (Cevilla) Sloan. The cost was 15 cents an hour from 2 o'clock to 5:30.

In February of that year they discussed "The Celite Quarries and What they Mean to Lompoc." The Alpha Club's dahlia show accepted the show rules of the American Dahlia Society. Also one of Marguerite's Hall's girlhood friends, Dale Laubly, joined Alpha Club.

In 1924–25 Clara, "Toots" Sloan was president of Alpha Club, even though she was forced to take several months off when her son Jim was born in February 1925. Clara was busy that year; getting used to married life, being a step-mother to a teenaged girl, joining Alpha and almost immediately assuming the Presidency while she was pregnant and having a child. Maybe that's where she got the nickname "Toots." She seemed like a train on the fast track with a whistle that warned everyone to step aside.

Around 1924, some members of Alpha put on a play that must have had a marriage in it, as the picture shows Marguerite as the bride in an elaborate gown and veil holding a big bouquet of flowers, "Toots" Sloan as a bridesmaid, also in a lovely gown with flowers and little Dale Laubly dressed as a gentleman. Two other "gentlemen," are present. The groom is short and the other is very tall. There are two small children sitting on the ground in front of them. They are all laughing and it looks like they had great fun.

In September 1925, the minutes show that a "Miss Sloan (Stella Cevilla,) gave a very interesting paper on 'Life in a Girl's Camp' (summer) making many of her hearers wish they were girls again." She was 16 by this time. There's a picture of a group of Alpha Club members standing in someone's back yard "all decked out in the splendor of their drop waist dresses."[2] taken that summer showing Margaret McCabe, Anna Moore and Ida Sloan with Mrs. L. E. Heiges and Mrs. Orlean Poland plus some others. In December, Ida Sloan presented the club with an entertaining presentation of her trip from Lompoc to Rome, a much-deserved vacation.

In 1926, the flower show was well on the way to including many types of flowers, not just dahlias. In fact, that year there were no dahlias. Awards were given for the best roses and sweet peas and children were asked to contribute wildflowers. Perennials were also included. Admission prices were up to 25 cents for adults, 10 cents for children. The chairman, Mrs. J. M. Smith, (Hattie Rennie) suggested that Alpha Club members "act as hostesses and take our visitors on excursions to seed farms in the valley." Those members who had automobiles and could drive them were excited to show off the many fields of flowers in bloom. The show was moved that year to spring and a decision was made to hold the show as an annual spring event, because there were always more flowers in bloom in springtime.

At the September 4, 1926 club meeting, Mrs. Rios of the building committee, reported that some members had made remarks regarding buying of lots. At the September 18 meeting, Hattie Smith reported for the building committee, "the lots desired by the club were still in litigation." At the October meeting Mrs. Rios reported again on the lots, saying, "the court had decided that desired lots were a Mr. Wesley Shelling's but on writing to him, the committee found that he had not been so informed." The committee had also heard of three other lots priced at $750.

In 1927–28, Hazel McCabe served as president of the club. The music section of Alpha reported that Lompoc was to have a Choral Society and it was voted to sponsor this group. In later months, they were interested in beautifying their homes, learning how to have a better garden and how to properly set a table. Martha Stewart has nothing new to offer Alpha Club members.

It wasn't all work and worry about having beautiful households. In the summertime, when Alpha was resting, her members were busy having fun. For some who liked to fish, there was the Santa Ynez River and the possibility of a great catch for a day spent at Lompoc fishing grounds, piling up the Steelhead, or trips to Ocean Park out at Surf to play in the lagoon, or on the beach itself. Sometimes the ocean breeze would make it difficult to stay warm at Surf, and so local friends would pack up a picnic lunch, take the afternoon off and travel in their Model T's, or the new Model A's, over to the Solvang area, where summer afternoons could be blistering, to enjoy a swim in the Santa Ynez river in that warm inland sun. Pictures of Marguerite and a friend in the River with their children have a caption she wrote saying, "Real Pleasure!" There were not yet any dams on the River, so even in summer it was quite full and pristine, after flowing down the mountains into the valley.

Anna Moore lost her husband in 1927 and that meant she took on more work at the store. She worked with her two sons, Howard and Ernest, after Frank's death, working a total of 40 years in Lompoc, while remaining a busy member of Alpha and other women's clubs in town.

On October 21, 1927, after much discussion and determination of members, the club took a big step. After 29 years of meeting in each other's homes, in the IOOF hall and now the library, at a special meeting, the members approved going forward to purchase three lots at Ocean Avenue and B Street. They would use the money they had raised so far. They had put on shows, plays, musicals, dinners for the chamber and others, afternoon socials, card parties and received donations to raise the necessary funds.

The Light and Power Co. held a demonstration on how to cook on the modern electric range at one of the meetings. Just a few months ago, in 2011, Alpha's program was a demonstration on the difference between incandescent and compact fluorescent light bulbs and energy efficiency.

There is a picture showing a group of twenty Alpha members on the front porch of Marguerite's home including Mrs. Poland, Margaret McCabe, Anna Moore, Ida Sloan, Dale Laubly, Hattie and, of course, Marguerite who still looks fairly young, not more than thirty-nine or forty. The home and garden sections of the club were very popular at this point with Marguerite, Hattie or their friend Dale Laubly chairing it. With talent like theirs, how could the club go wrong?

By December 1927, Mrs. Oates of the building committee reported that the lots for the clubhouse had been purchased, paid for and a guaranteed deed placed in the bank. Now they had the plans and property, *all* they needed was *more* money to build.

The year 1928 saw the most ambitious flower show yet. Twelve classifications of exhibits were to be judged, with blue and red ribbons going to the winners and second-place finishers. Commercial exhibits by valley farmers, Lloyd Callis, Bodger Farms, Zvolonek Seed Farms and W. Atlee Burpee's Floradale Farms were the highlight of the show, where no admission was charged. "Alpha Ladies again gave tours of several of the seed farms, delighting visitors with the sight of over 500 acres of sweet peas in full bloom."[3]

In 1929, the club members were concerned by some problems with the young people in the community gathering after dances late in the evening, so they endorsed the closing of all public dances at midnight. In September of that year, a resolution was sent to the supervisors thanking them for closing a dance hall that was objectionable. One program discussion in 1929 was, "The Next Step in World Peace." Little did people realize what was ahead. First, the "Great Depression," then World War II ten years later. That was only the beginning.

Club members continued with their efforts in raising money for a clubhouse. But with banks closing and jobs disappearing, as the country headed into the Great Depression, and a flower show as the only large fund raising effort, there was a prime concern. A large performance that year netted $151.21 for the fund, swelling its coffers to $653.83. Still, at that rate, none of the present members would live to see it.

In 1929, it was brought to the club's attention that it would be advisable to look into incorporating as a non-profit organization, in order to avoid being taxed as a business operation and all agreed. Non-profit organizations are incorporated for the "purpose of public or mutual benefit, other than the pursuit or accumulation of profits.[4]

In December 1929, Mrs. Oates asked the status of the incorporation of the Alpha Club and Mrs. Poulson advised that the preliminary steps for this incorporation had been taken and she would follow it up closely and have it consummated.

In January of 1929, another interesting plan to make money was endorsed, in which 12 members, (representing months of year) will pay a certain sum and then ask 48 members (representing the weeks) to pay a certain sum, who would in turn ask 336 others (representing number of days in a year) to pay a certain sum, hoping "they would make a considerable sum that might be added to the clubhouse fund." (Sounds like a Ponzi scheme.) They hoped to raise $1,000 during the year. The 'plan' didn't work out as well as they hoped, but with additional donations there was $956.59 in the clubhouse fund by September 1929.

They did have success with fundraising that year at the flower show because members served meals and added a music program, making $200 for the clubhouse fund. Alpha Club members hold a true optimistic spirit that has existed from the very beginning. They never give up. If we believe in something, it will get done eventually.

Incorporation of the club was moving slowly, because in May 1930 Mrs. Oates urged, "the business of incorporation of the club should be hastened." We don't like to pay taxes! By September of 1930, the club was holding their first meeting of the club year as a luncheon at the La Purisima Inn.

In October, the club received an assessment of $41.23 for street paving and the club activities were divided into three sections. Each section was assigned a quota of money they needed to raise and do whatever they decided, to raise it to add money to the club -house fund. We sense some weariness in the fund raising department. But Alpha Club never gives up, remember? They kept on going in more creative ways, trying out whatever worked.

In 1930, the club established a "Ways and Means" committee to focus on getting the clubhouse built. They also added a legislative committee to assist in keeping up with world events. They focused on international relations, law observance and citizenship. The club continued meeting the first and third Saturday afternoons from 2:30 to 4:30 p.m. in the library meeting room.

Margaret McCabe was still serving as a hostess and giving presentations until around 1930. She celebrated her 80th birthday in 1932 with a big party. Most of her sister club members were present and they enjoyed an afternoon of shared memories with a few old friends from Alpha Club past. There's a picture of Hattie, Mrs. Poland, Mrs. Rios, with Margaret McCabe standing in the center of the group. On her left is Anna Moore and Marguerite along with two others we can't identify. They are all standing in front of someone's home dressed in clothes that would denote the early 1930s. We wonder if this was taken at that birthday party?

Early group of Alpha members taken in the 1920s. Margaret McCabe is on the left, third woman on left is Anna Moore and fifth from left is Ida Sloan.

Marguerite's daughters; Harriet, about six years old and Margaret, about two. Taken about 1925.

Taken possibly on Margaret McCabe's 80th birthday in front of Hattie Hall Smith's home at H and Hickory Street. Hattie is on the immediate left with Margaret in a dark coat in the middle and Anna Moore standing next to her. Marguerite is standing second to the right next to the woman in costume on the right end.

CHAPTER 7

The Clubhouse

By 1930, the club had added new officer positions; that of trustees, with three members appointed. Their job was to assume responsibility for affairs involving large sums of money, audit books of the secretary and treasurer at end of each club year and exercise a general supervision over the affairs of the club. An annual report of their work was given at the first meeting in September.

Alpha Club members learned from experience and their flower shows got better and better. Members learned how to market like experts in their day. In 1930 they really put on a show. It started with displays of furniture and flowers in local stores and outdoor areas as a perfect lead-in to the flower show on May 10 and 11. Succulent and cacti exhibits were also added to the show for the first time. The clubwomen had taken a garden tour in Santa Barbara earlier and benefited from what they saw. Hattie and Marguerite, along with Mona Merriam headed the committee. The show of annuals, perennials, roses and sweet peas, along with delphiniums and children's cut flower arrangements was enjoyed by hundreds of out-of-town visitors. A donation of $100 was made to the clubhouse fund, which would equal about $1,550 now.

By 1931 it had become the custom to include many lovely displays by Lompoc commercial seed companies in the flower shows. They filled the auditorium with scented rainbows, as visitors were entertained by the Lompoc band and high school orchestra.

Ida Sloan became a widow in 1928, but remained a member of the Alpha Club until about 1933 when she was 74 years old. She was tired and wanted to retire from her long years of service to Lompoc. She knew that the clubhouse was about to be built and felt she had worked hard to help accomplish this. Ida moved to Santa Barbara, a place she had always admired and decided that was where she wanted to live out her old age.

Alpha members got down to business after 1930. Like marathon runners, they could see the light at the end of the tunnel. They came up with many creative ways to raise the money for the clubhouse. They set up a trust for donations with many of the members donating money, some giving large sums. They continued putting on plays, and providing entertainment, and held many other events resulting in a lot more fundraising. We think they also took out a loan, as we see it mentioned after the fact. In any case, the members managed to gather enough money ($2,500) to build the clubhouse, and at a special meeting on "April 29, 1933 they gave the contract to build to Mr. Peterson."[1]

In 1928, a new concept was born nationally for many women's clubs. The idea of starting junior clubs for young women ages 18 up to a certain cut-off date became popular. These younger women worked specifically on children's issues and education. Since in that time most women didn't work outside the home, Anna Moore being an exception, they were always eager for interesting activity. Young women liked the idea that clubs were including junior divisions focusing on their issues and needs. The state and national federations promoted the idea and so Alpha started a junior group in 1933.

Prior to the development of their junior division, members of Alpha Club included women of all ages, some who were married and some who were single. Additional amendments to the clubs by-laws were written:

> Section 1, Young women between the ages of eighteen and thirty years may become members of an auxiliary group to be known as the Junior Alpha Club. Application for membership in the junior club shall be made ... and accompanied by the stipulated initiation fee, and after acceptance by a balloting committee of which one member shall be a junior advisor the applicant shall be admitted to all privileges of membership.
>
> Section 2. The members shall determine amount of dues and fees....
>
> Section 3. At any time, members of the Junior Alpha Club in good standing shall be eligible for membership in the Senior Alpha Club without payment or fees, and Section 4. An Advisory committee consisting of two members of the Senior Alpha Club shall be appointed...."[2]

Thus the Junior Alphas were born.

Membership in the new auxiliary group counted 28. Meetings were held in the evening so that busy wives and mothers could attend. The first president was Dorothy Rudolph, the wife of H. S. Rudolph's grandson, Richard. One of their first issues was to set the age limit for juniors at 30. The meetings were brief and to the point, the meetings started with the flag salute and junior pledge. The Junior Alphas usually picked a project to work on, either a social event or doing something for charity. After brief discussions they were adjourned for refreshment and entertainment of some kind, either musical or a reading. The members focused on Christmas baskets for charity that first autumn.

Lompoc was growing and for young women moving to town it was very exciting to be invited to join Junior Alpha Club. The club was considered to be the finest in town and joining provided the new resident instant status and friends. The juniors met the first and third Wednesdays at 8 in the evening. From the beginning of Junior Alphas, all meetings were held in the brand new clubhouse.

One young woman who would never become a Junior Alpha was Minnie Rennie, Marguerite and Hattie's younger sister. There are pictures of Minnie as an infant and small girl. She attended Mills College and graduated in 1918. There's a lovely graduation picture. There's also a sweet picture of her in 1923 in formal wear. She was tall, like Marguerite. She, like her oldest sister, became a teacher. Her first teaching job was in Westwood, California near UCLA.

There's a family picture of Marguerite and Will, who's holding their youngest daughter, Margaret, Robert Rennie, and Minnie who's standing behind Harriet, who's about seven. At the bottom of the picture Marguerite wrote, "Our household." Looking back we realize that Marguerite and Will had only a few years alone at the Hall Ranch before the girls were born and they moved back to live with her father, Robert. Almost all of Marguerite's married life was spent with extended family as part of their "household." The last picture of Minnie in any of the albums shows her with Marguerite's daughters. She's holding Margaret, who's only a baby, standing with Harriet at the train station before leaving, maybe for Westwood. Minnie never married and died suddenly in Los Angeles at the young age of 33. Marguerite held a deep sorrow in her heart. She had been a second mother to her little sister. Hattie and Marguerite had wept in each other's arms. It took some time to get past their grief but as usual they carried on with the business of the day.

On July 10, 1933 Alpha Literary and Improvement Club was incorporated as a 23701e, business leagues, chambers of commerce, etc. tax exempt club. On July 26, R. M. Adam turned over $230.75 from the San Julian opening fund to be used for Alpha clubhouse furnishings and the Santa Maria Gas Co. "loaned the club a gas range for keeps."[3]

The 1933–34 club book has a picture of the new Alpha clubhouse inside the cover. Construction was completed by September just in time for the first meeting of the new club year, September 2, 1933. Completed in less than 5 months! They sure did things a lot faster in those days! Today the clubhouse still looks the same. The outside is white stucco with a red tile roof. The main door faces Ocean Avenue to the north, and enters into a small hall. To the right is a large meeting room with wooden beams; a back hallway off the entrance hall goes down the left side, with two restrooms off of it, ending at the kitchen. The kitchen was fully furnished with stove and oven, sink and cupboards. A large "Tea Room" was added later.

On September 13 Alpha members held an "Open House" to show off their lovely new home. Margaret McCabe was there to see her dream come true. She didn't take part in the club's projects anymore, but she was proud to be present at the Open House.

Gertrude Rudolph was very excited about the new clubhouse and the fact the club had started a junior division. She invited her nieces who had married grandsons of H.S. to join Alpha Juniors. Helen had married Kenneth, and Dorothy had married his brother Richard. Helen proved too old for the junior group after they decided to cap their age at 30, so the next year she was accepted into the senior Alpha Club.

Helen A. Kessler Rudolph

We couldn't find much information about Helen except that she was born April 10, 1894. She married H. S. Rudolph's grandson, Kenneth, on February 29, 1919, during World War I, when she was 25. Helen lived the next years in Lompoc with her husband and family. She joined Alpha Club in 1933–34, when she was 39.

In January 1934, as if opening a new clubhouse wasn't enough for the club year, Alpha Club decided to put together a float of beautiful sweet peas for the Rose Parade. These women were not just small town; they wanted to be in the big time as well.

Margaret McCabe remained a member until she died the next year, September 28, 1934. It was announced at the Alpha meeting on October 6, 1934 by Hattie Smith that, "flowers were sent for the funereal of our deceased member, Mrs. Margaret McCabe. Mrs. McCabe had been a charter member of Alpha Club and her passing was deeply regretted."[4] Margaret had worked diligently for the club from its inception. She had been a good friend, a hard worker and dependable member of Alpha Club and her spirit was greatly missed.

It's interesting that after Alpha Club started their junior division, their senior club began opening their meetings, as the younger women did, with a salute to the flag by autumn of 1934.

That year, the club's executive committee started holding separate board meetings at the call of the president. We could find no record of any earlier board meetings. The board meetings were sporadic, taking place only every few months at first, with discussions on the usual subjects; money, who would attend Federation meetings, and fundraisers (this subject never gets old!) By the new club year, 1934–35, the president announced that she would be holding board meetings at the clubhouse on the first Tuesday of every month during her term of office. Marguerite Hall, along with four others, served on the reception (today's membership) committee. With a new clubhouse, they must have been anticipating a lot of new members.

There's a picture of Marguerite with her father and her oldest daughter, Harriet, in the dining room of her home taken, March 26, 1935. Marguerite is sitting and the others are standing behind her. Harriet is 17 but looks older and Marguerite is only

48 but like most women at that time, also looks older. Fashions in the mid-thirties were drapey and made women look dowdy. Now the saying is, "sixty is the new forty," and that may very well be true.

Bertha Seaman Moore

Even as Margaret McCabe passed on, Anna Moore's two daughter-in-laws, Bertha Seaman Moore, (married to Howard) and Donalda Huyck Moore, (married to Ernest) came into Alpha in 1934–35. Bertha was born in January 28, 1896 and Donalda was born November 6, 1893. We know little about Bertha but we know that Donalda was born in Lompoc. Both were married here.

Helen Rudolph joined her aunt, Gertrude, in the senior club and was on the music committee the first year. In 1935–36 Helen chaired the program committee and Bertha Moore joined the telephone committee.

In 1936, Hazel McCabe and another past president entered and won a writing contest held by the State Radio Division (south) club minutes reflect, "The members of Alpha Club are proud of their talented members and regretted very much that the ladies would not be present at the state convention (SFWC), to receive their rewards in person." Alpha Club has always been very active in district and state federated women's club affairs, sending delegates as often as possible to state events and even to national events, at times. At this point in time, there was the General Federation of Women's Clubs (GFWC— national) the California Federation of Women's Clubs (CFWC—state) and county federation meetings. Sometime later, the county groups were dropped in favor of district groups. Travel was getting easier and it had become possible to travel to distances 70 to 80 miles away and back, and spend several hours at a luncheon/meeting in one day. There are now 13 federated women's districts under the California Federation, which is under the General Federation.

In the minutes from the Executive meeting on May 2, 1936, we see "the report of finances of Alpha Club led the executive committee to hope that additional funds of $200 could be advanced from Alpha Club to ensure two years payments on loan." This seems to be another reference of a possible loan to help pay for the clubhouse.[5]

In the photo used on the cover of this book, club members are shown standing in front of the clubhouse, some dressed in costume some not, in a photograph taken at another club party in 1936. Marguerite is in the back. Helen Rudolph is sitting on the grass with a group in front. She has dark hair and is turned laughing at a woman in a face mask. There are two small girls in the picture in the front the group. Most women are smiling, unlike earlier days when everyone looked so stiff and serious in a picture.

The flower show had been held in various places since it started in 1922—the high school auditorium, the Opera House, the Forester's Hall and the Legion Hall. After 1931, it was held at the high school auditorium until 1937 when a big change took place. The chamber of commerce, who were usually helpful in getting the word out and promoting the flower show for Alpha Club, suggested that they hold the show in the new Veterans Memorial Building, which was going to be finished in time. "The chamber prepared a brochure which brought over 1,000 visitors to the Lompoc Valley for the 'Great Artist's' show … worth seeing at the new Veterans Memorial Building" thus, insured a long tradition for the flower show."[6]

Ida Sloan missed her friends in Lompoc, especially Alpha Club, so she came up to visit occasionally, especially at flower show time. She managed to come from Santa Barbara in 1937 to enjoy the lovely new venue and visit old friends like Anna Moore. It was always good to see Marguerite, and Hattie too. She was pleased her friend Appie's girls were so involved. Ida found she missed being close to her family, especially Stella Cevilla, who was married and had small children. Harry and Clara had a young son, too, who called her Aunt Ida.

Hazel McCabe continued as an Alpha member until two years after her Aunt Margaret died in 1934. In 1936–37, for some reason, she resigned from the club. That same year, 1937, some of the club's older members, Gertrude Rudolph and Anna Moore, suggested that the club consider holding only one general meeting a month as there were also a number of sectional meetings being held at separate times each month, and it was difficult for some to keep up with everything. Possibly, they were just getting tired. The members decided to change the meeting day to the first and third Wednesdays at 2:00 p.m. instead of 2:30, but continued meeting twice a month.

Interestingly, Gertrude Rudolph dropped out of Alpha Club later that same year, in 1937 at age 59, but her nieces, Helen and Dorothy were members, and carried on the Rudolph name in Alpha Club.

Dorothy (Dot) Riggs Rudolph

Invited to join Junior Alpha Club at its inception in 1933, Dot wasted no time in getting involved. She was born September 11, 1911 in East Prairie Missouri, coming to California as a young child. She grew up in Lompoc and married Richard Rudolph, Kenneth's brother on June 25, 1932 in Reno, Nevada. Richard was nine years younger than Kenneth.

Dot was only 21 when she married and just 22 when she joined Junior Alpha in 1933–34. She was a "little bitty thing,"[7] but it sounds like she had a great spirit. She loved life and was always laughing. She was eager to take on whatever came her way so, of course, took on the presidency of Junior Alphas in 1934–35, the year after she joined. Dot was very active in the Junior Alpha section where she stayed for 20 years, coming into senior Alpha Club in 1953–54.

It was reported, early in 1937, "Yearbooks of 1913–14, 1927–28, 1928–29, and 1929–30 were missing from the files, also several of the minutes books." We were sad to find this true, as we were starting this project, but also grateful that so many were still available and in good enough condition to read!

In 1938–39, when Helen Rudolph was president, many of the executive meetings were held in her home. It seems they held a monthly executive meeting, a board meeting and the general club meeting. (Too many meetings!) Even so, they still took time for fun as "Hattie Smith announced at the first meeting of the new club year, that plans were completed for the 'Members and Escorts' dinner to be held on September 29, 1938. A 'Bit of Sweden' would be the theme for the evening."

At the May 6, 1939 meeting, President Helen Rudolph explained a letter she had received asking members to lend every support and assistance to the securing of the 1940 convention of the California Federation of Women's Clubs at Santa Barbara. Alpha Club continued to support and be very involved in the federation in addition to all those Alpha meetings.

In 1939, Anna Moore resigned from Alpha at age 72. Members reluctantly accepted her resignation with an invitation to become an associate member of the club, which she did. She continued to attend some of Alpha's programs and teas. Anna retired from the store that same year. She switched to an Honorary Member of Alpha in the late 40s, as it became apparent that she was suffering from dementia. She would come to special Alpha functions with Bertha from time to time.

In 1939, the executive committee discussed appointing Anna's daughter-in-law, Bertha Moore as flower show chair. It's different now. We never appoint a chair but sometimes its difficult to get one. Bertha was nervous, but did a great job serving along with Mrs. Clarence Ruth. The theme was "The Valley Beautiful." "The show saluted the California Exposition on San Francisco's Treasure Island, with Hazel McCabe winning sweepstakes.

Visitors enjoyed a tour of the 'marvelously restored' buildings of the La Purisima Mission, as well as the tours of flower fields." At this time, most contributors and winners of flower show entries were Alpha Club members

Ida Sloan decided she was missing too much, living away from Lompoc, so she returned in the summer of 1939 to live in her family home again. Ida rejoined Alpha Club for three more years, serving on the reception committee that first year and taking part in plays and presentations, parties and teas. She was happy to be back and Alpha members were very happy to have her with them again.

In 1939, Jennie Dimock died, after serving the Alpha Club as secretary from 1905 to 1938. Marguerite Hall took over the job from 1938 to 1940. During that club year 1939–40, along with Marguerite as secretary, Hattie continued to serve as treasurer, as she had since club year 1925–26. Helen Rudolph was Federation secretary and Bertha Moore was on the board of directors. These daughters and daughters-in-law of some of the charter members were always willing to do the 'dirty' work; the jobs that keep a club like Alpha going but don't get any special acknowledgment. They were the female version, of the "company man."

Part 2

The Middle

CHAPTER 8

Our Civic Duty, WWII

Alpha Club has always been about education and hard work, but we can never forget the fun. No matter what else was going on in the world, Alpha women always have time for a little fun, sometimes a lot!

On March 20, 1940, "gowned in fashionable costumes of early days, a skit, 'Meeting Of Alpha Club in 1900,' arranged by Mrs. Lilley and Mrs. Adam was presented before the largest attended meeting for the year. All the material for the skit had been gleaned from the minutes of Alpha Club meetings from 1898 to early 1900." To continue with the theme of yesteryear, "a brief explanatory talk on the early club programs and projects was given by Mrs. Lilley and a presentation of a corsage to the club's only surviving charter member, Mrs. Anna Moore, was made."

"Mrs. Grace Rios presided as president in the skit and Mrs. James Larsen as secretary. The cast of characters included Mrs. Lilley, Mrs. Adam (Linda) Mrs. Riggs, Miss Laura Meals, Mrs.

Hall (Marguerite) Mrs. Gaggs, Mrs. Maimann and Mrs. James Sloan (Ida). Mrs. Henderson sang, 'After the Ball' and 'Sweet Bunch of Daisies' accompanied by Mrs. Lilley at the piano. Mrs. George Harris gave a reading on 'Women's Rights.'

"In keeping with the atmosphere, old fashioned bouquets were used and antique table service for the tea. The tea committee was composed of Mrs. Max Wilson, Mrs. Harry Sloan (Clara) Mrs. Bates and Mrs. Betaque."[1]

The long years of the "great depression" were hard on everyone, especially folks in small towns where jobs were scarce. Unlike today however, the town's commercial enterprises were owned by local people, (mom & pop stores, not big corporations) and they did their best to stay in business. It was in everyone's best interest to do so. Anna Moore and her sons kept their business going. Anna, of course, retired in 1939, toward the end of that difficult period. Her sons, however, had no intention of closing up shop and moving on. Of course, they didn't have stockholders to answer to, so they could tighten their belts and do without everything but the bare necessities, in order to keep the store open.

Surprisingly, Alpha Club seemed to keep right on going, making great progress during the depression, building the clubhouse and continuing to put on successful flower shows that brought hundreds of people to Lompoc every spring making the town and especially the chamber of commerce, happy.

"War and rumors of war came close to home when David Burpee, of the W. Atlee Burpee seed company introduced 'Queen Wilhelmina,' a rose and white sweet pea named after the brave, beleaguered Queen of Holland."[2] Burpee also opened the vast and lovely acreage of Floradale Farms to flower show visitors, stating, "The war has made the Lompoc and Santa Maria valleys the seed house of the world. Fields in many European countries which supplied gardens everywhere with seeds have been devastated by bombs and armies … and when the war is over those torn fields and gardens will probably be replanted with seeds now being grown in this country." It probably never occurred to anyone, at that time, that there would be a threat to this country. Shortly after Pearl Harbor, Japanese submarines were spotted off the central coast of California, near where all these seeds were to come from.

The Alpha Club got plenty of publicity in 1940. There are clippings from the San Francisco Chronicle (June 17, 1940) the Los Angeles Times, the Fillmore Herald, the Santa Barbara News Press, the Santa Maria Valley Vidette and of course, our own Lompoc Record. Lovely pictures of young high school girls in flower fields and others showing them arranging flowers were in all of these newspapers. The press committee certainly did a good job.

The executive committee continued to meet infrequently, only if called to meeting by the president. By this time the general club meetings included a luncheon at the beginning of each club year. The executive committee decided to have it catered in September 1940. At the December 18, 1940 meeting, "it was suggested that the ways and means committee prepare one large affair early enough as to not interfere with the annual flower show and that this be sufficient for funds for the year." Oh, if only that would work!

The theme for the 1940 flower show was "Old Colonial Plantation." It was held in the Veterans Hall with an elegant stairway leading to a colonnaded platform embellished by hundreds of begonias and lush greenery. A patriotic buffet dinner was served to hundreds of show-goers.

1941 began as any other year. There was notice of an antique show for a Los Angeles Federation District benefit, in which members were asked to exhibit their antiques and give interesting stories about them. Club talent was invited to participate at the show. It's remarkable that, in those days, when there were just narrow two lane roads, often switching back and forth up and down any mountain, club members would even care to travel down to Los Angeles to be involved with other clubs' events.

Club records show a Mrs. C. D. McCabe (Hazel) back in the club in 1941–42. Maybe she felt a need to reconnect because of the rumors of war, so she would be able to be involved, as she knew Alpha would be. Hazel's son, Malcolm, was old enough to be drafted. He had grown up in Lompoc and was away at college when he did get his notice. Malcolm served in WWII. Hazel's daughter, Betty, grew up here and eventually married and had two daughters and a son. Hazel jumped in where she had left off in the thirties and became very active again. Hazel was a down-to-business sort of woman, who never hesitated to make herself understood. Alyce Martin remembers how Hazel would come to meetings and put a "No Smoking," sign in front of her place at the table. She was way ahead of her time, considering that many people smoked in public, meeting rooms and dining places. Alpha Club was happy to have Hazel back because she knew how to get a job done.

The club continued with their talented presentations by members at every meeting. Hazel McCabe entertained the group at a fall meeting in 1940, with a motion picture report. She loved theater and the movies, any part of the acting experience, often writing plays. On the evening of February 19, 1941, the Junior Alphas presented a program consisting of many delightful musical numbers for the general club.

At the April 4, 1941 meeting, Marguerite Hall, chair of the garden section, announced a special flower arrangement event for the next regular club meeting, April 16. The club tried to ensure that members were able to enter winning arrangements in the flower shows by offering arrangement classes from time to time. But at times, several years might go by without them. Younger members would not feel as skilled as their elder members when this happened and there would be fewer entries as time passed.

(At this time, in spring of 2011, we're giving arrangement classes for six weeks to encourage more members to enter the show.)

The flower show in 1941 was delayed due to late, heavy rains that spring, which also caused the flower fields to be late in blooming. Anyone putting on a flower show knows that some things just can't be helped and one is the weather. Too much of it can cause the whole business to be disappointing.

On October 19, 1941, Marguerite's oldest daughter, Harriet, married Linda Adam's son Kenneth, much to the delight of both old friends.

Harriet Hall Adam was born in 1918 at the Hall ranch on the Honda and grew up in Lompoc, at the Hall house on North H St. and Central Avenue. She was Marguerite and Will Hall's oldest daughter. Her younger sister, Margaret, was born January 1923, at the Hall home in town.

Harriet attended Lompoc Union High and Pomona College and studied music, becoming a piano teacher until she married Kenneth Adam on October 19, 1942.

Ida Sloan felt she was truly ready to make a permanent move to Santa Barbara. She was 83 years old now and knew she just couldn't stay in Lompoc, where it was so hard to resist being involved. She submitted her letter of resignation to Alpha Club again and it was regretfully accepted. Harry's son, Jim Sloan, remembers visiting her in Santa Barbara during her last years. She was always happy to see him and hear about things in Lompoc, and would often give him an heirloom to keep. Ida lived to be 94.

The December 3, 1941 meeting was all about getting the city to put up street decorations and Alpha had to promise to pay for a share of the electricity if they put lights on Mrs. Heige's tree. The club voted to pay $5 as their share. Just a few short days later, on December 7, 1941 the Japanese bombed Pearl Harbor and the United States entered the Second World War.

At the December 17, 1941 meeting of Alpha Club, Christmas took a far distant second place. That meeting certainly was all about the war. Marguerite Hall announced that the Alpha Juniors planed to send cookies and candy to soldiers and called for a motion asking for senior members to assist. It was approved. Marguerite also gave a talk on Red Cross work with information regarding the great amount of sewing to be done and plans for the much-needed help required. Although Hattie was the nurse, Marguerite was instinctively a caring person as well, and the sisters worked tirelessly for the Red Cross and other causes.

By January 1942, plans were made to omit the usual "Members and Escorts" dinner party and purchase a defense bond instead. At the suggestion of Hattie Smith, the club would hold in reserve all money raised by the ways and means committee to be used as an emergency relief service, as the committee might see fit. This was also approved. Later that month, members were appointed to serve on Alpha's new home defense committee.

Junior Alphas were busy doing their part toward the war effort by hosting a party for young officers stationed at Camp Cooke in Lompoc. As difficult as times were for the country, Dorothy Rudolph had to admit to herself that she really enjoyed all the entertainment and dances the juniors were putting on. Life was certainly not boring!

A dance was held in May, 1942 at the Veterans Memorial Building, put on by and for Junior and Senior Alpha Club members and their escorts, as well as officers and their wives stationed at Camp Cooke. The event featured a live orchestra playing Benny Goodman, Duke Ellington and that new jitterbug music. By this time the club had set up a war service fund and the Red Cross had set up two emergency or casualty stations, one at the memorial building and the other in the grammar school. Alpha members helped furnish cots and old clothing that could be made into blankets as requested by Hattie Smith.

There were many slogans and ads on billboards and posters all over the nation to encourage personal sacrifice and effort toward the war. One said, "*Do less so that they will have enough!*" The poster showed a service man having something to eat. Too often we forget the sacrifices people made during WWII. We don't see that kind of sacrifice anymore.

"This Pacific Coast" was the theme of the 1942 flower show held in the Lompoc Grammar School auditorium, due to the war. The Alpha Club was very involved in the war effort as the year 1942 went on. It was a primary concern for the Alpha Club women in this first year of World War II. "Although it was the 20th anniversary of the flower show, the main concern of the floor committee was an effort to keep them (entries) patriotic. Arrangements of red, white and blue were encouraged; and the Burpees introduced a new sweet pea named for Mrs. Douglas McArthur, wife of the general.

The new bloom had only been shown once before, at the International Flower Show in New York"[3]

At the June 1942 meeting, a motion was made and carried to send flowers to sick members, Anna Moore and Mrs. Heiges. They were the club's oldest members and deeply respected. Anna recovered and continued coming, occasionally, to meetings.

At the first meeting of the new club year, September 2, 1942, it was announced that "a day nursery would be opened in Lompoc, primarily for children of working mothers, but at present anyone may send their children at a maximum cost of 25 cents a day." The first and last club meetings of the year were luncheon meetings, with all others being a tea, but at this meeting it was moved that the club hold a luncheon on the third Wednesdays as well. Bertha Moore served on the clubhouse committee with Hattie.

After Marguerite's daughter, Harriet and her husband were settled in their new home, their mothers suggested that Harriet join the Junior Alphas. They really didn't have to try hard to get her interested because like her mother before her, Harriet was happy to join. Harriet became a Junior Alpha the same year at age 24 and served as president in 1946–47.

During WWII, many women entered the work force for the first time. It was a necessity for them to keep things going financially for their families, while their husbands and sons were off fighting in the war, as well as provide the needed labor in our factories and fields. For some it wasn't difficult, as older women in the family helped out with childcare. But some, who had no one to help, learned to manage all alone, factory job, home and children. The result was an awakening. They found out they could do it! They could do a man's job! "Rosie the Riveter" became familiar to all. Farm wives had always known this, but it was a revelation to women as a whole. At the time, most women only thought of this as their patriotic duty to the country. But it was an awakening of a different sense of self.

In January 1943, Hattie Smith made a plea on behalf of the Red Cross, for knitters and those who could help with sewing and other work. She also announced that the home nursing class would start on January 11 at the Walnut Street USO. Hattie and her husband had no children of their own. He had a daughter from his first marriage, who was grown before Hattie and he married. Hattie was happy to take on this cause. She was 53, in good health and nursing was her calling. She took her job seriously, working relentlessly for the Red Cross during the war, as a volunteer.

That same month "there was a discussion about, whether the club should meet only once a month being that the attendance was so small at the other meeting date. Not reaching any definite decision it was left to the executive committee to decide at their next meeting."[4]

By spring of 1943 the junior club was putting on a lot of card parties and donating some of the proceeds to the Red Cross. At the same time Helen Rudolph was installed as vice president of the county federation for a two-year term.

The flower show was held June 12 and 13 at the Lompoc Grammar School auditorium. It was called "Flower and Victory Garden Show." Along with arrangements, a victory garden basket full of fruits and vegetables was arranged. A "Who Done It?" contest required contestants to guess the identity of the entrants of several arrangements.

At the beginning of the club year in September 1943, the Alpha Club changed to only one general club meeting a month on the third Wednesday. We have been meeting at that time ever since. Marguerite Hall and Clara Sloan served the luncheon and Marguerite also reported on the Red Cross committee. Bertha Moore served on the clubhouse committee again with Hattie and Clara "Toots" Sloan served as liaison to the Junior Alpha Club.

Throughout club year 1942–43, the Junior and Senior Alpha Club were asked to help at the USO, the Red Cross, and with getting people to purchase war bonds. They donated sums of $25 and $50 to Red Cross, and to buy war bonds. They held dances at the USO and sometimes the clubhouse, where they danced the Jitterbug, which livened up any dance in no time. They gave parties at the clubhouse and other events for soldiers and their families and put on special entertainment whenever needed for the launching of each new government loan drive. Loan drives were very popular and encouraged by GFWC. The government sold war bonds and people bought them to help the war effort. Alpha Club even helped with a "Bonds for Babies" contest.

In November of that year the club voted to "sponsor filling two traveling chests each month for boys of the Coast Guard. Twenty-five Service men were invited by various club members to share Christmas in their homes."

In 1943, Lompoc's first hospital opened after years of evolution: from a small Sanitarium in 1908, to Susan Henning Van Clief's Maternity home opened in 1914, to Nellie Sperber's surgery room added onto her home. The town finally had a fully equipped health care facility. Robert Rennie was a charter member and Harry Sloan was on the board of directors. That the hospital opened during WWII was no small coincidence.

At the January, 1944 meeting, Alpha members were requested to decide whether to hold the annual flower show that year, due to the war's demands. After much consideration and debate it was ultimately decided in April that the club would hold a tea with floral exhibits for members only, in order to maintain the tradition of the flower show, while dealing with the realities of the war. The tea was held from the hours 2 and 5 p.m.

By this point Alpha Club members were inviting outside entertainment for their meetings. We suspect that the demands of the war effort on members allowed little or no time for them to arrange their own entertainment as they had always done. One can only imagine the immense amount of time they were spending doing the additional work it took to be of service to their country, as well as the club and local community. At the April meeting, the club enjoyed the performance of the high school glee club and orchestra.

The flower show tea went unexpectedly well with hundreds of visitors attending the tea and a show put on by local youngsters, in appropriate colorful costumes who sang flower songs.

Club year 1944–45 opened on September 19, 1944 with forty members attending and a delicious luncheon served by Mrs. Henderson and her committee, Marguerite Hall among them. The speaker was Josephine Lacey, Supervisor of the new Lompoc Community Hospital, who gave an informative talk on the hospital and its relationship to the community. Marguerite and Hattie were two of the first women to become members of the Lompoc Hospital Auxiliary.

A motion was made and approved at that meeting, that junior members could have a transition year when they reached the age limit, which would allow them to remain a junior, while trying out the Senior Alphas, as Associate members. Therefore, they wouldn't be required to take part in any duties or pay dues to Senior Alpha until they decided to move up. They were also invited to attend club section meetings during that transition year.

Bertha Moore was elected to serve on the board of directors for three years. New club yearbooks were ready and had been completed as usual by the Lompoc Record. The club made plans for another junior/senior dance for service men and wives. Members were asked to go to Camp Cooke the next Monday to sew for the boys. Clara Sloan called for knitters for the Red Cross, to knit army sweaters and socks. Everyone, back then, was involved in the War effort. Even in grade schools, Girl Scouts knit for soldiers.

An example of the club year, 1943–44 is given in a letter from President Jane Swartz, written at the end of her term in June, 1944, when she gave a brief account of the year saying, "Due to members working an average of 938 hours per month on the war service the meetings have been held only once a month.... Members of the executive committee and the board of directors met regularly the first Wednesday afternoon of each month. Luncheons were served by club members at seven meetings and tea and coffee at two meetings. In October of 1943, the county federation council met in Lompoc with Alpha Club hosting." Donations for this year were: $5 to the district clubhouse fund, $5 to AWVS, $5 for a tuberculosis bond, $5 for cancer control, $10 for Save-the Red-Woods-League and $25 to the American Red Cross.

At the October meeting, a guest speaker gave a presentation, including a motion picture about training and services of the women's auxiliary corps. Movies were extremely important during the war years. One could see for oneself the devastation and ugliness of war, on the big screen in movie theaters, when they ran the newsreels between every movie. We remember watching the horrors of the concentration camps, even the ovens, and not quite believing what we saw as children. But everyone loved to go to the movies and watch wonderful stories of adventure, mystery, romance and especially cowboys acting tough in the early West. It took us out of the reality of the world we lived in for a little while and let us forget, while we traveled to the South for "Gone With the Wind" the Pacific Islands for "From Here To Eternity," or to the old West for "The Outlaw." Now we have television and computers that allow us to live more and more in a virtual world, every hour of every day if we so desire, but we still have the movies when we want to go out.

Harriet Adam gave the juniors' annual report to the Alpha Club in June, 1945 "which was received with enthusiastic approval." Everyone was always pleased when a second or third generation Alpha member took part in affairs of the club, but Marguerite was 'bursting her buttons that day. Aunt Hattie Smith was also very pleased as she made a motion that a note of commendation be sent to the junior club. Harriet continued to serve in the juniors until she moved up to Alpha in 1953–54. Kenneth Adam became Managing Editor of the Lompoc Record in 1946.

On June 5, 1945, a declaration that the war had ended was signed in Europe, and on August 14, 1945, President Harry Truman announced that Japan had surrendered and had signed a peace treaty. The country felt optimistic and Alpha Club was no exception. Club members could get back to just club business and everyone breathed a sigh of relief!

There are several pictures taken that year at the Hall home, showing Marguerite and Will standing in their yard together and one with Marguerite's father, Robert Rennie, and Margaret their youngest daughter. Robert Rennie was about 84 at this time,

Will was 66 and Marguerite was 58. Robert lived only two more years, but had looked the same, in pictures, for 20 years.

The flower show that year was done "as in the previous year," and held as a member's only show with a tea. Profits were donated to an emergency fund for hospital patients at Camp Cooke.

Besides helping with The Lompoc Youth Welfare Program, chaperoning teen-age dances, working with the high school girls' Tri-Y club, conducting the Young people's choir and many other duties, the Junior Alpha Club raised money by selling stationary, holding a rummage sale, and a blanket raffle to send the money made to "The Women's Veterans Home in Yountville." The club staged a 3-act musical comedy, the "Victory Vanities." They made a huge profit of $250. Keeping $150 they gave $100 to the Lompoc Youth Recreation Program." That last year of the war, 25 junior members also put in a total of 2,555 hours from September 1944 to March of 1945, working for the USO, AWVS and the Red Cross.

In addition to serving meals, refreshments, providing dances, being hostesses, playing piano, hat checking, helping to make records, buying contents and filling stockings for servicemen at Christmas, providing other numerous services, club members also helped sort clothing for the United Nations Clothing Drive. Such unlimited energy these young women had. Now, young women usually must work full-time outside the home either because it takes two salaries to survive or even more problematic, some are single moms. After a long day of work and sometimes a commute, they barely have enough energy to fix a meal and do a load of laundry. Consequently, there are very few young women's clubs left and no one to take on all those civic duties.

By spring of 1946, the country was booming. Men were back to work and women were back in the home. Many were "barefoot and pregnant," as well. Everyone was full of great hope for the future. The flower show that year was dubbed, "The most ambitious show in Lompoc Floral History." Alpha Club was celebrating, just like everyone else, with the United States flag reproduced in flowers on the stage of the Veterans Hall. Well over a thousand people attended the show "enjoying for the first time exhibits in shadow boxes." Later that summer, the kitchen and the clubhouse exterior were re-painted.

By autumn of 1946, the junior club was back to planning garden parties and style shows, inviting all senior members. It was good to be back to these kinds of affairs. It was reported at the December 1946 meeting that the executive committee favored putting the flower show money, a sum of $350, into the building fund. Motion made and carried. Things were looking up!

In February 1947 Robert Rennie died. Marguerite and Hattie had never experienced separation from their father. He had been their rock when they lost their mother. Marguerite had actually lived with him, with the exception of her time away at school and the first few years of her marriage to Will, all of her life. She felt such a deep loss at his passing. It took months before she stopped sensing his presence in the garden, carriage house workshop, or when she walked into the living room. He was a small man in stature, but his presence was missed in all of Lompoc.

At the 1947, Spring flower show, something different was tried. "Favorite blooms were accepted from people's gardens, flowers could be placed one of a kind in a container, which was the prelude to specimen entries. There were also numerous entries from children that year so that they had to be displayed on the balconies of the auditorium."

The Junior Alphas put all their considerable energy back into club work and were always busy raising money for some good cause. They gave a fall fashion show and dance, which went into the club's Christmas philanthropy fund. At Christmas that year, a large party was held by the women of both senior and junior Alphas, the AWVS, the Lompoc Woman's Community Club and the American Legion, so that everyone in Lompoc would have a happy Christmas.

The juniors gave their usual rush tea in autumn of 1948. A picture of the officers standing behind the tea table shows Alyce O'Neal who had joined the club by invitation in 1947–48.

Alyce O'Neal Martin was born in Hixson Tenn. in 1927 and came with her parents to Santa Barbara when she was two. They had a restaurant in Montecito for four years, but later came to Lompoc when Alyce was ready for high school, in 1941. They felt that with Camp Cooke being constructed there would bring more opportunity. Alyce attended Lompoc Union High, graduating in 1945. Lompoc was still very small and it was not hard to get to know almost everyone, which she did. Alyce was invited to join the Junior Alpha Club and did so in 1947. In younger days, she was small with dark curly hair and a dusting of freckles. She has always had a deep mellow voice and has never lost her Irish sparkle. She served as treasurer of Junior Alpha in 1948–49. Alyce was not related to anyone who had been in Alpha Club, but her new mother-in-law was a dear childhood friend of Marguerite Hall's.

Alyce married Perry Martin in 1950, at the age of 23 and had five children, as well as remaining an active member in Junior Alpha. She "flew up" to Senior Alpha in September of 1963, after having her youngest child the previous June. Alyce had no problem becoming friends with her new mother-in-law, Emily Deitzman Martin. This can happen, we understand, but must not be taken for granted.

"Emily Deitzman Martin was born on her father's ranch, and grew up next door to Marguerite Rennie Hall. Their ranches adjoined and they spent their girlhood playing together, jumping back and forth across a large drainage ditch that separated the properties. Both grew up to be avid gardeners. Living next to Robert Rennie's ranch, with all of his beautiful flowers would have made it next to impossible not to love them as much as Marguerite did. Marguerite of course, went on to join Alpha, but Emily did not have an interest in women's clubs."[5]

Emily married William Thomas Martin in 1917, in Lompoc and lived the rest of her life on the property where she grew up, just as Marguerite lived most all of her life at her childhood home.

Emily was delighted with her oldest son's choice of a wife and Alyce got to know a lot about her mother-in-law and her friends. Marguerite's daughter, Harriet Adam, was in Junior Alpha when Alyce joined and the two older women hoped they might be friends.

Emily and Marguerite stayed friends to the end of Emily's life. They had a birthday group that always got together for each woman's birthday. Sadly, Emily died of cancer in her 50s, leaving her family and Marguerite to grieve.

Betty McCabe Morris was born in Lompoc, November 20, 1924. She married James Harry Morris on February 6, 1943 in Lompoc. Betty had her first child, a boy in 1946 and a daughter, born in July 1948 at the end of her first year in the club. Her second daughter was born in December 1951.

She was a newcomer to Junior Alphas in 1947–48 club year and was Hazel McCabe's daughter. In pictures, Betty looks quite a bit taller than her mother. She looked thin and had dark hair. She immediately began doing her part in the club by serving on the hospitality committee that first year. In 1949–50 Betty served as parliamentarian. Hazel was very proud of her daughter. In club year 1949–50, Betty served as home and garden chairman and was responsible for the program in March 1951. Betty took it a little easier in club year 1951–52 as she was pregnant with her second daughter, who entered the world in December.

Clara "Toots" Sloan was chair of the flower show in 1949, which featured musical table titles. Having friends like Marguerite Hall and Hazel McCabe gave Toots confidence with flowers that she hadn't grown up with. "There was even a special train to and from Los Angeles to accommodate the throngs of Southlanders wishing to attend the Alpha Club Flower Show and tour the flower fields." The flower festival, which came later, wasn't even thought of yet; so having such a popular flower show was a really *big* deal!

In the late forties, the club began to put on more programs at their meetings, dealing with the arts; painting, writing, music, literature, travel and any other interesting self-improvement idea. Alpha seemed to be recharging, to be nurturing their body of members after the strenuous war years. They went back to their roots as an "Improvement" club, always a good idea. Going back to ones roots that is.

CHAPTER 9

Boom Town

Lompoc's Camp Cooke served as an Army training camp during WWII. At its peak, Camp Cooke boasted a 1,500-bed hospital, fire stations, chapels, warehouses, theaters and 36,000 troops. After the war, the Camp served as a Prisoner of War Camp for German and Italian prisoners. Sixteen branch POW camps grew from the Camp nucleus and eventually housed 8,700 prisoners in a maximum security Army Disciplinary Barracks, later to become a federal penitentiary constructed on post property adjacent to Lompoc. The Camp itself lay idle after 1945 until it was reactivated in August 1950 for two and one-half years during the Korean conflict.

Over 200 potential sites were considered by a select committee before Camp Cooke was chosen, in 1956, for its availability and location, to be a missile base. Camp Cooke was renamed the Cooke Air Force Base. Within 18 months, the old Camp was refurbished and missile launch and control facilities began to appear as tons of steel and concrete transformed the base. The name was changed yet again to Vandenberg Air Force Base, commemorating General Hoyt S. Vandenberg, second Air Force Chief of Staff and early proponent of aerospace preparedness. On December 16, 1958, Vandenberg launched its first missile. The big change began in 1957 when there were only 6,665 people living in Lompoc. By 1962 there were an estimated 18,500 Lompoc citizens due to military and civilian contractor personnel working on the new military base.

In 1950, there were over one hundred members in Senior Alpha Club and about fifty-nine junior members and that was before the huge increases in the town population began later in the decade. Alpha Club was certainly the popular place to be! Senior Alpha Club started having monthly luncheons at 1:00 p.m., before their business meeting, which was catered and seemed a good idea, except for the crowded clubhouse meeting room. Of course not all members attended each meeting, but still they needed more space.

In February 1950, a committee was appointed which included Hazel McCabe, Clara Sloan and a Mrs. James Larsen to administer the student aid fund, changed from a student loan fund. A request from the Lompoc branch of the California Alumni Scholarship Aid Fund was read and it was moved and passed that the club give $10 to that fund. Club dues that year were $2.50 for a regular membership!

The sweepstakes prize for the 1949 and 1950 flower show was won by Hazel McCabe.

The theme for 1950 was the official state song, "I Love You, California."

Request for items needed for the soldiers were again met by willing club members as well as blood donations given when the Red Cross Mobile Blood Bank came on November 28. A dance was given on Thanksgiving at the Community Club Center and a big Christmas party was planned in 1950 for the soldiers at

Camp Cooke. We were at war again, even though we weren't calling it one.

In January 1951, Marguerite moved that Alpha take part in a flower judging class that would be sponsored by Federation. The motion carried. Of all the clubs taking part in this idea, Alpha was certainly the most experienced. These days only a few club members even enter Federation Arts and Crafts Day floral arranging competitions.

Hattie Smith was still the Alpha district director for Federation, but managed to have some time for flowers. Dale Laubly, Marguerite's friend, was chair of the garden section and announced that their next meeting would be at Marguerite's home to discuss camellias. Hattie always saved time for these meetings.

In March of 1951, a tea was held at Hattie's house and it was decided to consolidate the three committees: art, literature, and music into one and meet 3 or 4 times a year. With so many war-related activities the club had taken on, they needed to lighten the burden of meetings.

The flower show's theme was "Flowers on Parade." Hattie Smith was chair and the show realized $469.04 in profits.

In January 1952 Alpha Club was asked for representatives to attend a meeting held by the school board of trustees for the purpose of discussion of the tax rate. The club was also involved in "efforts to prevent bill boards on our highways."[1]

At the February meeting, several topics were discussed, including the usual concern for volunteers for the Red Cross and members who had attended the school board meeting spoke of the necessity for maintaining the present school tax rate in view of increase in the cost of operating the schools. That seems reasonable.

Anna Moore was the last surviving charter member of the Alpha Club. Even though she became ill and experienced dementia, which necessitated that she receive 24 hour care, she remained an Honorary Member of the club until her death, March 22, 1952, at age 83. She had spent her last days in a convalescent home in Fair Oaks, California near family. At the April club meeting, Marguerite Hall gave a talk in memory of Anna who had been Appie's good friend. Anna had been an Alpha Club member for 54 years.

At the end of that club year, Hattie finally resigned as treasurer, after serving for 17 years in that capacity, all the while taking on many other tasks as well, especially her work with the Red Cross during WWII. She didn't stop with the other tasks, as the in the next club year she served as fine arts chairman as well as being on the program committee. There have always been a few members who were willing to carry more than their share of work for the club, like Cevilla, Ida and Clara Sloan, Margaret and Hazel McCabe, Emily Bissinger, Anna and Bertha Moore, Marguerite Hall and Hattie Smith, to name a few. (And there are always those who seem only interested in coming to the club luncheons.)

In September 1952, when Harriet Adam (Marguerite's daughter) transferred from juniors to Alpha Club, her husband, Kenneth Adam, became owner and Editor of the Lompoc Record upon the retirement of his father, Ronald.

At the October 15, 1952 meeting, it was recommended that Mrs. Richard Rudolph, (Dorothy) a junior member, be accepted into the Alpha Club. She joined her sister-in-law, Helen as a member. In November the focus of the club meeting was "Art in the Home" and "Fulfilling the Goals of the American Home."[2] After WWII, women were re-focused by the media and society to their jobs as mothers and homemakers. "Rosie the Riveter" had disappeared and maternity wards were full. But some seeds of change had been planted.

In 1953, Dale Laubly was appointed as chair of the schedule committee for the flower show, with her friends, Marguerite and Hazel, volunteering to be part of the committee. A men's table was featured along with a "First-Timers" table to encourage new entries.

We find it somewhat interesting that there was so much less to do about the war going on in Korea. Yes, Alpha was involved in some of the same ways it was during WWII but generally; it did not affect the country as a whole nearly as much.

There were none of the major sacrifices being made, as had been during the war ten years prior. Our routine lives didn't change as much, unless we were directly involved because a loved one was in that war. It's as though most people just wanted to forget about wars and the pain and sacrifice they bring. Many were just so busy going about their business, having children, working, buying homes that they barely noticed when, shortly after the flower show in 1953, the Korean Conflict ended. Some of the women in Alpha breathed a sigh of relief, as their sons came home and began to get on with their lives. One thing that Alpha started during the Korean Conflict was the blood bank that ran at the clubhouse, with some members assisting. It started in 1952 and replaced the Red Cross committee. Alpha ran the blood bank at the clubhouse until 2009. At that time the Red Cross began using a Blood Mobile, which was easier for their staff.

In May of 1953, Will Hall died, leaving Marguerite alone in her home for the first time in her life. He had been ill for a short time, so his death was not a shock. However, the loneliness was very difficult. What helped her was the full and active life she led outside her home and she was thankful she was able to still be very much involved with all of it. She had joined the hospital auxiliary after the hospital opened in 1943, and in addition to all her other activities she played in the Tuesday bridge club. Later, she joined the Lompoc Historical Society, Lompoc Republican Club, and the Robert R. Young Iris Society.

Marguerite's friend Linda Adam's husband Ronald, also died in 1953, so the two women had each other to lean on while they adjusted to widowhood.

That same year Clara Sloan became an honorary member of Alpha Club but still came to meetings and served on committees. She was only 61 at the time. Marguerite was 66 in 1953 and still going strong. She had every intention of remaining an active member for many more years. That club year, Marguerite was chair of the home and garden committee and her daughter Harriet served as second vice president.

At the January, 1954, meeting, a discussion was held regarding the possible change in our flower show date to coincide with a proposed flower festival to be sponsored by the chamber of commerce and other civic organizations, on the Fourth of July. A hand vote gave consensus to go along with the community, if and when the plans for it materialized. Alpha president, Mrs. DeGroot and several other appointed members were to meet with the chamber of commerce."[3] It was decided that the chamber of commerce festival committee would serve as the overall sponsor for the event, with individual organizations taking over various phases of the event.

At the club's May 1954 meeting, "Mrs. DeGroot spoke about our great need for a tea room and called on Mrs. Lawrence Schuyler to report on costs for same. She reported that figures obtained, to date, were between four and five thousand dollars. It was suggested that the members think about it and a possible idea might be forthcoming as to how best to obtain the much needed tea room."[4] The club had outgrown its clubhouse in just 21 years.

Lompoc's first flower festival took place on July 4, 1954 with the theme for the flower show being, "Festival of Flowers." Festival events included a community breakfast, kiddie carnival, parade, tours of the flower fields and Mission, Mass at the

Mission, Gymkhana, and a band and choral concert." Hazel McCabe won sweepstakes, again.

Many enjoyable slide shows were given for Alpha members during this time. People were beginning to travel more, in spite of the Cold War taking place between Russia and the rest of the Western World.

The main business of the day at the club meeting, January 19, 1955 was "a discussion of the proposed addition to the Alpha clubhouse to be used as a tea room. A vote was then taken, with 63 members present and a unanimous affirmative vote. Those not present will be contacted as according to the by-laws all should vote and an affirmative vote obtained from three-fourths of the active membership before we can proceed. The room was to be 20x30 feet and was to be built adjoining the south side of the present building. It was to be used as a dining room and arranged so that food could be served directly from the kitchen ... estimates received from four contractors ranged from $4,500 to $6,500." The balance in the Alpha building fund at the time was $2,514.26. The additional balance owed was to be borrowed at two percent interest and payable in installments the first of September of each year.[5] Such a deal!

In March, the club members learned that another older member had passed away. Gertrude Rudolph died on March 6, 1955 at age 77. Gertrude was remembered as a faithful member who had joined several months after the club was started and although she dropped out for 12 years she came back in to Alpha from 1914 to 1937.

Flower show chairs included Bertha Moore and they again staged the show with the Fourth of July celebration and flower festival. There was some discussion in the Lompoc Record's "Party Line," concerning the complaints heard from time to time on why some people can make so many prizewinning arrangements. The answer is planning, according to the article. Hazel McCabe won the sweepstakes again.

Hazel McCabe had been chair of the scholarship committee for some time and had suggested that the club raise the amount given to $100 from $50, which was done, but it seems that they ran a little short at times and she would call for members to contribute. On March 15, Helen Rudolph thanked everyone for the flowers sent on the club's behalf for Gertrude's funeral.

Apparently several women's groups put on a fall party for the district's teachers as the May 1955 minutes note that "Mrs. Henning and Mrs. Marguart will represent the club."

Maybe we should do that now. It has to be so much harder to be a teacher these days, with shootings at the schools, pay cuts and pensions threatened.

At the end of the club year, in June of 1955, there was $2,637.47 in the savings account and $326.54 in the clubhouse fund. The tea room committee had arranged for the loan and the tea room was added to Alpha Club that summer. That's right, in just two months time "Presto-Chango," a new tea room and it's still standing today!

In August of 1955, Marguerite Hall, Linda Adam, and two other widowed friends took a trip to Hawaii. There is a picture of them "cruising" aboard the Lurline and standing together with leis around their necks. Marguerite wasn't the type to feel nostalgia or sad returning to the spot she and Will had spent their honeymoon, she was just happy to get back to such a beautiful place.

On September 26, 1955, a Note was secured by "Deed of Trust" for $3,000.00, to Hattie R. Smith. Payments were to be made annually, at the sum of $100 with 2 percent interest per annum. Sometimes there is a "Fairy Godmother" who swoops in and gives a big helping hand to Alpha. This time it was Hattie.

In autumn of 1955, the club prepared for its annual Escort party, a potluck that would officially open the new tea room. A fall chrysanthemum show was held at the clubhouse, chaired by

Marguerite Hall, which also provided an occasion to show off the new addition.

In January of 1956, "the speaker was the Superintendent of the Lompoc Schools. His topic was the forthcoming Bond Issue for new school facilities." The Superintendent was concerned because he knew that Lompoc was about to be hit with a huge increase in our population. By 1960 (in just four years,) the population of school children would nearly double what the entire population of Lompoc was in 1956. The club members were urged to help get voters to the polls. It was announced at that meeting that "the local papers had printed that the chamber planned to hold the flower festival the last week-end in June and if so, that the Alpha Club would coordinate its annual flower show with the festival."[6] It's worked like that ever since.

On April 1, 1956, Marguerite held a tea at her home, but it wasn't an April Fools joke. Everyone looks very cordial and proper, dressed to a "Tea," literally. Some of those invited were: Linda Adam, "Toots" Sloan, Elsie Sperber, Alice Lowary and Irma Henderson.

In May of 1956, Officers were elected for the next year. Dorothy Rudolph was elected secretary. An offer was made from the Junior Alphas to cater the Senior Alpha's luncheons, and was accepted. Thirty dollars was allowed them for additional equipment for cooking. By this time, meetings were preceded by a 1:00 p.m. luncheon, priced at $1.25 each. So the juniors had found a way to fill their coffers. In 1996, the price was still low at only $4.50 each for lunch, but soon went up rapidly. Now, in 2011, we pay $10 plus a dollar extra for the building fund, and our meals are catered by a local restaurant. For a number of years however, the club members set up committees and took turns preparing the food and serving the membership. In recent years, we have gone back to catering because we have so many older members. We still have our committees however, for decorating, making desserts and serving the lunch.

In 1956, a play in three acts was prepared by a Mrs. Thomas F. Gibson at GFWC in Washington DC and distributed to all federated clubs for reading to commemorate "Jennie June, Mother of Clubs." The prologue states in part:

> "History records that the woman's club movement played a quiet but powerful role in the recognition of woman's independence. As members of the General Federation of Women's Clubs, it is fitting that we become better acquainted with the founder of this movement, Jennie C. Croly, lovingly known as "Jennie June, Mother of Women's clubs."

Jennie Croly was a journalist living in New York City, "who applied to the president of the New York Press Club for admission to hear Charles Dickens speak. She was rudely refused, solely on the grounds that she was a woman." She decided to take on the "attitude of the day of masculine superiority." "Her plan was not to be militant, but to form a unified group to help bring about a proper recognition of womanhood." The goal of the new women's club was to "remain feminine, but not femalish, to meet to improve our minds, but not to 'preen' we will obey the 'Golden Rule'." The play told the story of the first meeting held by women, in order to form a club, in 1868.

In 1890, Jennie Croly invited women's clubs throughout the United States to attend a ratification convention in New York City. Sixty-three clubs attended on April 23–25 and took action to form the General Federation of Women's Clubs (GFWC). Eight years later the Harmony Club was born.

At the June meeting in 1956, members were informed that there would be several interviews on television, showing the flower fields, (although TV was in black and white then) and also several radio programs about the flower show. On behalf of the general federation, a Mrs. Arreguy presented Alpha Club with a certificate of 50 years membership in the GFWC. (As of 1954!)

Someone else did win the sweepstakes at the 1956 flower show, a Mrs. Earl Ross. The highlight of the flower festival that year was an Aquacade at the dedication ceremonies for Lompoc's new Municipal Pool.

At the same time, hundreds of acres were annexed by the city and thousands of homes were being constructed to provide for new residents connected with the two new missile bases at Vandenberg. At the end of that club year, Donalda Moore resigned from Alpha Club. She had not been very active, participating only on the telephone committee for several years. We think, maybe, she stayed in the club out of respect for her mother-in-law, Anna, but unlike Bertha who really liked being in the club, Donalda didn't seem to enjoy it.

In January 1957, Helen Rudolph also withdrew from Alpha Club along with five others, which would have devastated the club in earlier days but with so many newcomers in town, membership seemed abundant. Helen and her husband Kenneth had decided to retire in Long Beach and had purchased a new home. Helen lived out the rest of her life there.

The club also voted to pay Hattie Smith $500, plus interest, on the loan for the tea room. Hattie had made the club a better offer than they would have gotten from the bank! Marguerite was legislative chair at the time and "gave a report on billboards in our county."

Around this time, early 1957, the club minutes begin to identify members less formally, now we begin to find just Mrs. Hall instead of Mrs. Will Hall in the club minutes. By March of that year, we find a combination of usage of Mrs. Hall, Mrs. Marguerite Hall and/or Marguerite Hall. The problem with using just Mrs. Hall is when there is more than one woman with the same last name, as there was with the Rudolph's. We really have to guess who is being referred to. Somebody's first name needed to be in the notation. It's interesting how long it took women to claim their own identity. It was like peeling onions, one layer at a time.

At the March, 1957, meeting, it was announced, "The garden section is to hold a series of 3 meetings ... for anyone interested in flower arrangements."[7] We noticed that usually the club was very diligent about holding these meetings/classes, to keep up the interest and abilities of its members.

Dorothy Rudolph served on the telephone committee that club year, but she was not able to be very active in the club, unlike when she was in the juniors. By this time Dot's (her nickname) three sons were grown and she had gone to work with a prominent realtor in Lompoc, Harley Craig. Dot was a very gregarious and happy person and it was a great time to sell real estate, especially homes. "In those busy days, acres would be bought up and houses built as fast as possible to fill the need of all the new people moving to town. They couldn't get the houses built fast enough, that's why some people had to sleep in their cars until their house was ready."[8]

Anyone who has ever been a real estate sales person during boom times, knows you eat, sleep and breathe selling houses, with no time for much of anything else. Alpha Club met on the third Wednesdays at 1 p.m., so it was hard for Dot to even get to meetings. She knew she was probably the last of the Rudolph's to be in Alpha Club. Even though she tried, when her new daughter-in-law, Cathy, moved to town, she couldn't get her interested in being a club woman.

The flower show/festival theme, in 1957 was "Under the Big Top." In an unusual undertaking the exhibition hall was transformed into a circus "big top," with a moving carousel and a "live animal act."

Hazel McCabe's daughter, Betty, wanted to stay in Alpha Club but was getting divorced and realized she needed to find work to help support her young family and herself. By club year 1957–58 she'd resigned from Junior Alpha. Hazel was so disappointed for her daughter, but always practical she determined to continue on with her life as an active clubwoman. Betty later re-married but she had no interest in re-joining Alpha Club.

In 1958, Alpha Club was very involved in the Tierra Adorada District, which had been formed at the beginning of club year 1956 to take the place of the county districts. Our new district included all of Ventura, Santa Barbara and San Luis Obispo Counties. Alpha had become interested in mental health issues, no doubt with suggestions coming from Federation. The club invited speakers from county mental health and our state hospitals who showed films previewing tours of Camarillo and Atascadero State Hospitals.

The flower show theme in 1958 was, "Yesterday, Today, and Tomorrow." It was obvious that the "Tomorrow" of the theme had to do with Space, as the grand marshal of the flower festival parade was Maj. General David Wade, Commander of the 1st Missile Division at the Air Force base. Marguerite's friend, Dale Laubly won best of show and Mrs. Vern Duncan won the sweepstakes.

At the September, 1958 meeting, Harriet Adam, program chair, introduced the guest speaker as Captain Brady from the Air Force base who "very efficiently explained SAC and its place in our defense program, describing it as a deterrent force primarily. His talk was illustrated by informative slides."[9]

In November of that year, a "letter was summarized, from Tierra Adorada District, requesting us to let radio and TV station managers know our individual opinions of radio and TV programs, if we want to be a constructive factor in getting better programs."[10] About the only way to do that now is to set up a huge boycott against a particular program. It can still work.

In 1959, Alpha was still very much involved in trying to get roadside signs removed and members were urged to write to officials. They were also actively writing protest letters to our council about a parking lot. Have we lost some of our civic courage over the years?

In March 1959, Alpha had the superintendent of schools speak again, this time about the demands being made on the school system. Mrs. Arthur Batty read a letter addressed to Lompoc City Council to be signed by Community Women's Club, Junior Alpha Club, Women's Chamber of Commerce, PTA and Alpha Club, if agreeable, in regard to having a traffic policeman direct traffic at H Street and Ocean Avenue, especially during peak hours. Alpha signed the letter. Sometimes women need to be reminded of the power they can have when they join together for a cause.

In March the Wakands Camp Fire Group sponsored by Alpha Club presented a playlet called "Let There Be Harmony" which depicted one of the first meetings of the club. The girls played roles of charter members, including, Mmes, F. D. McCabe, F. B. Moore, J. C. Rudolph, Holton Webb, George Bissinger, Hensen Poland and president, Mrs. C. A. Farnum. The play was a riot and was to be given a number of times over the years by Alpha members.

In the fall of 1959, Hazel McCabe went on a European trip and later showed slides at the home and garden meeting at the clubhouse on October 28. The decade was drawing to a close, no one understood yet, but things were about to change, big time. Some believe the next decade was the downfall of our society. It's certain that we lost some of our innocence in that next few years, even in Lompoc.

CHAPTER 10

Decade of Change: The Sixties

Bob Dylan had a very popular song released in 1964 titled, "Times They Are a-Changing," and wow, were they. Change is not immediately perceptible. It seeps into life, little by little, like smog that grows thicker year by year, until one day you look up and can't see the sun.

One could not say that things were like they used to be in Lompoc by 1960, with the enrollment of over 10,000 students in the schools. But still, like most of us, people in Lompoc didn't realize the numerous effects that such a rapid, large increase in population would have on the town.

In 1960, the number of women who voted equaled the number of men, for the first time, and the FDA approved the use of the birth control pill.[1]

The Alpha Club started out the new decade, as they had so many others, going about the business of the club. The home and garden section met at Marguerite Hall's home in January 1960.

The Senior Alphas made plans to entertain the junior club at a February 3 potluck.

The theme of the flower show was, "Show Time" and the Commander of the US Navy facility at Point Arguello was the grand marshal. In keeping with the theme, the best arrangement at the show won an "Academy Award." Children's arrangements titles were "Bambi" and "Dumbo," among others.

The club held its usual potluck "Escort Night" in October at the clubhouse and a good time was had by all who attended.

In 1961, Hazel McCabe and her daughter, Betty, attended the presentation of a bronze plaque by the city in memory of her late husband, Carl.

May 29 to June 11, 1961 was declared clean-up time for the city and the Alpha Club was doing their part by serving sandwiches and cookies to the men who were volunteering to help collect trash. The juniors distributed 5,000 leaflets to homes to remind people of this project. All club members were urged to cooperate. In June the clubhouse was painted and repaired and on June 20, 1961, the club had paid Hattie Smith the $3,000 plus interest in full for her loan to add the tea room.

The flower festival in 1961 was highlighted by the grand marshal; Jayne Mansfield accompanied by her husband Mickey Hargitay, former Mr. America. The flower show theme was "A Garden of Verses." Another big attraction for the festival was an Aunt Jemima pancake breakfast held on Sunday morning. Over 2,000 people attended. The price of flower show tickets was increased to $1 for adults, students and children free. Alpha also joined the chamber of commerce, which allowed the chamber to sell flower show tickets as part of their advance tickets sale.

Since shortly after WWII, the La Purisima Mission Association had put on the "Annual Mission Day Fiesta" and Alpha had always been asked and agreed to, you guessed it, help bring and serve food. In those days it seemed like something was going on in town almost weekly. There was no way to be bored!

Newcomers certainly found this to be true. If you moved to town because your husband was going to work in the Aerospace industry, you were most likely to be invited to join Alpha Club. At the September club meeting, Clara Sloan introduced eight new members. Members also began planning to hold a Tierra Adorada District meeting in Lompoc in the spring of 1963. Marguerite Hall and four others served on the hospitality committee. With that many new members coming into the club, they needed a whole committee. Harriet Adam served on the music committee that year. In October, there were two more new members. Marguerite had taken on the responsibility of making up corsages for new members every month, and continued to offer her home for various occasions. She was in her mid-seventies by this time. At the November meeting five new members were introduced by Clara Sloan. Thirteen new members joined in three months!

Hazel McCabe, with her newspaper background, continued to keep herself well informed and offered information to the club from time to time. She spoke at that November meeting on a Water Bond issue to be voted on.

At the January 17, 1962 meeting, "the following recommendation by the board was read and unanimously adopted, that the president appoint a committee of five to investigate assisting the hospital."[2] It seems that Mr. Thomas, the administrator of the Lompoc District Hospital, came to the board meeting and asked for assistance from the Alpha Club. It's interesting that in earlier times, committees were appointed frequently, to deal with a special project. Appointees may not always be 100 percent agreeable, but they seemed to get the job done that way. At the next meeting of the board, it was reported that the committee appointed to help the hospital had voted and passed a recommendation to purchase a Stryker Circomatic bed, at the cost of $1,000.

In April, 1962, members got very excited when the club president presented a report by a state appraiser, which showed that the lot and clubhouse together would bring around $43,770, if it should be sold. You guessed it, another committee was appointed, with Clara Sloan as chair and four others including realtor, Dorothy Rudolph, to investigate another site for the clubhouse. Several board meetings later they hadn't decided what to do and had gone on to worry about needed bathroom repairs and the paint job for the clubhouse. Twenty-nine years with the same sinks and toilets is a pretty good record with all that usage!

In 1962, housing was booming around Lompoc. As Vandenberg grew, the need for off-base housing grew. Personnel wanted housing closer to the base than Lompoc, which was 5 miles away. A group hired a large company, Utah Construction, to do the job. A decision was made to build a Village and building started immediately. As the need grew, the idea to put a golf course around the Village became popular and rumor had it that some of the new managers at the base were offered free membership in the golf club if they bought a home in the Village or the country club area. The area was lovely, with warm sunny skies most days, scrub oaks, chaparral and manzanita growing on the sandy rolling hills. There was flowering ice plant along the roads, and of course, always the cool ocean breeze in spring and summer. Who wouldn't want to live and work in such a place?

The flower show celebrated its 40th birthday in 1962. The Theme was "Halls of Ivy. "There were bands such as "The Fluorescents," "Ten Tones," and Finney's Combo Band rocking and rolling in Ryon Park." Dr. W. B. Jamison won the chamber of commerce women's division silver trophy for his sweet pea arrangement.

In January 1963, the club put a pay telephone in the hallway between the restrooms. In May of 1963 "Dorothy Rudolph of the building committee gave a report of possible sites for a new clubhouse. She gave facts and estimated values of both commercial and non-commercial property, as well as zoning regulations. In June, the board was advised that Dorothy Rudolph had a building site in mind and would contact and advise the board."[3]

In June 1963, Dot heard on the radio that a couple, who were good friends of one of her sons, who had been missing for several days, were found at Surf Beach. They had been murdered. Dot was understandably upset and called her young daughter-in-law, Cathy, to tell her about it. While she was speaking on the phone, she paused suddenly, and then told Cathy that all of a sudden she had a very bad headache and would have to call her back. Cathy did not get a call back, so when her husband got home from work she told him that she was worried. When he went over to check on Dot, he found that his mother seemed to have had a stroke. Apparently she had a brain aneurysm that left her aphasic (unable to speak) and in need of care. She was only 51. Dot lived through the summer, with nursing care at home and assistance from her family. By September she seemed to be getting better, but then the aneurysm burst. She was taken to Santa Barbara, Cottage hospital, but she died on September 14, just 3 days after her 52nd birthday. Alpha members were saddened to hear the news, as they had hoped that Dorothy was on the way to recovery.

In October 1963 Hazel McCabe gave a colored slide presentation to the club of her Mediterranean journey. She even arranged a table with items she had purchased, such as a hand-woven skirt and shift dress, miniature dolls in native costumes and a Greek urn. A note of appreciation was read from the Rudolph/Riggs families, that day, for the spray of flowers the club sent for Dorothy Rudolph's funeral. After that we could find no more references to selling the clubhouse or building a new one. We know it didn't happen, as the original still stands today in its original location.

In November 1963, "Escort Night" attracted 90 Alphas and their escorts. That month a group of Alphas put on a matinee for the club, impersonating stars of stage and screen. Among them was Louisa Van Ausdal as Charlie Chaplin.

Louisa Van Ausdal tells us that she was born on August 4, 1918, in Plymouth California, on the edge of the beautiful Shenandoah Valley in Mother Lode Country. She went to Grammar school in Plymouth and High School in Sutter Creek, a small town nearby. When she graduated from high school she did office work. Her first job was in the office of Wheeler's Department Store, in Plymouth. Louisa's father was the Methodist minister in Plymouth.

Louisa met Max through his two girl cousins who came from his hometown in Utah with their father, Max's, brother who had a restaurant in Plymouth. She tells that she was dating another guy, but then she met Max. That was it! They were married on June 11, 1939. Max died just one month short of their 70th anniversary, in May of 2009.

Max was in the Air Force, as a pilot in WWII, and shortly after the war, Louisa's niece, Charlotte came to live with them. She was only seven. Louisa's sister was having problems and asked Louisa if she and Max would take her little girl, as she just couldn't provide for her. They jumped at the chance, as they had no children of their own. When Charlotte was in high school, Max was assigned to Germany and they weren't allowed to take Charlotte out of the country, as they weren't her parents or legal guardians. She stayed with someone else in the family, then, until she was grown.

After Germany, Louisa and Max were assigned to Vandenberg Air Force Base. They moved into a new little house on North M Street, in Lompoc where they lived for 10 years. Louisa liked Lompoc. People were friendly and there was a lot to do here. She was invited to join Alpha Club in 1962 and became a devoted member, who has added a lot of sparkle to the club. She loved flowers and saw Alpha as a way for her to do things for her community as well as have fun, and have fun she did.[4] Louisa had dark hair and dark shining eyes. She was tiny, dress size and all; she was no more than 4'10" at her tallest. She has always worn extremely high heels and, even then, she had to look up when she talked to someone. Now in her nineties, it makes things pretty wobbly and she does fall sometimes.

Another new member, who joined Alpha Club in 1963, was Gene Holmdahl (Mrs. Walter) She and her husband had a ranch in Miguelito Canyon, just out of town.

Gene Holmdahl (Evelyn Genevieve) was born June 3, 1913, in Elliott Iowa, where she attended high school, grew up and got her first job selling men's clothing. She met Walter, who was a farm boy, and went with him to Dodge City, when he took a load of horses to sell, on April 24, 1937. They decided to get married while there, and when they came back her parents weren't too happy. Her German father was especially unhappy when she moved to Kansas after her marriage.

She had a restaurant in Kansas, but things were slim during the Depression and when Walter got an offer to work in Los Angeles, they moved. Soon after the move, their youngest son, who was just an infant, died. They stayed in Los Angeles until 1944 when Walter had the opportunity to work as a Ranch Foreman in Solvang. They loved the Santa Barbara area, but moved again to Watsonville for another job for Walter, as a Ranch Foreman for Angustora Angus Ranch in 1948.

In 1950, Mr. Max Wilson, owner of Riverview Angus Ranch in Lompoc, was hospitalized for TB and Walter was asked to take over as Foreman, otherwise Mr. Wilson would lose the ranch. Gene and Walter hated another move, but were also anxious to get back to Santa Barbara County. The ranch was near the Santa Ynez River. Gene got a job working in the men's department at J. C. Penney Co., which was in the Moore building on West Ocean. She worked there for 10 years.

In 1952, they purchased Rancho San Miguelito from the Talberts. It was located one and one-half miles down Miguelito Canyon, south of Lompoc. Gene helped on the ranch until 1962, when she went to work at Stalkers Men's Apparel, located in the old Rudolph building on South H Street. Gene worked there until 1972. While she was always busy, Gene was never too busy to take on something she liked. She loved flowers and had always wanted to join Alpha Club. So she did in 1963.

Gene was hearty and strong and could do the work of three people. She was middle-aged when she joined Alpha, at 50 years old. She was friendly and a can do person. We couldn't help but like her from the start.

Gene was also a member of the Hospital Auxiliary, Santa Barbara Cowbells, a 4-H leader and trail rider, Committee to Beautify the City, past Mariners Club president, president of Presbyterian Women's Association, served as deacon for the church, and last but certainly not least, she cooked and served Presbyterian Church harvest dinners for over 25 years. In her spare time, Gene worked in her garden and painted scenic pictures.[5]

The January 24, 1964 home and garden section of the club held their meeting at Hazel McCabe's home. A speaker demonstrated how to furnish the home. Louisa Van Ausdal, another flower lover, was chair of the group.

Harriet Hall Adam was chair of the music section again in 1963–64. She often played piano at the meetings to entertain or as accompanist. A hat program was scheduled for the March meeting of Alpha Club. Basically the subject would be "Ideas for Easter bonnets and the art of creating fabric-covered hats."[6] What is that old saying, "What goes around, comes around?" Especially in small towns, where we have written memories like these and can compare with today's life. This year, in 2011, at our Easter luncheon meeting, we were all asked to wear spring or Easter hats, just for fun. At times like these, we can walk into

Alpha Club for a meeting and it's as though time is standing still for us. For a brief moment we're still back in the 40s.

Around this time, a small group gathered at Marguerite Hall's garden for a picture, standing in the Marguerite Hall Iris Test Garden, Lompoc. In the picture are Dale Laubly, standing next to Marguerite, Harriet on her other side and Irma Henderson next to Harriet with two other women in back.

The flower show theme in 1964 was "Bridal Memories." Dale Laubly was judge's chairman for the show. The show was so successful that the club's net return was over $1,100. Members felt so affluent that they purchased containers for 20 cents each, to replace the old painted milk bottles and beer cans that had been used for almost half a century.

In club year 1964–65, when Gene Holmdahl was first vice president, there were 144 members in the Alpha Club, and among them was Alyce Martin who "flew up" to Senior Alphas after having her fifth child in June. She was one busy woman.

That September, the home and garden section held a "Hawaiian inspired garden clothes and gadgets fashion show at Louisa Van Ausdal's home. The comic highlight of the show was when Mrs. William (Pat) Boone and Louisa Van Ausdal modeled original home-made 'muumuus' for 'mommie' and daughter, with Pat Boone, who was tall and ample licking a lollipop, as the daughter, and tiny Louisa as the mother, wearing a crazy hat and gloves."[7]

At the October home and garden meeting, a dramatic program on color planning for the home was presented. We were really big on home design and planning in the 1960s, even though the "Baby Boom," was slowing down, women were still very much into being happy homemakers, and wondering why their Boomer daughters were turning their noses up at that idea. It wasn't clear to us, but we could see abundant changes in the younger generation.

In late 1964, the Alpha's were busy hosting the Officers' Wives Club, and visa versa. Some women belonged to both. Many newcomers who had come to Lompoc because of the new Air Force and Missile Base were, or had been, in the Service.

In April 1965, Louisa Van Ausdal presented a check for $117.49 to the chamber of commerce beautification committee from the Alpha Club garden section. Louisa's garden committee was also responsible for the guest speakers at the April luncheon meeting, with a program on "Antiques."

Women's federation had begun to encourage a number of projects, among them was conservation. The 1965–66 Alpha's district federation report states that Alpha Club became a charter member of the Lompoc Valley Historical Society, in order to help preserve the history and landmarks of the Lompoc area. Alpha Members also serve on the beautification committee and, that year, they were responsible for "alley clean-up." Alpha Club had never stopped being responsible for the planting of trees around the city and they still do to this day.

Marguerite Hall "was given special mention in the annual report of the Historical Society as chairman of library committee, for organizing pioneer pictures in suitable books." It's because of Marguerite that we are able to write much of this story. She indeed, organized some of the large picture albums of Founding members of Lompoc and their families including genealogy, which made it possible to get some of the vital information on charter members of Alpha. Marguerite also wrote papers on the history of Lompoc, parts of which can be found in this book.

In a picture in the Lompoc Record on Monday, May 23, 1966 are eight Alpha members dressed up in former flower show theme title costumes that they presented at the luncheon meeting. Alyce Martin is dressed as a Space person. That month the juniors took in the largest new membership total ever, 20 new members in a month!

For a number of years, the flower show and festival had two different titles, which could be a challenge at times. In 1966 for example, the flower show theme was "This Is Our Valley" and the festival theme was, "Valley of Missiles and Flowers" which fit together nicely. Gene Holmdahl co-chaired the flower show with Mrs. William Boone. It was the beginning of years of involvement for Gene.

Members were requested to make four dozen cookies each for the tea room during the flower show and leftovers were donated to the fire department. When Gene Holmdahl was installed as first vice president in June of 1966, she knew she could use more polish. Gene was a farm woman and felt unprepared for the job so she signed up to join the Toastmistress Club and Parliamentary Law Group. She wanted to learn how to run a meeting! In 1967–69, feeling confident after Toastmistress experiences, Gene served two years as Alpha Club president. In addition to Alpha and the Toastmistress Club, Gene was busy helping her husband run the family Feed Store at their ranch from 1967 to 1977.

On July 27, 1966 Harriet Adam's husband died, unexpectedly, while having surgery at Stanford University Hospital. They were married for only twenty-five years. Kenneth was 50 years old and in the prime of his life as publisher of the Lompoc Record. Marguerite was able to support her daughter during her time of grief, as she had supported others so many times before with the loss of loved ones. Harriet had her mother's strength of character and knew she had to step in and take over the newspaper. She became the CEO and ran the paper until 1973, when she remarried. She continued her membership in Alpha Club, in spite of her demanding job.

In 1966, members continued to knit or crochet at least 50 pairs of slippers for women veterans at the Sepulveda Veterans Hospital in the San Fernando Valley. Alpha made and furnished many decorations for events in Lompoc, such as the pioneer's tea, the chamber of commerce luncheon and other luncheon meetings. Members donated many handmade items to the hospital gift shop and many worked as Girl Scout leaders, Cub Scout mothers and 4-H leaders.

At the February 19 meeting, a speaker from Covair Management Club gave a talk to members on his ideas of "What Inflation Really Means," saying, "Inflation is really a tax on our money."[8] It seems that we spend as much time and energy trying to get our economy to balance, as we do our personal bank statements. It's the same old story, too much and we get inflation, too little and we get recession. Alyce Martin and Mrs. Raymond Clifford reported that they would manage a fashion show on International Day in March, and asked for club members with available costumes of foreign countries to model them or allow someone else to do so.

Later that same month, Alpha Club gave four checks to "the Lompoc Hospital, the WMCA, the Boys Club and the Lompoc Valley Association for Retarded Children." The International Day in March was successful with eleven Alpha members dressed in foreign costumes representing different countries. Alyce Martin represented Hawaii, and Hazel McCabe, Greece. Alpha members won 20 awards at the district federation conference in April. In pictures of the conference, we notice that out of the ten women pictured only four are wearing hats. A big change in the past few years!

On another Hat day, April 19, the club's guest speaker was an expert on hats. An article in the Santa Barbara News-Press on April 23, 1967 states, "One of a woman's well-known weaknesses are her absolute madness for a pretty hat." The speaker gave a presentation on "Hats in History" and most Alpha members wore their favorite hat. There's a picture of all of those who wore their hats and although we're sure they seemed quite lovely at the time, some seem rather silly looking now. We had our "Hat" day for the year at our luncheon April 20, 2011 and only about eight of us even wore them. These days you can barely find a hat; usually you have to look in an antique store. Most of us seem to have gotten over our "well known weakness," and never looked back!

Marguerite celebrated her 80th birthday on May 10 1967, with both her daughters and all of her friends present. Pictures show an older thinner Marguerite but still vital and able to be involved. She had no intention of retiring anytime soon!

In the first week of June 1967, the General Federation of Women's Clubs (GFWC) held it's 76th national convention in San Francisco and several women went as delegates from the Tierra Adorada District, including Gene Holmdahl and Mrs. W. Boone.

A number of articles have been cut out and pasted into the Alpha scrapbook, one of special interest is entitled: "Club Women Facing Membership Decline." The article states that the number of club women in America is declining and gives several reasons; "one is that there seems to be a club now-a-days for everything, and another reason is 'senior fallout and junior dropout.'"[9]

We see the phenomena from hindsight and wonder if it is a problem or part of the solution. We have to remember why women's clubs were started in the first place. Women at the end of the nineteenth century had very little independence; they had so much to gain from these "improvement clubs." They wanted the right to vote, to improve their knowledge, and to better their communities. Some even dared to hope to accomplish something in their own right. Moving into the last part of the twentieth century, some of those things had been accomplished and women were beginning to discover themselves as individuals. In the 1960s and 70s we see a big movement to organize women, so they can go farther than voting rights. They wanted equal rights!

There was, of course, a backlash from some of the younger southern women, who felt that the GFWC as a whole was getting too militant and may have lost some of their femininity! One was quoted as saying, "Women are taking control of businesses, replacing men in boardrooms and asking for complete equality, and men have no place to go. They're becoming more feminine … letting their hair grow long, for instance."[10] We don't think GFWC was to blame for this, we remember the goals of the very first group to organize. There are always people who are afraid of change and probably didn't have the good fortune to study women's history (her story). That's one good reason to write this book, so women can get a better idea of what HerStory was all about!

The theme of the flower show that year was "Just Imagine." For some reason the show was held the last weekend in May, a few weeks after the club celebrated the 80th birthday of Marguerite who had been the first co-chairman of the flower show. That year admission fees went up to a whopping one dollar for adults and fifty cents for students.

Gene Holmdahl was president and Louisa Van Ausdal was first vice president in 1967–68. In August, Gene announced that Alpha would initiate a newsletter.

By this point in time, the juniors held a Brunch for new members instead of a "Rush." Gene held the event at her home and gave a talk, "What a Junior Club Can Offer You." The article in the paper even describes what was served—coffee cake, watermelon shells that were scalloped and filled with colorful spears of melon, etc. It didn't hurt to have the publisher of the local newspaper as an active member of Alpha! It all sounds so lovely and enticing; it would be hard to resist that kind of presentation. We are still capable of putting on these kinds of affairs, but not as frequently.

A past presidents tea was held on October 10, 1967, an event held every year at the clubhouse to show gratitude to the past officers. That year 34 past presidents attended. The picture shows Marguerite with a huge smile grasping Gene Holmdahl's (the current president) hand with two other former presidents standing with them. Marguerite is wearing a hat in keeping with her era as president in 1916–17.

Every year the club sponsored an essay-writing contest for eighth grade students. It was a citizenship essay with the title: "What the Stars and Stripes Mean to Me." In 1967, the focus of the garden club, in late November, was holiday suggestions, especially learning to make festive table settings. It looks like the group had a lot more fun doing it together at the clubhouse than we do watching Martha Stewart on TV.

A New Year's 1968 resolution, made by President Gene Holmdahl, was to catch up on her 1967 ironing and to try to stop the influx of pornographic materials into Lompoc. This was prompted by the club receiving "promotional brochures for a series of films which, by description, could only be classified as pure pornography under the guise of education. Alpha and other organizations took up a letter writing campaign to national, state and local representatives which proved to be a lesson in futility." [11] We are sure this wasn't just happening in Lompoc. The courts, as we remember had taken the position that the matter "Cannot be excluded from the Constitutional protection of freedom of speech and press." Attitudes were changing, that's for sure! The Boomers were challenging all the old norms and rules!

A talk on fire prevention was given at the February Alpha Club meeting. It's interesting to note that in the same article new members are introduced with only their married name. Club books still listed members names as Mrs. Will Hall, but at least the woman's first name was listed in parenthesis after her formal name, even though, as in Marguerite's case her husband had been gone for over 10 years by this time. In every newspaper article, the woman's name is Mrs. Will Hall. It's going to take another decade before women feel comfortable with their own identity.

In March, Alpha donated a $700 check to the hospital for an oxygen tent. At the club luncheon, Louisa Van Ausdal dressed in Spanish costume in keeping with the honored guest, an exchange student from Spain, who was the speaker at the Alpha meeting.

A picture was taken in June of Linda Adam, Marguerite Hall and Dale Laubly, looking over a lovely dahlia garden in town, as they reminisced of the early dahlia show they were involved with, the one that started the whole tradition of putting on flower shows.

About this time Louisa and Max Van Ausdal moved into a lovely new home in the country club area that was very popular for many newcomers. Louisa was first vice president in 1967–68, but never president. She was dean of chairman in 1968–69. She chaired the flower show in 1970.

The flower show seems to have reached its apogee during this year, 1968. The theme was "Melodies in Flowers" and Les Brown and his Band of Renown played at the Queen's Ball. It was said that crowds of around 100,000 attended the flower festival and Alpha Club listed 168 members. Marguerite is seen in a picture pouring tea for a specimen judge at the flower show tea.

At the club membership tea in September 1968, members had some fun using paper dolls and purses to depict club duties, all hand made of course. Gene Holmdahl served as president again and that fall the Alpha Board discussed expanding the facilities and appointed a long range planning committee. Lompoc was still growing, due to Vandenberg, and Alpha Club hadn't begun to experience that membership in women's clubs was on the decline, not yet anyway.

Alpha's luncheon honored the past presidents on October 16, 1968 with 17 past presidents attending. In a picture taken that day, actually dated and with names written on the back, (for the first time) all wearing corsages, we see Hattie Smith sitting on the right and Hazel McCabe sitting on the left. Marguerite is standing behind Hattie and next to her is "Toots" (Clara) Sloan. Seven are wearing hats, Toots and Hazel among them. It's a great picture. Hattie looks very frail. Marguerite looks thin and does not seem quite so tall, but is still regal. Hazel looks healthy and serene and "Toots" looks stunning. She is wearing a dark hat and a three-string pearl necklace on a two-piece crepe dress.

That fall, Alpha Club gave the hospital a check for $800 to purchase an anesthesia ventilator for its anesthetic machine. As usual it wasn't all work. The club was still up for fun times and always enjoyed entertaining each other. At Christmas time, the juniors gave a fashion show that interpreted styles in most ultra-literal manner. The show, "Kooky Kostumes," was a hit with senior members. At the same time, club members continued to provide gifts for women in the Veterans Hospital in Los Angeles, as they had for many years.

In February 1969, a "Way Out" dinner party and hilarious program was given by the senior club for the juniors. There's a picture of the "Grannies' Band" with several members dressed like hippies. Tiny Louisa Van Ausdal is wearing a short-skirted dress with a wig, sunglasses and black boots, calf high. She is playing the string bass, the biggest instrument of the group. Guests were advised to "Do your thing."

Marguerite hosted the garden section, at her home, several months in a row and in March the subject was orchids. Members were told the blooming season is December through June and their questions were answered about home growth of the plants. We had a similar presentation five or six years ago and we're thinking maybe we should do that again, so our orchid plants will start blooming next year. That spring Alpha Club donated books to the libraries of the Boys and Girls Clubs to promote reading. On Arbor Day, Alpha Club planted another tree.

Another milestone was accomplished in Lompoc, when on March 9, 1969; a newly built modern library was opened on North Avenue. The old Carnegie Library sat empty for a year, while a committee made plans to turn it into a Museum.

In April 1969, Alpha Club earned the name "Love Club" at district federation when Gene Holmdahl gave her president's report "appearing in a wig and mini-skirted dress." The report of each club project was prefaced with the phrase, "Love is—".

In May, Alpha had a triple theme program; mothers, hats and gardens. Members voted for "mother of the year," as usual and then there was the annual hat contest with a touch of silly. Members were urged to wear hats, as usual, but told if they didn't wear one they would be forced to wear a dunce hat all day and a prize would be given for the "craziest" and the most suited to advertise the club's flower show. Of the six women pictured who won awards, Louisa is wearing a very silly flower hat and Dale Laubly has on a bird's nest with eggs in it. Always laughter.

The 1969 flower show's theme was "Lompoc History In Flowers." Some of the table titles were: "Temperance Colony;" "Lompoc Landing;" and "Tragedy at Honda." Five previous winners were competing for the sweet pea trophy, but someone new won. For Louisa and Max Van Ausdal it was a double win, with Max winning best men's entry for his entry "Steelhead," and Louisa winning best shadow box, the beginning of a long tradition for both of them.

Every July during "down time" for Alpha Club, some members just couldn't resist entering the Santa Barbara County Fair with flower arrangements and often they were winners. One, Mrs. Donald Cameron, (Evelyn) served as Superintendent of Floriculture, managing displays and judging the floral entries in 1969.

Alpha announced its plans for the new club year at the first meeting, held on September 17, 1969. The meeting included a fashion show, "Getting to Know You," modeled by members, Hazel McCabe, Gene Holmdahl, Alyce Martin and Dale Laubly, to name a few. The clothing was furnished by Moore's, Stalkers and Fashion at the Inn. Gene stepped down from her position as president, but took the job of chair of home and garden section. Toots Sloan continued as chair of the duplicate bridge group that was franchised to Alpha. You wouldn't think that would be a hard job for someone who loves bridge, but like now, the chair has to call players and match partners, get there early and set up cards, take in the money, and always be sure there will be plenty of food to munch on.

Later that month, the home and garden group met at Louisa's lovely home. The subject was "set the tables." There were displays throughout her home and garden of table settings arranged by Mrs. Kammeier of Kammeier's Hardware & Gifts. We can just picture how lovely it all was in Louisa's French provincial style home. We can't help a little nostalgia, as we write all this. Lompoc had so much more in those days, Moore's Department Store, with it's up to date fashions and everything else and Kammeier's, which also made shopping so easy back then.

In October, Alpha members worked to plant a vacant lot in downtown Lompoc, a continuation of a beautification program originated by a local business owner. Gene Holmdahl is on her knees, planting with assistance from "a host of women." In November, Alpha celebrated National Art Week with a guest speaker showing his "bird and elf" sculpture. Harriet Adam participated in the program as well.

On "President's Day," October 1969, there are only eleven past presidents in the picture, but Hazel McCabe, Marguerite Hall and Toots Sloan; the three old friends are there as usual, smiling into the camera.

Marguerite Hall's Iris Test Garden: taken at her home in 1964. Front row, left to right: unidentified gentleman, Dale Laudby, Marguerite Hall and Irma Henderson. Back row: unidentified woman, Harriet Adam, unidentified woman.

Past president's day in the late 60s in front of the club house. Marguerite is seated in the front row on the extreme left and "Toots" Sloan is next to her. In the back row, second from the right is Gene Holmdahl.

Lousia Van Ausdal (kneeling center) and Gene Holmdahl (kneeling right) looking over a few specimens in 1970.

CHAPTER 11

The New and the Old

The club starts planning the flower show in January now and has since the 70s. Unlike in the very early days it takes that long to get everything to come together. There have been a few times over the years, when things didn't get started as early as January, but this can cause a little panic toward show time. Louisa Van Ausdal was the flower show co-chairman for 1970. Always efficient, Louisa wasted no time getting started.

Alpha sponsored an art talent contest for seniors in the high schools and entered the winner's art into the state level 1970 art talent contest, sponsored by General Federation in cooperation with Hallmark Cards. The company, annually, awarded a total of $3,000 in scholarships to national winners.

Alyce Martin began her service as crafts chair in 1970. She loved doing crafts and had a real talent. Her enthusiasm brought in some new members to the group. Alyce continued as chair for the crafts section until 1977.

Among the annual reports written for district federation for the year 1969–70, at the very back, is a status of women report, which was filled out by our president. Questions asked were:

> Question: Does your club have a Status of Women Chairman?
>
> Answer: No.
>
> Question: What has your club done to inform and interest the members in the Status of Women?
>
> Answer: Announcements are made at regular meetings as to what our women are doing in the community.
>
> Question: What projects were undertaken to help the young women desiring to go back to school or to work?
>
> Answer: Many of our women have gone back to school or work and we encourage them to do so.

We don't think Alpha members really understood the questions. Pasted on the next sheet after the questions and answers is a position paper from the Public Affairs Department of the Department of Labor, Washington DC on the STATUS OF WOMEN. It defines status as:

> The position of an individual or a group in relation to another of like class.

It goes on to say: STATUS OF WOMEN could be defined as:

> How women rate in ability, in judgment and importance when comparing them to men. We outnumber the men so why have we elected so few women to government position? Why is the major part of the higher paying positions in education, industry and professions held by men?

The paper then states a purpose:

> To develop our California Clubwomen into an INFORMED, INVOLVED WOMAN POWER dedicated to helping all

> women increase their STATUS by making it possible for each to realize her potential.

It goes on to say that:

> CFWC is on record as supporting the existence of the Advisory Commission on the Status of Women in California.

It is obvious that CFWC *did* understand and was moving forward!

The chamber of commerce asked for members of Alpha Club to be represented on the committee to establish a museum in the old library building. The museum was ready in just a year. It took a lot of planning and a large donation by a retired school-teacher, Clarence Ruth. Mr. Ruth held a large collection of local Indian artifacts at his home that for 30 years had been open to the public. He is shown in a picture supervising workmen as they set up the exhibit in the "new" museum. Gene Holmdahl was on the incorporation committee and was a charter member. Doors to the Lompoc Museum opened for the public on February 15, 1970.

In the spring of 1970, a general beautification of Lompoc took place by the "Flower Power" group organized, of course, by Alpha members. The group represented seven civic groups and they planed to plant, clean up and put up large metal flowers on light standards in the commercial sections of Lompoc. There's a picture of Gene Holmdahl, standing on a stepladder fastening one of the large flowers to a lamppost. "Be careful Gene!" The whole idea is "beauty creates business." The old saying, "some things never change" really applies as for several years now, up to and including 2011, our city has taken part in the National America in Bloom effort and actually won the Championship two years ago with Alpha Club winning an award. Unfortunately, this happened during the early part of the "Great Recession," so it didn't do much for business.

By 1970, some women are wearing slacks at public events, but most are still wearing dresses. We wouldn't think of getting up on a ladder with a skirt on now, especially in windy Lompoc. In March, Alpha Club presented a check to the hospital administrator for purchase of five wheelchairs.

"Spirit of The '70s in Flowers" was the theme for the 1970 flower show with Louisa as chair. Organ music was played softly throughout the exhibition. Max Van Ausdal, (Louisa) and Robert Sech (Rose Marie) constructed dividers for the arrangement tables so that the arrangements could be separated and easily viewed.

In October 1970, for the Presidents Day photograph, Marguerite is sitting in front looking sharp and happy but Hattie isn't there. She had become very frail and wasn't able to get around by this time, not like her older sister, who just kept going strong.

In 1971, the clubhouse was the chief concern. A new roof had been installed and now the members had to come up with the money to rewire, fix a sewer problem and remodel the kitchen. The president, Mildred Joy, convinced the members that the club could at least remodel the kitchen; remove the "pantry" which just took up space, install a swinging door into the dining (tea) room to accommodate members serving each other, rather than catering the luncheons. The idea was to have members each pay $25, if they could or more if they wished, and they would get a promissory note to be paid back by Alpha Club by 1978. They needed the sum of $2,525 for kitchen and door improvements. Alpha Club members, optimistic as usual, agreed to this plan and the work was done.

Immediately after the work was completed, members began forming committees and preparing their own luncheons, desserts and decorations every month, as a way to save money for the clubhouse. Another way to make money was by starting Marathon Bridge in the fall of 1971. Funds received monthly from that bridge group went to pay off promissory notes. Where there's a will, there's always a way!

On February 13, 1971, Harriet Adam is shown in a picture in the Lompoc Record, breaking ground for a campfire ring at the Kenneth L. Adam Park, for the use of 23 Girl Scout Troops of the Lompoc Neighborhood. Harriet had been publisher of the Record for five years by then and was doing well. She still maintained her membership in Alpha Club and attended meetings when she could. Her biggest contribution, at that time, was getting almost everything noteworthy that Alpha Club did into the paper.

Another issue the new president, Mildred Joy, planned to tackle was "to bring better fellowship among the members." "Our membership had dropped off and lack of interest was apparent ... there has been some improvement ... however, most of the members are still reluctant to accept any office or chairmanship with responsibility."[1] I'm told that after the kitchen remodel and members started preparing their own luncheons, membership improved greatly. It appears a simple matter of good food and a few promissory notes can work wonders! A newcomer, who needed no persuasion to take on membership in the club, was Mary Lou Parks.

Mary Lou Parks was born during the Depression, July 10, 1934 in Yankton, South Dakota. She moved with her parents and baby brother to Sioux City, Iowa in time for kindergarten and grew up there, graduating from Heelan High School. She got her nursing degree from St. Catherine's School of Nursing, associated with Creighton University in Omaha Nebraska, becoming a registered nurse. She then married Tom, whom she met at Creighton. They married in January 1957 and had four children. Mary Lou was one of those young women who returned to school to work toward getting her college degree in the late sixties, but put her plan on hold to move to Lompoc. She was hopeful that she could continue toward that goal in California. Mary Lou was tall and thin (in those days) had brown curly hair, with just a hint of grey when she arrived, in Lompoc in May 1971.

Mary Lou was invited to join Alpha Club. The cut-off for Junior Alpha was 35 years at that time and she had just turned 37. Mary Lou and her husband had lived in Nebraska and moved for his new job as Economic Development Director of Lompoc. She was excited to move to Lompoc and remembered coming through the area when she was 15, on a family trip from Iowa. She had never forgotten the beautiful Central Coast area and felt like she had died and gone to heaven when they arrived. Seeing Lompoc nestled in its beautiful valley after traveling across the west to San Francisco and then down the coast, she could imagine how the pioneer families must have felt. Well sort of, the early pioneers didn't have motels and cars![2]

A new activity, organized in May of 1971, was a travel group that named themselves the "Roadrunners." Sometimes, as many as 45 members would go along for a pleasurable trip to a secret lake in an upper valley, an interesting ranch in a hidden canyon or a tavern on the upside of a high mountain. There would always be lunch or dinner and maybe even some live theater. There were always plenty of places to explore around the Central Coast. There still are.

A very active home and garden section continued to hold meetings on the fourth Wednesday at the clubhouse and occasionally someone's home. They served each other a lunch and did flower arranging, as well as entertained a few guest speakers.

The flower show's theme in 1971 was "Fairy Tales in Flowers." Irma Henderson made the record for chairing six flower shows. Louisa Van Ausdal won the arrangement sweepstakes. Mary Lou Parks attended with her family, amazed at all the beautiful flowers. She had always liked flowers and planted them whenever possible, but they grew for such a short time back in the midwest. Driving around the flower fields was unbelievable. She and her husband kept raving to people back home.

In September 1971, the regular garden party and style show featured at-home costumes and lingerie. It was held at a member's home and garden. Some of the club's oldest members were models, including Dale Laubly. Alpha always enjoyed a good fashion show and why have young models? We're more interested to see how older women, like us, look in these clothes. We can dream, can't we? Marguerite, who was 84 years old by then, continued to make up corsages for the new members and the president each luncheon.

At a membership tea for the new club year in September, 1971, each chair of a committee or section was made up to depict a famous television or movie star and gave a short speech describing the project she was chairing. Also in September, Marguerite went on a Roadrunner trip to Mattie's Tavern with Dale Laubly and a number of other members, even though she was worried about Hattie who was not well. Marguerite was always willing to have a good time. She knew how to keep her life balanced.

When Mary Lou entered the Alpha Club that first day as a luncheon guest, she was sure she had somehow time traveled back a few decades. Club members didn't seem to be so rushed. They were very friendly and interested in each other and all the things she hadn't had time for as a young nurse and mother. There was a garden section, a literature and drama section, the travel group and art appreciation. There was a whole room full of potential new friends. She knew immediately she was going to love living in Lompoc.

In fall of 1971, a committee was working to update the by-laws and they would read them and ask for approval of each new change at meetings. This had to be done from time to time. Over the years, many members had taken the time and interest to revise and re-write the club's by-laws just like Emily Bissinger had all those years ago.

In late December of 1971, Hattie Smith died at Lompoc Hospital. Marguerite was relieved. It had been hard to watch

Hattie grow weaker, becoming so frail. She would miss her terribly, but knew Hattie had been ready. It was her time. Marguerite hoped she would go quickly, when it was her time. She still felt strong and vital at age 84. We are grateful she did because it gave old friends more time with her and some of us newcomers a chance to meet and get to know her a little. Enough so that she was never forgotten.

For the January 1972 club meeting, a play was presented from Sir Walter Scott's narrative poem, "Marmion" that inspired the characters and plot of "Lochinvar." According to the Lompoc Record article, "Costuming proved half the fun, the 'slapstick' approach, the rest. Playing the lead role of Lochinvar and directing rehearsals was Mrs. Tom (Mary Lou) Parks." (Even the paper is now including our first names!) "Others in the fast paced play were: Joy Batchelor; the bride, Theo Clayton the jilted bridegroom; Sandra Johnson and Claudia Short; the brides parents, Norma Kertcher and Louisa Van Ausdal; her brothers, Laney Kahler: the bridesman, Betty Palmer and Alyce Martin; bridesmaidens. Fairest Decker was the announcer and narrator."[3]

When Louisa Van Ausdal was being interviewed for this book, she recalled the fun we had when shown the picture of this play. It was crazy fun; we knew how to enjoy each other back then. Now, we seem to rush though everything so fast, we wonder if we could slow down a bit, we might enjoy ourselves more.

Now that Gene Holmdahl was not Alpha's president anymore, she decided to take on the chairmanship of the flower show for four consecutive years, 1972–75.

The March meeting entertainment was the popular fashion show that members put on for themselves. Clothes were from Moore's and models, this time, came from a local modeling school. It took some time for Alpha Club to start putting on a large fashion show for the public. We have a great fashion show now, and it is $30 a person for lunch and the show.

Spanish Doll dancers lent color and interest as decorations on the tables, at the April, 1972 meeting. Décor was furnished by Louisa. The Librarian, Paul Thompson displayed topical books available at the library in honor of National Library Week and Alpha promised fresh flowers would be delivered all during the special week. Guests were special Spanish speaking students, who showed slides of their recent trip to Mazatlan.

In May, Gene Holmdahl's husband Walter, "roasted a whole pig for Alpha Club's luau feast, which was the piece de resistance for the Luau, hosted by Alpha Club. Other treats were fresh poached salmon salad, baked chicken in wine sauce, yam casseroles, watermelon baskets filled with fresh fruit balls, broiled bananas, hot breads and coconut spice cake. The evening was attuned to the island theme with a profusion of flowers, and guests dressed in Hawaiian attire. . . ."[4] We wish we hadn't missed that, as it sounds absolutely divine!

The California CLUBWOMAN for April and May announced the 69th Annual convention: THE GREATEST SHOW ON EARTH, for May 8–11, 1972 at the Disneyland Hotel, Anaheim, California. The president's page contains her contemplation, a part of which that says:

> Today a woman's club must of necessity wear the new look of a service organization, dedicated to the task of making a reality of the American dream of equal opportunity and a satisfying life for all citizens in every community of the nation. —Carolyn Cunningham, President, CFWC.

Even in Lompoc, it has always been difficult to find equal opportunity, so that all of our citizens could live a satisfying life. Lompoc has never seemed as segregated as in some other places, however. When Camp Cooke grew into a large Air Force Base and Aerospace complex, and people came from all over, many stayed to retire here. The community's multicultural citizenry grew and integrated fairly well to outward appearances. There were, however, problems that appear to come in waves. It seems we are in the middle of another wave now, due to the large immigration of our neighbors from Mexico, which has caused some hostility. In writing this story, we have discovered that as the nation goes, so goes the town. So we were not surprised to find just how much segregation there had been in Lompoc, over the years.

Working with Gene Holmdahl on the flower shows was quite an experience. One year, 1972 or 73, it was extremely hot the week of the flower show. The day we were setting up, Thursday, it must have been about 98 degrees, which is very rare in Lompoc. Everyone was afraid the flowers would wilt in people's gardens before they could bring them to the show and/or wilt when they were placed in the Veterans Hall, because there wasn't (and still isn't) any air-conditioning. Some of us were wearing shorts and that was almost unheard of then. As some of the youngest members, (Alyce and Mary Lou) we tried to do most of the heavy lifting and carrying to set up the show, so none of the older women would have a heat stroke or heart attack in the dreadful heat.

To start the day off, Gene and a few other members, had brought in plenty of food to snack on. There were fried chicken parts, small sandwiches, bowls of fruit and plenty of cold soda and of course, coffee. To Gene it was like working on the ranch, just keep the workers fed and they will get the job done!

That June of 1972, Alpha Club celebrated "50 Years of Sports and Flowers" the golden anniversary of the Alpha Club Flower Show and the 20th anniversary of the flower festival. Gene Holmdahl co-chaired the flower show with Mrs. Dale Batchelor.

A Golden Anniversary Award was presented by Gene Holmdahl to Marguerite Hall, chair of the first flower show in 1922. There is a great picture in the Alpha scrapbook of Marguerite, who is all smiles as usual, presenting an award to the local Catholic priest, Father Andrew McGrath, the winner of the best dahlia bloom, reminiscent of that first flower show.

Another picture, in the Lompoc Record, shows Hazel McCabe walking amongst a dahlia garden reminiscing about the first flower show. She entered the very first show and continued to enter every year for those 50 years.

In July, a picture of the usual summer picnic of the home and garden section shows Hazel McCabe, Marguerite and two other older women. One, a Mrs. Florence Talbert, was a special guest of Gene Holmdahl's' who bought Mrs. Talbert's ranch 19 years earlier. Hazel has gone modern and is wearing slacks, but Marguerite is still wearing a dress.

In October 1972 the literature and drama section decided to hold a creative writing contest for senior citizens over 50 years, announced by Mary Lou Parks and Angeline Weil, co-chairmen of the group. (It's amusing to us, now, to think we thought anyone over 50 was a senior. Our own children are mostly over 50 these days and they are still so young!)

President's day on November 22, 1972 finds fourteen past presidents grouped in the clubhouse. Marguerite and Hazel are sitting in front with three others and Gene is in the back row, standing behind Hazel. All are wearing dresses for the occasion.

The Roadrunners took a trip up to Santa Maria on November 27 to be guests of Allan Hancock College Drama Division. A conducted tour was given of the backstage area to see how a production is put together. We remember how much fun that trip was. Most of us were interested in theater; putting on our little plays, but we had never been backstage in such a prestigious place as the PCPA (Pacific Conservatory of Performing Arts)

On Wednesday, December 20, 1972, we presented a one-act play, "Good Will Towards Women," at the general meeting as part of a special Christmas program. The cast was made up of Junior and Senior Alphas including Alyce Martin and was directed by Mary Lou Parks. The play was "filled with bright dialogue, good characterizations and excellent philosophy."[5] We had a great time working on this play. We would rehearse during school hours so that those of us who had school age children could be home when school ended. Most of the characters wore the popular Christmassy long plaid skirts and/or vests of the day. Some wore slacks.

In January 1973, junior and senior members celebrated a party designated, "Twelfth Night." It was a version of the Escort potlucks of the past. At the board meeting, plans were made for the month. At the general meeting the program would be "Jewelry Art." The Roadrunners planned an evening of contemporary music and dance on January 26. Selections from modern musicals such as "Hair, Curlie and Jesus Christ Superstar were to be the fare at the Timbers Restaurant, Winchester Canyon Road off Highway 101 in Goleta with a great dinner planned of beef-en-brochette.

At the March Alpha meeting and luncheon, a guest spoke on "Responsible Citizenship." A group planned to attend CFWC, Tierra Adorada District Fine Arts Festival, at the end of the month and a hat contest was to be part of the festival. Members met to be milliners for a day and designed creations for the competition. There we go with the hats again. It seems like an addiction. We just can't stop, until we finally did!

In April 1973, a group of members, including Gene Holmdahl, spent time preparing flower show brochures that included flower seed packets to take to the district convention on the 25th – 26th of April. On April 10, the winners of Alpha's writers contest for seniors, pictures and all, appeared in the Lompoc Record. They were to be luncheon guests and receive their awards the next Wednesday. "Mrs. Tom (Mary Lou) Parks, literature and drama department chairman of Alpha Club, directed the contest. Following her introductions, Mrs. Harry (Mildred) Joy, Alpha president, will make the presentations. Courtesy judges for the contest included Bernard Moulton, Mrs. Kenneth Adam and Mrs. R. L. Snyder." We can't remember what the awards were, but the contest was a lot of fun for those who entered and even those who put it on.

On June 16, 1973, the week before flower festival, Harriet Hall Adam married James McCollum. The groom was a former newspaperman, who in 1973 was manager of the Public Information Department of Pacific Gas and Electric Company at their headquarters in San Francisco. The couple planned to make their home in Piedmont.

Harriet's mother, Marguerite, and the groom's father, gave the couple in marriage. In the article that goes on to describe Harriet's dress and the music played at the ceremony, which was held at St. Mary's Episcopal Church, there is as much to say about Harriet, her life and her career, as the groom's. A very balanced report of the new couple, we think. But then, she was the publisher of the newspaper! Harriet resigned from Alpha Club, but planned to come to Lompoc frequently to keep her eye on the newspaper, as her son Rennie Adam took over.[6]

"Heroes of the West" was the theme for the 1973 flower show. Gene Holmdahl was chair again. Dahlias were making a comeback at this show and Gene encouraged members to plant them. Her husband Walter decorated their buggy with the fringe on top with flowers and pulled it by mules for the parade, with such passengers as: "Sitting Bull," "The Hanging Judge," "Diamond Lil," "Calamity Jane," and "Will Rogers" portrayed by club members and their husbands. What a fun way to advertise the flower show.

The membership tea in October, 1973 was held at the home of Mrs. Joseph (June) Schwartz. Her neighbor and sister member of Alpha, Louisa, did floral arrangements throughout the house that uniquely depicted various interest groups and sections of the club: bridge, home and garden, travel, literature and drama, religion, music and art.

There were 151 members in the senior club, but only 26 members in juniors! Louisa Van Ausdal must have been planning to travel again, that year, as she is listed as an associate member.

Gene Holmdahl had become an expert on chairing the flower show and gave a talk to the home and garden section in October on how to plant and grow bulbs.

Sunday, October 28, 1973 was proclaimed "senior Seniors Day" by the current mayor, E. C. Stevens. Anyone over the age of 80 was considered worthy of honor at city hall. A committee served sandwiches, cookies, coffee and a specially decorated cake. Alpha Club members made corsages and boutonnieres for the guests of honor, as well as furnishing fresh flowers for table decorations.

On November 2–3, 1973 the Alpha Club held its first boutique at the clubhouse. Alyce Martin was one of the members who made the many items for sale; knitted clothing, baby sets, pillows, Christmas decorations, jewelry, and much more. We always enjoy a craft boutique and are happy that Alyce has started up the arts and crafts committee again in 2010–11.

New Year's Eve, 1973–74, the City of Lompoc held a centennial ball at the Veterans Hall. A committee was formed that included Alpha Club members and others from the community. It was a costume ball and we remember wearing a 1920s flapper dress and accessories. It was attended by everyone who could get tickets and was a huge success. We remember a long line formed to do the "Bunny hop" all the way through the big hall, down through the foyer, to the left through the tea room and back. It was a magical night. What fun we all had!

Marguerite Hall was chosen by the city as Lompoc centennial year "First Lady." She held the honor for the entire year with a lot of fuss and bother, which she somewhat liked. She missed her daughter, Harriet, and even though she came often that year, it wasn't the same as having her right here within shouting distance all the time. Getting all that attention as "First Lady" didn't hurt.

February 16, 1974, Alpha held a gala night at the Royal Coach restaurant. The evening included a cocktail hour, dinner and a program. At the monthly meeting, a Humorist spoke who said, "She has addressed over 500 clubs and has always managed to be funnier than a treasurer's report."

Alpha usually puts months of work into getting ready for each year's flower show every year, and it shows. In the Monday April 22, 1974 Lompoc Record, there's a picture of Max Van Ausdal, who has returned with Louisa from places abroad. He's holding his planned entry (a bottle of whiskey and some flowers) for the "Men's" table at the flower show. The theme was Temperance, which was always fun. In the picture, everyone is "hamming it up" as Max discusses his entry with Mrs. Frank Anderson and Mary Lou Parks. An expert from Seal Beach, who was a qualified professional flower show judge, came to teach flower arranging on a weekend in early April.

For several years, Louisa Van Ausdal rounded up children in her neighborhood and taught them flower arranging in her garage. She is quoted as saying, "Flowers bring me so much joy and I like to see them used. That's why I like to help the young people who are interested. The children are learning to love nature, when they see that just a few sprigs of greenery and two or three flowers can make a full arrangement, it becomes fascinating. I think they like the competitive nature of the show, too." Louisa's method with the children was to let each workshop progress until the "feel" of flower arranging was accomplished.

The flower festival's theme was the celebration of "The First 100 Years" of Lompoc. The parade marshal was David Burpee, son of W. Atlee Burpee and owner of the W. Atlee Burpee Company. The flower show's theme was "A Floral Salute to the Centennial." Terrariums were introduced as a new category in the specimen division. Admission prices were still only $1 and Alpha Club gave 10 percent of its profit to the festival association, as it had for the past several years. Gene Holmdahl was chairman again and Louisa won best of show.

In October 1974, Marguerite is shown receiving an invitation from Nell Poorbaugh, who is chair of gerontology for Alpha

Club. As Lompoc centennial's "First Lady," Marguerite received the first invitation in person at her home for the "senior Seniors'" annual party. There's another picture taken around that time of Marguerite holding one of her great-grandsons, and a few others of her with two granddaughters, sight seeing somewhere. She was 87 by this time! Marguerite represented the flower seed industry in those days. She was a highly respected citizen of Lompoc and one of it's oldest.

Another person involved with the flower seed industry arrived in Lompoc shortly after her September 1974 wedding to William Scott, president of Denholm Seed Company.

Marjorie Scott was born on July 19, 1925 in Genoa, Nevada, where she spent her childhood. Genoa was originally known as Mormon Station, Utah Territory, founded as the immigrants were coming to the gold and silver mines of Nevada. Marge went to work for the Farm Bureau Office, when she graduated from high school in Genoa, but soon moved to Reno to attend Business College. After Business College, Marge went to work as an executive secretary for an attorney, with whom she worked for thirty years.

Marge married William Scott in Reno in September 1974, and immediately moved to Lompoc. Marge was a beautiful woman of 49, tall and slender with dark eyes and a lovely complexion. She wore her platinum blond hair in a very fashionable sweep and dressed like a model. Being the new wife of an executive in the flower seed business was exciting in a small town like Lompoc. It offered immediate status and, of course, invitations to join many of the women's clubs in town. Marge was more than happy to join Alpha Club so she could meet new friends and become part of a club that put on renowned flower shows. After a thirty year career working in the law business, she also felt it would be a nice change to be working with flowers instead.

Marge was skilled and confident, and got right to work learning all about the club. Even though Marge spent a good share of time entertaining the many foreign visitors who came to see the flower fields and traveling with her husband, she took on responsibility as a club member quickly. Marge, like some of the other members along the way, was able to jump right into club affairs, contributing whenever she could.[7]

The following is a somewhat humorous feature by Stan Tulledo at the Lompoc Record from November 1974. It is but a small example of a typical luncheon and meeting in the middle seventies at Alpha Club. We wanted to share this piece with you because some of us were there and feel it gives the flavor of the club at that time. Enjoy!

> Now if you should ever have the opportunity to attend an Alpha Club meeting, you should do it. The Alpha Club is not what you think if you think they are only devoted to flowers and putting on the … flower show as they have done for the past 52 years….
>
> Last Wednesday, the ladies of Alpha Club finished lunch at their clubhouse and filed into the meeting room, carrying folding chairs and the din of 40 to 50 conversations. They turned the chairs to face the front.
>
> I had the good fortune of having Mrs. Lucille Baker sitting next to me. She answered my questions.
>
> In one corner was a table. It was covered with sundries—knitted hats, Christmas decorations, stocking fillers, various novelty items—all handmade.
>
> "What is all that for?" I asked.
>
> "Oh, that was left over from the bazaar," Mrs. Baker said kindly.
>
> What bazaar I didn't know, but I asked, "What do you do with the money made?"

"It goes for scholarships."

The meeting had already commenced and Mrs. Tom Parks, (Mary Lou) eventually stood up with a red coffee can in her hands. She told how money was needed to buy ingredients for Christmas and Thanksgiving pies for senior citizens in Lompoc. The Girl's Club has agreed to make the pies if others provide the makings.

"Most of these are little old men who don't have wives anymore, and all they'll be getting for Christmas is a pie," said Mrs. Parks.

That was enough. The room of well-groomed and handsomely dressed ladies popped open their purses and coins began to jingle.

"Anything will be appreciated, a dime, or a quarter," she continued. "Fine if you can, if you can't that's alright too."

Other business transpired. Fourteen beaming new members were presented to the membership.... Big applause.

Next, a member stood up and announced that Friday is the day to give blood at the Alpha Club .... "Please give if you can," this member urged. "Last month we had 28 donors and usually we get more than that. You only have to be between the ages of 18 and 60...." She hesitated, looked around the room, and smiled. Someone suggested aloud, "Maybe that's the reason." A burst of laughter from everyone in the room punctuated the comment.

After the laughter subsided, Mrs. DeAtley, (the president,) reminded the membership that a chair was "desperately" needed to "tie up the ends and run with the ball" for the 1975 flower show. No lady to date had volunteered. "That's an awful lot of work," Mrs. Baker whispered to me.

> As if to change the subject, a member asked if Alpha Club was going to help the veterans again this Christmas. Mrs. Max Van Ausdal (Louisa), chairwoman of the veteran's affairs committee, answered the question and startled the room. She reported the female veterans in some wards in Southern California hospitals received so many gifts last year that nurses were known to have taken gifts home. So, she, Louisa, was going to investigate where the need is and then inform the club.
>
> See! The Alpha Club ladies quietly donate time, blood, and money to help others when all you think of them doing is arranging a flower show.
>
> Senior citizens will have Christmas pie, the Tri-Counties Blood Bank will get blood, and women veterans will receive holiday gifts because of the Alpha Club ladies.

On the next page in the Alpha scrapbook, there's a picture of a little girl taking pies out of the oven with two senior gentlemen watching. The pies were served by the Girls Club for Thanksgiving and Christmas.

By September 1974, Mary Lou Parks had taken on a job at the local level of a newly funded national aging program for senior citizens over 60. It involved a hot meal program five days a week, outreach, information and referral and transportation services. A local office had been set up and the program was administered under the Community Action Commission. The pies were served at the Lompoc Senior Congregate hot meal site.

In late January 1975, preparations began for Alpha Club to celebrate its diamond jubilee as a charter member of the California Federation of Women's Clubs, with a tea. City and Vandenberg AFB officials and dignitaries would be invited guests, as would officials of the state and district federation and past presidents of the club. Members went all out preparing favors, tea sandwiches and petit fours. Marguerite is pictured with the current president looking on, at an assembly of pictures of club past presidents, set up on an easel. She and Dale Laubly, long time members, were both special guests. Marguerite was one month short of 88 years old, at the time.

In February 1975, the Lompoc Record ran a series of articles that included some minutes of Alpha Club meetings from the early days, all the way up to the present.

In April 1975, Alpha Junior members made it their job to attend to elderly seniors on their respective birthdays by baking and serving them a cake and having a little party for them in the Long Term Care Unit of the hospital.

Gene Holmdahl was flower show chair one more time in 1975 when the theme was "Happiness is." The theme for the flower festival was "Good Old Golden Rule Days," so we at Alpha just combined the two: "Happiness is: Good Old Golden Rule Days." We remember the fun we had going all over town, the Village and Vandenberg Base taking pictures of each and every school in Lompoc. We fastened the pictures up on the bulletin board at the back of the classroom we had fashioned in the foyer. We put an old-fashioned school desk in the middle of our exhibit and stood a mannequin from Moore's Department Store next to the desk. We dressed the mannequin in 1900 style clothes; a long black skirt with a white blouse that had a high collar ruffled at the top. She had her hair pulled back into a bun, wore nose glasses and held a pointer toward the bulletin board of school pictures with the combined themes lettered on the top.

There was something missing we thought, oh yes, flowers! Marguerite was especially interested in the display as it reminded her of her own early days as a teacher in Lompoc. She wanted to help so she offered any flowers we wanted out of her front yard. We picked Matilija poppies, those lovely large floppy white poppies with the yellow centers that grow so abundantly here in Lompoc in the spring. We put them in white buckets and enclosed the whole scene with a small white wooden chain fence.

There's a picture of two Alpha members, sitting at the desk with the newly installed President Laurel Beaudry, standing next to the "dummy" teacher. Below that picture, there is one of Louisa serving tea with Irma Henderson and a third one of Gene standing next to an award winning shadow box with the winner.

It was early in the summer of 1975 that we began to hear on our local radio station about some vineyards being planted in the Los Alamos area. Remember when we actually had a local station? The idea of vineyards this far south was new. Everyone was used to traveling north toward San Francisco and Napa Valley to taste California wines, but this was enticing. We could have wine *and* flowers, how delightful!

It was a bittersweet time for Mary Lou, as she would soon be moving to the Los Angeles area, where her husband was now working. There were no words to describe how badly she wanted to stay in Lompoc and with Alpha, but like so many other women, Nina Rudolph for one, she had no choice. The Alpha members held a going-away party at Arleen Harris' home at the end of July and the movers arrived the first week of August.

Club year 1975–76 began with Marge Scott's friend Laurel Beaudry as president. Alyce was craft chairman and Louisa served as Community Improvement Program chair. Gene Holmdahl was elected first vice president of the Tierra Adorada district. The September program at the club was: "All the Flowers of Tomorrow Are in the Seeds of Today."

The November program for the club was given by Mr. Stanley M. Roden, district attorney of Santa Barbara County, speaking on consumer fraud, which was starting to become a noticeable problem.

By club year 1975–76 the junior club was down to only 18 members and three of those were now Associate members, trying to hang on to their membership while getting into the job market. So many younger women were dropping out of junior clubs due to the desire to try their wings in what was known as the "real world." They were determined to try "bringing home the bacon."

There are not nearly as many articles in the Lompoc Record in 1975–76. We knew all the publicity would run dry fairly soon, after Harriet Hall Adam McCollum left the area.

In January, 1976 DeWayne Holmdahl, Gene's son, gave a presentation for the club on African Farming with movies. Dale Laubly hosted the home and garden committee's meeting on January 28, which gave instructions on how to prune roses and shrubs by Mike Farcia from Pines Nursery. The Roadrunners went to the Atascadero Museum, plus visited the shops at the Discount Mall. (Which was even more fun!)

In May there were three Flower Arranging Seminars given by Eunice Antosik. As usual, the Alpha members were always interested in staying sharp and helping out others in the community who wished to enter the show.

The flower show in 1976 celebrated the country's "Heritage and Horizons, "as it was the bicentennial celebration. Decorations in the Veterans Hall included "Betsy Ross in old-fashioned dress, dust cap and apron, in a rocker, sewing an American flag. A drop-leaf table held wooden spools of thread, and gold-fringed American and California state flags completed the setting," designed by Chuck's Nursery. Club experts, Evelyn Cameron and Louisa Van Ausdal tied for the sweepstakes award, so they tossed a coin and Louisa won the silver trophy. Back then, the prizes were silver; now they are crystal.

After the flower show, the club rests for two months, but some members never do. Under chair Alyce Martin, the craft section worked all summer building and furnishing a miniature scale model doll house. Alpha Club's "little house" contained six rooms and a sun deck. There was a living room, dining room, kitchen, bath, bedroom and attic rumpus room. Each room was cleverly furnished with hand made rugs, furniture, curtains and light fixtures, as well as wall decorations and miscellaneous items to complete the décor. The house itself was built by John Miller, husband of member Lois. Helping make all the tiny accessories and furnishings were at least 20 Alpha members.

What would they do with it when it was finished? Well, auction it off, what else? For $1 a ticket the profit would fund some of their many philanthropic projects. That summer Bertha Moore decided she could no longer keep up the pace as a regular member of Alpha, at the age of 80, so she became an Honorary Member like her mother-in-law, Anna, before her. She planned to continue attending meetings and special events when she could.

At the board meeting in early September 1976, it was proposed that Alpha hold an evening section for those who are unable to attend daytime meetings. It sounds like some members of Alpha were trying to accommodate younger members who were working outside the home so they wouldn't have to resign. It's interesting that in the early days, the club needed to hold meetings on Saturdays to accommodate members, but as time went on, and life gradually became easier for homemakers so it seemed logical to hold meetings on a weekday, during the daytime. In 1976 women's lives were changing again. Many were now working outside the home, at least part-time, and could no longer attend meetings or help with many projects. Life is funny it seems "the more things change the more they stay the same." We also think that what once seemed old can now seem new again.

The first meeting of the new club year was also a membership luncheon. Marge Scott was first vice president for the club year.

The home and garden section had a member guest speaker in October. Peggy Maraszek vividly described a trip to the Holy Land. The group was also treated to a slide show of a tour of the United States, and especially California, and Hazel McCabe displayed her paintings and encouraged others to take up one of her special interests. Hazel was involved in the Pioneer Society (later the Historical Society) and the Order of the Eastern Star, as well as Alpha. Like Bertha Moore, Hazel too, was 80.

In November, the Senior and Junior Alpha Clubs had an "Apple Frolic." The affair was held at the clubhouse. Apple cider punch was served by Gene Holmdahl, president of Tierra Adorada District. Dinner salads, hot dishes and apple desserts comprised the menu. The event was for members only. Apparently, there were no more escort dinners.

For the January 1977 meeting, the club was decorated in red, white and blue. The placemats were copies of the Declaration of Independence and a scattering of peanuts were strewn down each table. This was in honor of Jimmy Carter's inauguration that month. There were 77 attendees and three guests.

In February, the Roadrunners took a trip to Los Angeles to Descanso Gardens in La Cañada, and then to the Huntington Library and Gardens in Pasadena. Camellias were in bloom at both sites. They had lunch at a restaurant in between stops. What a lovely day they had. We're sure they came home with many new ideas for their own gardens. Especially interesting to try would be the amazing variety of succulents at the Huntington Gardens.

In March 1977, Louisa spoke to the American Business Women's Association in Lompoc. Her program was on flower arranging, with both a talk and a demonstration. Naturally, her audience was invited to enter displays for the flower show coming up in June.

It was time for some fun at the home and garden section's "Taste Teaser." A picture shows six members entertaining with a crazy fashion show including Marge Scott and Alyce Martin, Peggy Maraszek, and others. The event was a food judging of favorite recipes. Desserts were judged while they ate and watched the fashion show. It sounds like a hilarious afternoon, as everyone hammed it up.

Hazel McCabe is pictured with Laurel Beaudry in the Lompoc Record issue, April 26, 1977, as having served as presidents of Alpha. Hazel in 1927 and Laurel in 1977, a fifty-year span. Hazel was voted an Honorary Member of the club at that time.

At CFWC, Alpha won many achievement awards as usual, but this year seemed to be especially focused on the "happy homemaker," with sewing, cooking and, of course, flower design. Women are always interested in these creative activities no matter how busy they are. Martha Stewart knows this.

The flower show theme in 1977 was "New Horizons." Irma Henderson again chaired the show and is quoted as saying, "Fifty-five years of flower shows and there's always something to learn each time we prepare for Alpha Club's annual event."[8] Complementing the flower festival was the opening of the Lompoc Museum's new exhibit entitled, "The Story of Lompoc Valley's Seed Industry." You can bet that Marguerite helped with the story. She was a member of the Pioneer Society and wrote a story of Lompoc's early days, parts of which were used. Louisa was grand marshal of the parade, along with local cardiologist, Dr. Barry Coughlin.

Marge Scott was president for the new club year, 1977–78, and Alyce Martin was first vice president. Marge chose an international theme for the club that year because of her experience traveling all over the world with her husband and entertaining many foreign guests as well. At the September meeting, Robert Veers was the guest speaker and presented a program called, "Vagabonds." He showed a slide show that took everyone "Around the World." Many older members of Alpha could say they were or had been "vagabonds." Louisa certainly was a vagabond, as was Hazel. Travel has always seemed very popular for older persons who were employed at Vandenberg.

October 19 was "United Nations Day" at the club with Filipino-American dancers entertaining. Marguerite's name continues to be listed as an active member of the club and, in fact, she was on the February luncheon committee in 1978. But she had not been feeling well.

About the first of November, Marguerite went into Lompoc Hospital. Word got around that she was failing. Her daughter,

Harriet, left for a planned trip to Europe and Harriet's son, Rennie Adam, who was then running the Lompoc Record, remembers going to visit his grandmother every 3 or 4 days and they would talk about life in Lompoc. Rennie doesn't remember exactly what was wrong, but the family knew Marguerite was dying. She remained lucid, as she grew weaker.

On November 16, 1977, a club day, the Lompoc Record announced that Marguerite had died the night before at Lompoc Hospital at the age of 90. She was the oldest living native of Lompoc at the time. The next day at the club, members held a moment of silence at her passing. Marguerite had been a member of Alpha Club for 66 years and her contributions were immense. Harriet did not get back in time, but that's the way Marguerite would have wanted it.

A letter was written to the Safety Division of the Tierra Adorada District in response to their request from the safety chair to Alpha Club president, Marge Scott, to find out if the schools in Lompoc were using the "Mini Course on Alcohol." Marge reported that the course was available at the Auto Association office and that the schools had been notified of this, but neither school had responded. Alpha had another cause. Although the effects of alcohol were included in the schools' curriculum, there was no active program, so members of the club formed a committee to try to persuade school authorities that more needed to be done. Instructional programs were started after that and we would like to think that the modern version of teen age driving safety, "Every 15 Minutes," evolved from that nudge.

In the spring of 1978, the club was also asked to take on the issue of fire detectors in the homes and they pursued a project to get residents in a condominium development to install the detectors and get their group fire insurance reduced.

In May, word came that Helen Rudolph had died on May 11 in Lomita near her home in Long Beach. She was a month short of 84 years old. Another death took place just before the flower show on June 18, when Bertha Moore passed on. She died before the Alpha Flower Show but had somewhat of a flower show of her own at her funeral. So many people attended, that the church was filled with beautiful flowers in her honor.

The 1978 flower show theme was "Holidays in Flowers." Alpha members made long pale blue skirts with matching vests adorned with appliquéd flowers of their own design. They wore the "uniform" during the show, so that show goers could recognize who was in charge and who to ask questions. We like the matching outfits idea, but that's a lot of work for just one weekend. Who knows if the outfit would fit again the next year?

Gene Holmdahl gave an extensive report on a proposed clubhouse remodeling project to allow more room for activities and to upgrade safety features. The partial wall between the clubroom and the tea room and the double doors used for separation would be removed and replaced with a folding door. Two more outside doors to the clubhouse would be added for fire safety, so that each of the main rooms would have two doors without using the kitchen for an exit. The tea room door on the south west side would have steps and landing, with a wrought iron railing. This would be done to meet fire safety codes. The extra door on the northwest wall would have a ramp for the handicapped.

The work agreement was signed by Frank Signorelli on December 4, 1978. The cost would be $5,900. The job would be completed within two weeks! This remodel project was paid for the same way other work had been accomplished on the clubhouse, by using promissory notes. When there wasn't enough money in the treasury, club members always managed to pay anyway, even if it came out of their own pockets. It was a good investment!

Alpha Club had a membership coffee, instead of tea, in October 1978 at a member's home. Alyce Martin was president and Marge Scott served on the nominating committee and was co-chair of publicity. The home and garden section program was held on November 1, 1978 at the clubhouse and members were urged to bring some collectible object to display and share. Louisa brought her collection of steins from around the world. She is shown in a picture showing Irma Henderson a crystal stein dating back to 1881. Looks like Alpha Club had their own version of the "Antiques Road Show."

Alyce had her hands full that club year. Her husband retired the month after she took over as president. Even though Perry was a very patient man, he did remark at times that he could never get a phone call in because she was always busy with Alpha calls. Plus, there were two teenagers still at home, so we can just imagine how many times their home phone rang every day. It was almost unheard of for a family to have more than one phone line in their home. A friend we know did put in a phone booth at the end of the hallway with a separate line because they had five daughters!

A Halloween potluck was held October 27 and the annual Christmas bazaar was held on Saturday, November 4. That year the club decided to hold a Christmas potluck for members with surprise entertainment, instead of the regular meeting and luncheon.

The Junior Alpha/Alpha Club luncheon was held Saturday, January 27, 1979. A Gold Rush theme was used by the juniors, who hosted the potluck.

"Lets Go Hollywood" was the theme for the Alpha Club's Hollywood-type gala of days gone by on Saturday evening, February 24, at the Village Country Club. A 1926 Model T pickup was spotlighted at the foot of the steps to the club. Max Van Ausdal was in charge of the car, which was on loan. Dress was period, if one had something. Louisa wore a black evening gown from 1946 and was mistress of ceremonies, as well as having written the script for the program. The club gave out "Alfie Awards." Best actress Alfie went to club president, Alyce Martin and a "Wonder Woman" award went to Marge Scott who, in turn, presented Louisa with the best script writer award. Other "talented club members won awards also…."[9] It must have been a marvelous evening.

An interesting note: Although the local newspaper and others are now referring to women by their own first name and their married last name, we see in Federation's program for the fine arts festival in March, 1979, held in Lompoc, that some women are still being referred to by their husband's name only and some by their own names. It seems to be a toss up at this point.

In May, the club held its annual fashion show for entertainment during the luncheon, as they usually did, with Moore's Department Store furnishing the lovely clothing. Past presidents were also honored, including Marge Scott, Laurel Beaudry and Hazel McCabe who was still an active member of the club. Marge Scott also served as a model for the fashion show.

"Around The World in Flowers," was the theme for the 1979 flower show. Music paired with blossoms in this show. Louisa again won the sweepstakes. Titles included "Arrividerci Roma," "In Muenchen Steht Ein Hofbrauhaus," "A Little Bit of Heaven," Flying Down to Rio," and "Japanese Sandman." Junior entries were "On The Beach At Waikiki."

We can say that was a prediction of things to come for the Junior Alphas as they truly were "beached." They were down to just over a dozen members and although the new president, Lois Miller, worked with the remaining junior group over the summer, by August it was obvious there just weren't enough young women able to join. So many were in the work force they didn't have the time. The decision was made to cancel the junior section for club year 1979–80. It was sad, but wasn't this what the goal of federated women's clubs had been from the beginning? If women were going to be successful in getting the vote and having their work valued the same as men's, wasn't the fact that so many younger women were working, at least part time outside the home, by the late 1970s a good thing?

The new club year 1979–80 started with Lois Miller as president. Gene Holmdahl was serving as parliamentarian of the district and second vice president of the Alpha Club. Marge Scott was editor of the newsletter and photographer.

The membership tea was held on October 12 and the Roadrunners took in a dinner and a show to start off the new club year. Several local clubs, including Alpha Club, helped to fund the new Cardiac Care Unit (CCU) at the hospital.

Alyce Martin was home and garden's chair during Lois's term. She remembers touring Janet Begg's home to see her famous doll collection. Alyce has always had a beautiful home and garden herself, and can tell you the names of most every native plant and flower.

The Equal Pay Act had been passed in 1963 and was implemented in June of 1964, but even in the 1980s women were making only 59 cents for every dollar a man made for the same job. Women have been working toward equal "status," but even now we haven't yet reached it. Currently, in 2011, a woman still makes only 80 cents for every dollar that a man makes for the same job. Even women physicians and attorneys make less for the same work as their male counterparts. We've come a long way "baby," as they used to say, but we aren't there yet!

Part 3

Modern Times

CHAPTER 12

The Communication Era

A whole new way to "keep in touch" descended on us in the eighties. Things got simpler in some ways and more complicated in others. By 1980, there were 3.2 million pagers being used worldwide and by 1990 there were over 22 million. Pagers were liberating in some ways, annoying in others. Physicians and other professionals began carrying them so that they could be instantly contacted in an emergency. This was good. Many other people started carrying them so that they could keep in touch with their office or family while out and about, which was good but sometimes annoying. We experienced the frustration of being on a freeway or on a country road when our pager would go off and it wasn't always easy to get to a phone but we at least knew when someone was trying to reach us! For the first time we experienced the irritation of being interrupted in a conversation with someone when their pager would go off and they would have to excuse themselves to make a call.

The first generation of cell phones became available in the 1980s. They were large and cumbersome and you needed to be near a "cell" tower to receive or make a call, it was a lot like Dick Tracy in the comics, only better than his "two-way wrist radios."

We have had computers around since 1936, but it wasn't until the 1980s that the Personal Computer, (PC) became available. Many of us resisted some of these modern inventions. Why did we need them? We had telephones (land line) and typewriters. We do remember however, the frustration we had when typing a term paper. Every time something needed to be changed we had to start over or "cut and paste." Even trying to write this story using a typewriter was impossible. We are grateful for the typewriter now however, as we pick up on Alpha minutes again, all neatly typed.

The January 1980 club members took on a re-cycling project for the first time. They were reminded to take their newspapers and cans to the re-cycling center or to bring them to the clubhouse on meeting days, which would save gas at the same time. This was the beginning of some serious conservation efforts. After the gas shortage in the early 70s, the prices began to slowly go up and people were worried about supply and demand. Members had started carpools the previous year for out of town events and meetings. Renters of the clubhouse were reminded to keep the thermostat set at the level requested by President Carter.

In February 1980 there were 160 members in Alpha Club. For older women, the club was still the thing. Members continued with another "Antique Fair." This seemed very popular and was a fun way to raise money for club projects, that is, if the antiques held out. In April, Alpha held a "Gala Night," Gene Holmdahl was the chair. This was the beginning of great things to come.

Hazel McCabe died on May 5, 1980 at Lompoc Hospital. She was 84 years old and had been a valued member of Alpha Club for many years. She also contributed her talents and services to several other organizations in Lompoc. Hazel's daughter,

Betty, had been ill before her mother died and in August 1980, club members learned that Betty died as well. Hazel had always held out hope that her daughter would come back into Alpha Club after her re-marriage and her children had grown up but Betty died at age 56, only a few short months after her mother. It was the end of the line for the McCabe women in Alpha.

Only one older member remained. "Toots" Sloan had moved into the Solvang Lutheran Home as she felt she could no longer manage at home and didn't want to be a burden. These older women had given the club so much of their time and energy throughout the years. They would always be missed, but there were new younger members who had come to Lompoc, not as pioneers but as adventurers who had no problem carrying on Alpha's work.

Home and garden section held several flower arranging workshops during the spring months. Louisa was always involved and gave the one for March. At that point in time, home and garden gave an annual home tour in late May every year. This stopped when the hospital started doing their Christmas home tours. We recently started holding a home garden tour in May and it is very popular. People love home tours, especially garden tours in Lompoc. They are always lovely in spring.

"Hands Across the Border" was the theme for the flower show with an unwritten invitation to neighboring counties to participate in the flower show. Little did we realize that within the next 25 years other countries, especially those with similar climates and cheap labor, would take over much of the flower seed industry. Louisa won the sweepstakes again! At the California Federated Women's Conference for 1979–80, Marge Scott won the state award for communications.

There is a copy of an article in the Lompoc Record, July 30, 1980 with a lovely picture of rows of planted flowers growing in a field in Lompoc Valley. The headline reads: "Lompoc is the flower seed capital of the world." The article starts with, "In 1909, when

Robert Rennie … first planted a crop of sweet peas," [We found it was 1908] "the Lompoc Valley was found to have ideal conditions for growing flowers." The article goes on to name the four major growers, Anton Zvolonek, David Denholm, W. Atlee Burpee and Ted Holden. In 1980, three of the companies remained in full production in Lompoc. Things would change slowly over the next thirty years.

In July, Alpha had 42 members and guests at their annual summer picnic at the La Purisima Mission under the shady branches of the oak and walnut trees. After the picnic, a guided tour of the mission was conducted by a docent in full uniform of a Spanish soldier in the seventeen hundreds.

Alpha's October 1980 program started with a slide show by Mildred Joy's husband, Harry, "Seeds For The World." Lois Miller had stepped down from her term as president to become arts and crafts chair and Alyce Martin remained chair of the home and garden section. Alyce demonstrated how to multiply houseplants at her home for their first session.

In the fall, the arts and craft section worked diligently every Thursday morning making over 100 handmade items for the annual Christmas bazaar held in November. They planned on using their profits to pay off some of those promissory notes used to fund the clubhouse remodel two years before. A picture of them working on all sorts of interesting items includes one member with her little five year old pug, Ginger. Ginger was included in many activities with the exception of the regular club meeting, of course.

At the November 1980 luncheon, the guest speaker was Lt. Col. Aubrey Sloan, chief of management division, 6595th Shuttle Group at Vandenberg. He gave club members up-to-date information on comprehensive activation of the space shuttle and its future impact on the community and environment. The highlight of the meeting was honoring long-time members of the club. Those being honored were: Clara, "Toots" Sloan who joined in

1923–24 and Irma Henderson who joined in 1932. Others being honored for many years of membership included Alyce Martin who had been a junior/senior member for 32 years. "Toots" Sloan didn't make the meeting but was happy to be honored.

At the January 1981 Alpha luncheon and meeting, district and state officers were invited to be part of the program exploring the pros and cons of Federation. We're sure this wasn't the first time Alpha members had questions about continuing membership in the federation and we know it wasn't the last. Cost for dues and expenses were going up and some wondered if the club should continue as part of such a large group. Gene Holmdahl was politically savvy and understood what Federation meant to the club.

A high point in Gene's life was when she attended Ronald Reagan's inauguration in Washington DC, even though it meant she would miss this episode of doubt about Federation. Gene knew that some of the members were questioning the value of the federation and she felt newer members needed to understand the history of Alpha's accomplishments under Federation, and the importance of having the larger group to guide the club. Gene was back the next month, when the subject was addressed again at the February 18 club meeting and a two-thirds majority vote determined that members wanted to remain in the General Federation of Women's Clubs.

The March 1981 meeting was hat day again. Past presidents were also honored, a spring fashion show featuring clothes from Moore's Department Store was presented, and those wearing hats were eligible for a free lunch drawing—one way to get some hats at the meeting!

Louisa did a flower arranging class at the Officer's Wives Club on base on March 26 and Alyce Martin and Lois Miller took reservations for the fine arts festival of the Tierra Adorada District, which was held in Lompoc at the Elks Lodge again that year. About 175 women from Santa Barbara, Ventura, and San Luis Obispo Counties attended.

Alpha held another gala dinner and auction on April 11, 1981 at the Elks Lodge. Everyone was dressed to a "T" ready for a delicious dinner of chicken saltimbocca and a lot of dancing. One couple that especially loved to dance was Louisa and Max Van Ausdal.

At the June luncheon, Alpha had installation of new officers after the meal and the meeting. You can imagine how shocked everyone was when during the middle of the ceremony in marched Glen Newcomb (a high school music teacher) and his Big Bean Band.

"Island Memories," was the theme for the 1981 flower show. Harley Craig was grand marshal. He was one of the founders of the flower festival. Louisa won another sweepstakes trophy. Her house was filling up with silver trays, bowls and pitchers.

Dr. Barry Coughlin and Supervisor DeWayne Holmdahl were speakers at the first meeting of the new club year, September 1981. Dr. Coughlin, a cardiologist and hospital trustee, spoke about the expansion of the Convalescent Care Center and Supervisor Holmdahl spoke about the reapportionment of the supervisory boundary lines. We can no longer find anything in the club schedule about the "Roadrunners." The delightful travel group must have exhausted all possible trips or possibly as gasoline prices kept going up they decided that members couldn't afford to go "road running" anymore.

In October the club held their usual fashion show, but stores furnishing clothes were Peggy's Fashions, Village Fashions and Poppy Hill. Moore's Department Store wasn't used this time. It's surprising to us that the club hadn't decided to expand their yearly club fashion show to a public fundraiser. It took a long time for them to realize the great potential in doing that.

In November, the home and garden section toured the Denholm Seed Co. The hostesses were Marge Scott and her friend, member Laurel Beaudry. After a short business meeting with refreshments served, members went to Denholm's where Bill Scott and David Lemon conducted the tour and talk on the propagation of flowers and seeds. It was impossible to live in Lompoc and not learn something about flowers.

Moore's Department Store was the presenter at a home and garden section meeting in February, 1982 with a program entitled: "Setting a Pretty Table." Moore's china and table linens were displayed.

At the June club meeting, Gene Holmdahl was again installed as president of Alpha Club. Gene announced her ambitious plans for the coming club year. She wanted to hold a charity ball in November to benefit construction of the new wing at the Convalescent Care Center. Gene was on the committee to promote bonds for Lompoc District Hospital to add 36 additional rooms on to the Convalescent Care Center and thought it made sense to use the already popular gala ball as a fundraiser for the hospital. Club members loved the idea. Gene put the charity ball together and was chair of the event for the first five years.

Lois Miller, who had become a member of Alpha around 1972–73, was a very talented woman. She loved crafts, wrote poetry and became Gene's right hand woman. She was a clubwoman's version of an Executive Assistant for Gene. Gene was able to do as much as she did because of women like Lois who had her back.

In addition to all this, in 1982–83 Gene served as horticulture superintendent for the flower show at the Santa Barbara County Fair in Santa Maria. That woman was filled with such abundant energy!

The 60th Anniversary of the flower show's title was "Anniversaries in Flowers." Dahlias were the special in the show to honor the very first flower show. A special silver award was given for the "best" Dahlia. Louisa won the sweepstakes award again for best arrangement.

There are some pictures in the 1981–82 scrapbook of a beautiful grove of redwood trees entitled; California Federation of Women's Clubs' Grove. It is off of the "Avenue of Giants" in Humboldt State Park. The 40-acre grove was purchased with funds raised by the California federation in 1931 and was dedicated in 1933 in response to an effort by state federation that started in 1900 to stop lumbermen from cutting down those beautiful trees. In the same photo album next to those pictures, are more pictures of the state convention in 1982 in Palo Alto, with Gene, Barbara Cooperider, Laurel Beaudry and Marge Scott attending. As usual, the only thing written on the page is, "State Convention, 1982." The four women may have driven up to see the grove taking some extra days to enjoy their trip. Clubwomen had learned from men's organizations how to hold great conventions in and near beautiful places.

Marge Scott was publicity chair as well as in charge of Communications in 1981–82 and again in 1982–83.

In November 1982, the Alpha Club held its first annual benefit ball and auction, with profits going toward furnishing one new room at the Convalescent Care Center. Gene Holmdahl chaired the event, assisted by a committee that spent hours planning. Alyce Martin was ticket and reservations chair but also ended up as treasurer when that person quit. At first they planned to have simple refreshments, but knowing Alpha Club, there was soon a gourmet buffet planned. The hospital had been using a "$36 for 36 beds," theme for their bond drive and the Alpha committee chose to use the same theme for their ball.

The cost for the ball would be $36 a couple for the buffet dinner and dancing to a name band. The goal was to get 150 couples and place the entire amount in an investment account until construction of the new wing was completed. Alpha donated their own money to pay for the dinner and dance. The Veterans

Memorial Building was also donated for the event by the board of supervisors. Many donations from the community added to the profits and by the time the building was ready, Alpha had acquired $16,515. Enough to furnish four rooms! With such success it wasn't hard to convince the club to continue this event for a number of years, choosing different recipients each year.

At Christmas time in 1982, it looks like the club put on one of their fabulous plays. There are no captions as usual, but Louisa and Marge are dressed as angels with silver halos. Alyce is dressed as the devil all in red, tail and pitchfork included. It looks silly and fun and we wish we could have been there.

Alpha Club had started having a prayer breakfast in January 1982 and it was quite popular. In 1983 it was held on January 26. Gene suggested that the club hold Presidents Day in February instead of October, which made sense to Alpha members since February already had a designated "President's Holiday" weekend celebrating the country's famous presidents. We have held Alpha Presidents Day in February since 1983.

The 1983 flower show theme was "Yesterday's Headlines," which was fun to do using table titles such as, "Bicentennial," "Mt. St. Helens Erupts," and "Columbia Soars." People love to reminisce.

Alpha members heard by way of the Lompoc Record that Clara, "Toots," Sloan had died on June 22, 1983 in a nursing home in Apple Valley. She had been living at Solvang Lutheran Home but decided when she needed nursing care, to go to Apple Valley because her son's mother-in-law was there as well. Toots' death was the end of an era of Alpha Club Charter members and daughters, daughters-in law and nieces who had been such a vital part of the force that gave Alpha Club its energy and drive.

Alpha still had plenty of drive however, and after all the work that year, members relaxed at the Member's Picnic on July 6 at River Park.

At the September meeting for club year 1983–84, one member was missing from the club book membership list. Louisa Van Ausdal seems to have resigned over some kind of problem. There are always disagreements and contention among people who work together and this holds true for clubwomen. Some members may (in spite of the Collect for Club Women) hold grudges and become envious of other members especially when certain members are talented and seem to win all the awards at the flower show. Whatever it was that affected Louisa must have been perceived as hurtful or she wouldn't have left. In any case we know she was missed.

COLLECT FOR CLUBWOMEN

Keep us O God, from pettiness;
Let us be large in thought, in work, in deed.
Let us be done with fault-finding
And leave off self-seeking.
May we put away all pretense
And meet each other face to face,
Without self-pity and without prejudice.
May we never be hasty in judgment
And always generous.
Let us take time for all things;
Make us to grow calm, serene, gentle.
Teach us to put into action our better impulses,
Straight forward and unafraid.
Grant that we may realize it is
The little things that create differences,
That in the big things of life we are at one.
And may we strive to touch and to know
The great, common human heart of us all.
And, O Lord God, let us forget not
To be kind!

—Mary Stewart, Colorado, 1904

We don't know who Mary Stewart was, but surely she was a member of the federation of women's clubs. We are certain that she wrote that collect for a reason. We are also certain that even though we didn't include moments of friction mentioned in the minutes in earlier times, they did exist. Clubwomen had noble ideas and goals when they organized, but we know that it is not always easy to live life everyday with just those goals in mind. We get caught up in the issues and problems of the day and sometimes succumb to pettiness as all humans do. Every day is a new day and every club year is a new club year, so we can only try to live up to such a Collect.

November finds everyone gearing up for the second benefit ball to be held on the 19th of the month. There was a tremendous amount of planning and work for this size of an event. Club members prepared and served the food as well as arranged for the band, auction items, decorated and determined where the money raised each year would go so that information would go on the posters, tickets and in the paper.

Alpha never turned down a program that would entertain their members no matter how busy, so in November the luncheon/meeting included another fashion show. It was announced that four members would be attending TAD in Oxnard and that all members should keep saving Green Stamps, Betty Crocker coupons, and Campbell Soup labels. Remember when we all saved those? For some of us it was a way to purchase things we otherwise couldn't afford. For Alpha it was a way to raise money. It was announced that Alpha's bazaar and Country Kitchen realized a total of $3,891.79. With our recent start up again of the craft committee it may take a while, but we hope to catch up.

Home and garden reported on the progress of the grounds landscaping project. Removal of trees and roots would cost $300 with the nursery volunteering labor. We wonder how many times we have landscaped and removed and then landscaped again in the seventy-eight years we have been in the clubhouse to date?

A delicious Christmas luncheon was served to 104, with six being guests. It was reported that the benefit ball realized

$20,474.50! That may be the most money Alpha Club ever made from a single event!

Members were reminded that the next TAD meeting would take place on January 26 in Shell Beach. As we write this we realize how fortunate Alpha Club has been over the years. Our town has always turned out for our grand events. The support has been generous and has enabled us to give back in kind. Those of us so inclined get to travel with our friends around this beautiful central coast area to meetings where other club members share information and similar interests.

The club was back to having potlucks for husbands in January 1984. It was announced that the arts and crafts section would sponsor a Valentine's party at the Convalescent Care Center. Alpha not only raised a lot of money to help pay for a new wing at this center but continues to hold this party for the residents even today in 2011.

Members are encouraged to come to the potluck fun night and dress as they like. Hors d'oeuvres were to be served at 6:30 p.m. The club was now asking members to save their rummage items, deliver them to a local thrift store "Second Time Around" and ask for a receipt made out to Alpha Club. At the January meeting, the program was presented by a Linden's Furniture representative who spoke on current decoration trends in fabrics and home fashions. There's always something interesting we can learn to improve our homes.

We notice as we go along through the years that the members of Alpha Club loved to put on special "nights" for members and guests. These weren't fundraisers; they were just for members. They cooked a good meal, dressed up and enjoyed an evening at the club with their chosen escort and friends. For years there were "Escort Nights," then there were "Potluck Nights," then "Gala Night," and a few "Spaghetti Nights." The guests were usually husbands, but of course as time went on into the 1980s, older members began losing their husbands, as the Alpha population aged. Eventually there were fewer younger women coming into the club, so unfortunately these special "Nights" disappeared.

At the March 1984 meeting, $50 was pledged to give to the Hugh O'Brian Youth Seminar. An Alpha member, Ann O'Conner, had started collecting information in order to organize a MADD group in Lompoc (Mother's Against Drunk Driving).

In April 1984, Alpha Club was invited and joined the chamber of commerce, but at that same time a humorous reminder of our humble non-profit status occurred when the club decided to use Betty Crocker coupons to purchase 48 stainless place settings at half price. Members were reminded of the home and garden tour on May 26 at the price of $5 each, proceeds to be used for additional landscaping and sprinkling system. Gala night would be held June 1 at 7:00 p.m. at the Elks Lodge. The theme was "The Alpha Limited." We're not sure what that meant but we question if Alpha was "limited." What with the home and garden show, gala night and, oh yes, the flower show all held within a month's time!

The Alpha Board took up the recommendation of the 1984 planning committee of the benefit ball to donate $9,540 toward installation of new cardiac monitoring equipment in the Cardiac Care Unit of the hospital, as well as a telemetry transmitter and receiver to monitor patients who no longer need the Cardiac Care Unit. Alpha would donate $4,500 for this equipment.

"A Child's Dream," was the theme for the 1984 flower show. A local nursery won over the crowd with a floral depiction of "A Picnic in the Park." Visitors and locals were interested in touring the site where the space shuttle Discovery would be launched in 1985, as well as the flower fields that year.

A picture in the Lompoc Record on July 31, 1984 shows Gene Holmdahl swinging a rather large mallet at a retaining wall at the hospital to make way for the new two-bed addition to the pediatric unit that Alpha was paying for with the money raised at the benefit ball.

The Alpha Club held its first meeting of the club year in September 1984 with the theme: "Happiness is being a Friendly and Caring Woman." The goal of President Ruth Blunt was to encourage all members to be on a "first name" basis by Christmas. Alpha Club also planned to judge a poster contest sponsored by the Elks. The theme was "The Danger of Drug Use." As time goes on there are more and more problems to worry about. Alcohol abuse was bad enough, but in the 1980s drugs became a big problem in our country, even small towns like Lompoc.

It was a crime of neglect that Alpha members had been forced to let the clubhouse go too long without repair and paint, so on November 7, 1984 the board passed a motion to accept a bid of $1,000 to repair cracks, prime, sandblast and paint the exterior of the building, including the rails.

Another gourmet dinner was planned for the November 17, 1984 benefit ball. Esther Baker, chair of the committee and another great cook, planned baron of beef, teriyaki chicken, baked fettuccine, broccoli soufflé, California fruit bowl, layered vegetable salad, gingered pears, sweet and sour spinach mold, devilish egg salad, marinated mushrooms, homemade rolls and of course, a dessert table, all home cooked by Alpha members. That would be enough to get everyone in Lompoc interested in attending. Esther can no longer attend meetings but remains active on a few committees, holding the meetings in her home.

There are a number of pictures of the ball—people dancing, auction items, the committee—with Gene as chair, Marge Scott helping and Alyce Martin serving again. As if Gene isn't busy enough with the ball in November, she is also co-chair of the luncheon committee for that month's Alpha meeting, which requires planning a menu, organizing who would make what, going to the clubhouse the day before to decorate and then preparing the food in time to serve it by noon on the day of meeting. No small task to serve 70 to 80 members who attended. Gene's son, Dwayne, told us each time we spoke with him about his remarkable mother, "Mom loved to cook." We can say from experience that not only did Gene love to cook, but also people loved to eat what she cooked! It was no surprise to anyone in Lompoc that Gene was honored as "Woman of the Year" by the chamber of commerce in 1985.

On May 12, 1985 the Lompoc Record had a small announcement about Alpha Club's latest gala night, which would be a Hawaiian luau. The meal was catered by "Matter of Taste" restaurant. The menu sounded very tropical and tasty and included a fish course, fresh fruit salad, Hawaiian chicken and coconut pie. Entertainment featured Hawaiian music and dancers. Cost was only $10 a person. Sounds like the Alpha members had finally given in to treating themselves to a night out with someone else doing the cooking.

The next day, May 13, the Lompoc Record had a brief notice about the Alpha Home and Garden Section's tour of the Carpinteria greenhouse and visit to a cactus garden. On May 14, the paper had yet another article about the coming Alpha Club Flower Show and we can't leave out the June 8 garden tour announcement in the Record on May 29, 1985. We just had our 2011 garden tour on May 28.

The 1985 flower show's theme was "Favorite Movies" and Marge Scott was chair. There's an article in the Lompoc Record with a picture of a long time member, Irma Henderson, who told about the early days when she competed in 1924 when there were only 70 members. Irma, like members Marguerite Hall and Hazel McCabe, contributed every year since the beginning in 1922 until they died. This club year (2010–11) we have seventy-eight members listed in our club book, but two have died and about five more have become unable to come to meetings now. Back in 1985 the club had 131 active members.

About this time Alyce and Perry Martin began traveling around the country to his ship reunions in their RV. They visited many cities and parts of the country, sometimes being away for a month or two. Alyce had been a member of Alpha for 36 years by this time, her children were grown and she welcomed a break. She stepped back for a few years and let some of the other members do the work. She continued to attend meetings; of course the thought of resigning from Alpha never entered her mind.

Even before the first club meeting of the year, September 1985, there were articles in the Lompoc Record about the holiday benefit ball to be held on November 16 at the Veterans Memorial Building. Gene Holmdahl, the "Woman of the Year," was again chairing this big event. As November arrived there was plenty of publicity. One picture in the Lompoc Record shows Marge Scott and another member preparing their "bar maid" outfits and other members making centerpieces to reflect "Harvest Moon" the theme of the ball. Tickets were $20 each. Proceeds were divided between three community service organizations: the Food Pantry, Lompoc District Hospital and Shelter Services for Women.

In January 1986 another Student Art show was held by Alpha Club and on January 25 members held another of their fun night potlucks at the clubhouse. Lompoc was growing again with the expected West Coast's first space shuttle mission just months away. Alpha Club membership was holding steady at 128 active members and 29 inactive, continuing and courtesy members. The club was looking forward to even more members as the space shuttle program grew. On January 28, 1986, as we all remember, the Challenger with all seven crew members blew apart and all was destroyed.

The official cancellation of the Vandenberg shuttle program came months after the explosion but it was not a surprise. Lompoc had prepared for the space shuttle; the town had expanded. A number of new motels had been built to accommodate shuttle personnel who would be traveling back and forth from Kennedy to Vandenberg. Everyone was ready for boom times again. Instead there was a downturn in Lompoc's economy.

Because of NASA's Teacher in Space program, elementary school students had linked up in teleconferences with astronauts in the months leading up to liftoff, bringing the mission closer to home in the area. Some of the shuttle facilities have eventually been used by Spaceport Systems International. Many unmanned space flights are used to send up satellites, which have allowed the development of much of the technology we use to "communicate" in the 21st Century.

We think the Alpha Club Benefit Balls were just what the town needed to keep going and show that Lompoc's spirit had not died with the Space Shuttle program. Gene Holmdahl is quoted in the Record as saying, "The success of this year's 'Star Fantasy' ball pushed the amount of money that the Alpha Club has raised for the hospital and other local non-profit organizations during the past five years to $75,000. With the recent change of economy in Lompoc, this year's success shows that Lompoc is still interested in supporting its own needs. . . ." That year Gene was given another honor for her hard work. She was selected "Woman of the Year" by the Tierra Adorada District, one of ten women to represent GFWC as "Women of the Year."

May 1986 was a busy month as usual with gala night and the GFWC convention held in Anaheim but no garden home tour.

"Sunday Funnies" was the theme for the 1986 flower show, which proposed new challenges for the committee. Some of the categories were "Garfield," "Rex Morgan, M.D." "Beetle Bailey," and "Little Orphan Annie."

In club year 1986–87 Lois Miller was president again and Esther Baker as a member of the kitchen remodeling committee (yet another one) reported on the criteria established for the contractor: 3 ovens, dishwasher, commercial garbage disposal, re-plumb and rewire building to name some. A decision was also made to buy new blinds for the tea room. Women are always interested in new timesaving gadgets that make our kitchen work more efficient! All this time the current treasurer has presented all bills to the board for approval before paying them. For many years this was not a problem. Alpha had so little expenses and not much in the bank, but by now this procedure was becoming tedious.

The Lompoc Record had an announcement in September about the upcoming benefit ball. The theme for the November 15 ball was to be "Star Fantasy." It was now a community-wide holiday celebration with proceeds being divided equally between the Lompoc Hospital District and the Visiting Nurses Service of Santa Barbara County for the Lompoc Area. The donation that year went up to $25 a person. When you have a hot ticket item you can raise the price!

As usual, the club spent some time in the spring of 1987 with demonstrations and tips on flower arranging and specimens by a certified flower show judge and Al Thompson, a local gardener and journalist. Gene was chair at district convention that spring.

Gene, Norma Harrison and Lois Miller shared a room at the convention and when they arrived, they sat down on the beds to rest. Norma noticed a pair of dentures and sunglasses lying under the bed that Gene was sitting on and said, "You girls must not have had enough time to kick your boyfriends out." They looked down and saw what she was talking about and had a good laugh. Conventions were always fun for Alpha members. Traveling around the state, leaving husband and family behind was great for their egos!

The Los Angeles Times gave tips on how to get the most enjoyment out of the Lompoc Flower Festival and directions to get here. The theme for the 1987 flower show was "Golden State Memories." A local teacher won the best of show award with her "Wine Country" and Esther Baker from Alpha won the sweepstakes.

Club year 1987–88 started with the "Lompoc Junior Woman's Club" (a new version of Junior Alphas). Their theme was, "Juniors are a New Beginning." Symbolizing the new friendships, new experiences, new challenges and a sense of involvement that juniors offer. There were only 12 members including the Harrison twins, Judy and Janet. They had heard about Alpha for years due to their mother Norma's active involvement in the club. The plan was to provide activities and raise money to improve the community as well as host the kind of environment where friendships could develop.

This poem says it all, we think.

A FRIEND

Some people know the way to make each day
Seem more worthwhile.
They seem to take the sunshine and wear it in
Their smile,
They're kind and understanding, loving and
sincere,
Ready with a compliment or friendly word of
cheer.
They give with generosity that never seems to
end—
They know the lovely secret of how to be a
friend.

—Karen Raven

Younger women were clearly conflicted by the late 80s. Many had college degrees, even advanced degrees and were working as professionals in all kinds of careers. They had economic opportunities unheard of back in Margaret, Cevilla and Emily's day. But there was a backlash. Some women felt threatened. They really didn't want to "bring home the bacon," they were happy just "frying it up in a pan." Most of those women were economically secure in homes their husbands bought for them. Millions of women on the other hand, who had no such security, just wanted the opportunity to bring home enough food to feed their family.

The country was growing more conservative and many reasons were discussed as to why women would be better off without passage of The Equal Rights Amendment. Congress had passed the Act in 1972 after many decades of effort by women who actually started promoting equal rights during the suffrage movement. In order for the new Amendment to go into effect, it needed to be ratified by 1979. Many tried to stop the ratification especially, Phyllis Schlafly, a conservative women who ran a campaign against equal rights for women. Women were made to feel guilty by ludicrous statements suggesting they were "putting jobs before their families." Labor wanted to keep the status quo claiming women would no longer have "protection" on the work force if the Act passed.

Women have always worked as hard as men. We've worked along side of men in fields and factories. Sometimes getting paid, sometimes not and even when we are paid it has never been equal to men for the same work. We have done shift work, hard labor, worked long hours and no one ever questioned our ability as long as we didn't ask for much in return. We did all this work while having and raising our children and no one ever questioned our ability to get it all done well, as long as we didn't demand equal pay.

As the time limit set for ratification of the Equal Rights Amendment ran out only, 35 states instead of the 38 needed had ratified. It's no wonder some women felt like going back to the days of being homemakers and clubwomen.

On October 2, 1987, the membership tea was held at the clubhouse, and on the seventh, the home and garden section held their meeting there, also. Esther Baker, the chair, had announced at the board meeting that all home and garden meetings for 1987–88 would involve doing flower arrangements and critiques to ensure more entries for the flower show. Arrangements were to be in black and orange, a Halloween arrangement for October. Esther was one great flower arranger so who could refuse? In November, the arrangements were Cornucopias including making "your own vases and bases."

At the November board meeting, it was decided to have the wallpaper stripped off the bathroom walls and paint them. A new hot water heater had to be purchased when the old one broke the morning of the membership tea.

In November, another successful ball (this time calling it a holiday benefit ball) was held with proceeds going again to the Lompoc Hospital District and Meals on Wheels.

In December, a special board meeting was called to read a request from the Lompoc centennial committee regarding the centennial ball. It was moved and passed that Alpha Club would chair the centennial ball to be held at the Elks' Club on August 12, 1988. Alpha had proven themselves worthy of the job with their many successful benefit balls over the last six years. Gene Holmdahl reported on this request at the general club meeting.

Bids had come in for the planned kitchen remodel, but there were only two and they were high without including all the work needed. The major kitchen remodel was postponed and Esther Baker resigned from the kitchen committee. We all know how it feels to have great plans for a remodel, only to find out there's no way we can afford it!

In February, a bank account set up after a benefit ball in September 1985 was discovered. It held $2,950.99 and was named Lompoc Hospital Fund. The club donated part of it to the Convalescent Care Center, believing the account to be interest that was earned from the first ball's proceeds that had sat in an account until it was called for. Interest rates were high in the 80s! Found money would be every non-profit treasurer's dream!

At the March 1988 board meeting, it was decided to bring a written ballot before the general club to ban smoking at Alpha luncheons. The motion carried and ballots were prepared. The smoking ban motion carried on the written ballot 51 to 33."**Smoking Will be Banned at Alpha Luncheons!**"[1] It was too late for Hazel McCabe but we think she may have been smiling about this decision. She knew it would happen sooner or later.

Plans for the Lompoc Centennial Ball were announced by President Jeanette Laganas. It was to be held on August 12 at the Elks Lodge. The Elks would furnish the food and Alpha would furnish the desserts. A band from San Luis Obispo would play and Avenue Flower Shop would do the decorations.

At the March luncheon, it was announced that at the TAD convention in April, Alpha members would do a skit called President's Report. Mildred Joy announced that she, Marge Scott and their committee had prepared the first 20 years of Alpha history to be video taped at Comcast.

In April 1988, Alpha Club invited Mrs. Ronald Reagan to speak at either the May or June club meeting, but not surprisingly, they received a letter back from the White House thanking them but offering Mrs. Reagan's regrets, "due to her many demands of the official schedule, she would be unable to accommodate the request."[2] Well you never know; it never hurts to ask.

Guest speakers for the May meeting were former Mayor Andrew Salazar who showed slides and spoke on the proposed Western Spaceport Museum and Science Center. He challenged Alpha Club to sponsor the proposed botanical gardens. Here we go again, it seems the community never gives up on Alpha. We are always there, ready with a helping hand or money, but it never seems to be enough. At this same meeting, a speaker from the "Meals On Wheels" program was there to thank us for the $4,500 donation and Scott Rhine from Lompoc Hospital also came to thank us for the $4,500 donation that would purchase a monitor defibrillator. These gifts were the proceeds from the latest benefit ball.

At the June board meeting, it was announced that a request had been sent to the Secretary of State to change our IRS tax status from "501(c)(4) to 501(c)(3)." It was also announced that all our tax papers, the charter, current tax status and Articles of Incorporation would be put in Alpha's safety deposit box.

The 1988 flower show's theme was "Famous Women In History." The grand marshal was Jeanne Yeager, pilot of the Voyager airplane, which went non-stop around the world without landing or refueling. Table titles honored Cleopatra, Elizabeth Barrett Browning, Harriet Tubman and Pearl Buck and the Alpha page in the festival program featured past flower show chairs.

The club juniors continued their meetings through the summer but most of Alpha took a break. The crafts section was an exception because it never seemed to stop! We have noticed over the years that crafting can be somewhat of an addiction, much like bridge.

In August and September 1988, the club had a lot of maintenance and repair work done. An inventory of the clubhouse was taken, the roof repaired, the floors cleaned and sealed, the carpet cleaned, the piano tuned, new coffee pots purchased and the refrigerator gave up the ghost. A 1988 24 cubic-foot Hotpoint refrigerator was purchased for $725 plus tax.

At board meeting it was announced, "due to unavailability of many supporters of the benefit ball during the month of October 1988, because of election year commitments, the chair, Norma Harrison would like to postpone the event."[3]

By December 1988, Esther Baker had changed her mind about a kitchen remodel, realizing that it was better to get one thing at a time then to go for it all at once. She hadn't given up on more ovens and was working on the purchase of a new stove. She was given permission from the board to purchase two Maytag stoves at a cost of $438 each, plus extra oven racks, plus tax.

The same month, the club was sent a survey from GFWC asking that all members fill it out in order to "identify issues facing society and affecting women in particular … so that seminars could be conducted concluding with a "Forum for the Future." GFWC's hope was to set an agenda for its Second Century, "Our agenda must have a direct impact on society." The survey form asks each woman to rate six issues listed that they consider the most important. The following are the issues listed:

Adolescent Pregnancy
Care of the Elderly
Catastrophic Illness
Crime
Day Care for Children
Independent Living (Disabled)
Developing Countries
Education/Literacy
Employment and Training
Environmental Concerns
Equal Rights and Responsibilities
Family Law and Criminal Justice
Health and Health Care
Homeless
Human Rights
Income and Economic Opportunity
International Trade
Legal Rights
Nuclear Proliferation
Terrorism
World Hunger
World Peace

Information from the person doing the survey was requested, such as age, marital status, employment, family, education, area of country, type of community and club involvement.

Results of this forum for the future survey were as follows:

> Over 20,000 club members responded to select the top issues to be addressed as we move beyond our centennial into the next century.

Education proved to be the number one issue among all who voted. The following is a list of the top six issues picked:

1. Education/Literacy
2. Care of the Elderly

3. Environment
4. Crime (including drugs)
5. World Peace
6. Health

As a result, each Regional Conference would feature two panels, moderated by a clubwoman from the region. Panel topics were: "Our Families in Crisis," which would discuss elder care, health and catastrophic illness, teen pregnancy and day care for children; and The Global Perspective," which would offer insights into world health, world hunger, world trade, world population and world understanding. Panel discussions would then be followed by questions from the audience. These conferences would mark the GFWC entry into the twenty-first century.

As to the demographics of the survey, 73 percent of the women were married; 44 percent of the women were employed either full or part time; 22 percent were college educated and 22 percent had graduate degrees; 35 percent had some college; 46 percent of the women lived in small towns as opposed to 13 percent living in urban areas and 35 percent living in suburban areas. Only 14 percent lived in rural areas. Women 18 to 50 equaled only 31 percent and women 51 and older equaled 69 percent.[4]

Looking back, we can see several changes since that survey. The first is that women have now surpassed men by 57 percent as college graduates. They have widened the gap in all categories becoming college graduates and obtaining masters and doctorate degrees.

Second, in 1993 the GFWC took an active role in supporting the Family Leave Act which allows a family member to take an unpaid leave to care for another family member, such as an infant, child, ill, or elder family member without losing their job.

Third, GFWC has always been involved in health issues. They have supported the shingles vaccine and other benefits especially for women and children. GFWC has kept informed of Medicare and Supplemental Insurance issues and can offer a great body of influence in health care policy.

We all seem to be loosing the battle on keeping our environment safe, stopping crime and the misuse of drugs. As for world peace, that's a problem much too big even for an international women's group. Even with all the modern ways to communicate it seems impossible to bring everyone on the same page with any issue.

CHAPTER 13

The Color Question

Getting back to equal opportunity for everyone to live a satisfying life as suggested at a 1972 SFWC convention, in 1989 things still weren't equal even in Lompoc. Some people were barred from that opportunity.

On February 15, 1989, a special meeting of the executive board of the GFWC Alpha Literary and Improvement Club was called to order. President Edna Wright read from an article in the February 15 issue of the Santa Barbara News Press which stated the Lompoc-Santa Maria Branch of the NAACP called on the Lompoc Unified School District to sever all ties with the Elks Lodge over its rejection of a black man, Ernie Hutchinson, for membership. They also reported the Lompoc superintendent of schools said any district functions that were to be held at the lodge had been cancelled.[1]

President Edna also read a letter received from Arthur Hicks, former school teacher, school board member and chairman, civil rights committee of the NAACP and Smiley Wilkins, president of the Santa Maria and Lompoc NAACP, stating:

> the NAACP cannot condone the use of facilities owned by organizations which historically and systematically reject blacks or other minorities.

They urged Alpha Club to reconsider their planned use of the Elks Lodge. It was recommended by Freddie Weyl, moved and passed to postpone the benefit ball since problems were increasing as to where the ball would be held, and no other facility was available for the April date. It was clear that full support for the ball in the community was lacking due to the "Elks issue."[2]

An editorial in the Sunday, January 22, 1989 Lompoc Record was headed, "A moral decision" and stated:

> No one can argue that Hutchinson, a longtime resident, a Vietnam veteran, a former police officer, reserve deputy sheriff and housing manager for the Santa Barbara County Housing Authority was unqualified. He was blackballed pure and simple and for one reason—his color. He was rejected by 10 to 15 members solely because of a misguided belief Elks membership is for whites only.

That, sadly, was once true. But the national club first admitted blacks in 1973 when language limiting membership to "white male citizens" was changed to "male citizens." Nonetheless, not one of the 7,000 Santa Barbara County residents who belonged to the Elks at that time was black.

We understand from Edith and Art Hicks that this issue was taken to Chicago, the national headquarters of the Elks. Black groups in Lompoc urged the fraternal organization to repeal the "blackball" rule. The Elks did indeed change their national policy that excluded male blacks, and minorities but continued preventing women from joining their "Fraternal" organization. Women weren't allowed to be members of the Elks until a settlement of the ACLU forced the issue in 2005!

This was not the first time a federated women's club had been involved with segregation issues. Researching this incident made us curious whether the federation itself had ever discriminated against any race, or gender. We spoke to our contact at the general federation headquarters in Washington DC and she sent us quite a bit of information about the "Color Question." Back in 1900, even before Alpha Club had joined the GFWC, a number of problems arose around admitting black women to the federation.

It seems that a large number of clubs had applied for admission to the Massachusetts state federation during early June 1900 at the Fifth National Biennial in Milwaukee Wisconsin. As usual, all of the clubs' names were accepted by mail and were waiting for approval by the board. Among this large group was the "Woman's Era Club of Boston," but the state federation hadn't realized that this was a mostly black women's club. When this fact became known, the endorsement of the board was given to every club except the "Woman's Era." A motion was made to admit the club but after lengthy discussion the motion was "laid on the table," where no vote was taken at any subsequent meeting that week.

In the meantime, the state federation of Georgia was squarely against admitting blacks with the president of that federation writing to justify their position:

> While 'social equality' is now and always will be impossible in the South, yet history does not record a parallel example where a superior race with extremely limited means has done more for the moral, religious and educational training of an inferior race than have the people of the South for the negro.
>
> —*Annie E. Johnson, President of Georgia Federation.*

Not all southern women felt exactly as Annie did. Another letter written to the "Club Woman," the federation magazine, states:

> As this is a special meeting to discuss the admission of colored clubs to the federation, I wish to speak to the question and to record my views' with no uncertain sound.
>
> The daughter of generations of slave owners I have a strong personal abhorrence for the social equality of the African race. But as a loyal American citizen, as a representative clubwoman, I believe the Afro-American clubs in good standing and of intelligence should be admitted to the federation. This is a pivotal point in our national life. The future security of the republic lies in bringing its diverse races and classes to a high standard of citizenship, and in the eventual absorption of the colored race. Physiological statistics show there is not a pure blooded African in the United States today.... Women are the natural educators of their race, and their clubs should stand for something larger than social functions. Indeed, most of them are pseudo-political, literary and philanthropic.
>
> To take the stand some of the clubs are doing is elementary and childish. We may draw narrow lines in the hospitality of our homes, but a club has larger issues than personal prejudices. This is a far-reaching question. Political eyes are upon us. Classes are a menace to the republic. Clubs should level up, not down; like churches they should set standards of high living and thinking. Therefore I wish to record my vote in favor of the admission of educated colored clubs to the federation.
>
> —*Annie Hungerford White, M.D.*

So on the one hand, Georgia wanted the federation to "change the by-laws adopting a 'color line' in the membership rules" and Massachusetts asks the "committee to refrain from applying that 'color line,' saying that such action would be contrary to the avowed aims and purposes of the federation and that it is antagonistic to the earnest convictions of the great majority of its members."

Eventually, after much discussion and persuasion that the Negro wasn't ready, wasn't organized, wasn't educated therefore wasn't intelligent enough to be admitted in a Southern club culture, a decision was made. They would let the state federations sort it out because the general federation leaders were afraid that the Southern state federations would secede otherwise (keep in mind the Civil War had been over for just 35 years!).

"Believing that a disruption of the federation would entail serious loss on every side, Massachusetts deplores the necessity for such a disruption as would seem to be the inevitable resort of any vote upon the Georgia amendment." The federation was urged to "consider a proposition which would make the state federations the unit of organization, and give individual clubs membership only through their state or territorial federation. This would have the effect to remove the 'color question' entirely from controversy in the general federation, leaving each state federation free to make its own membership rules according to its own convictions." It only took six more decades to work all this out when the Civil Rights Amendment was passed in 1964. But even then some groups were really slow to catch on, like the Elks.[3]

It wasn't until 1984 that the first black woman, Louise Artis, joined Alpha Club. She was a member for 13 years, serving on the international committee most of those years. Hollie Farnum joined Alpha Club in 1986 and remained a member until June of 2009 Helen Jean Ward joined in club year 1991–92 and was a member until the end of club year 2003–04. Two others joined in 1992; Nanny Wilkins who joined in April and Ruth Hicks in September. Ruth Hicks served as treasurer for club year 1993–94 and remained a member until the end of club year 2001–02.

Nanny remains a member today, serving on committees and helping with the flower show.

Let it be noted that the GFWC constitution and by-laws stated in 1904 that: "no one of its members is affiliated with any organization which tolerates, either by practice or by teaching, violation of national or state laws, and it agrees to the constitution and by-laws of the General Federation"[4]

Alpha Club's by-laws have stated at least since 1990 "men are eligible under the same conditions as women provided representation shall be by women...."

Interestingly, we haven't seen any male members in the Alpha Club and we have had only a sprinkling of women of color. Maybe it's time to address this issue.

CHAPTER 14

The GFWC Centennial

In March 1989 CFWC sent out a legislative alert about the Volunteer Protection Act asking all members of CFWC to support this act by writing their Representatives and Senators and asking that they support this.

At the April 1989 meeting, a talk was given by Federation Chair Lois Miller about Federation Day, April 24. She noted that 75 percent of public libraries in America were started by women's clubs. At the May meeting, Gene Holmdahl and Alyce Martin received 25-year awards. The board recommended that the benefit ball committee find an alternate place for the 1989 ball in November.

Laurel Beaudry chaired the flower show. The Lompoc festival committee decided they could no longer afford to print a program but the Lompoc Record would print a special section instead. The theme was "Songs of the Century" and of course, songs were chosen for table titles.

Alpha Club's goals for club year 1989–90 were inspired by the celebration of the centennial of the GFWC in 1990. Alpha wanted to qualify as a federated, centennial club so they were required to meet some standards set up by Federation. The club would need to document at least one activity in each of the following:

1. Heritage
2. Celebration
3. Future

No problem, the club was already working on these standards; there was the committee continually working on Alpha Club history, writing and making videotapes and for the first time the club was planning a big fashion show in April using vintage costumes. It would meet the criteria for a centennial celebration and also be a money maker. As for the future, Alpha had been invited to put a bronze plaque announcing the federation centennial on it in the memorial grove at Beattie Park along with a tree to be planted that would have perpetual care. Alpha's final goal was to continue the clubhouse repair work and set up a continuing building fund. As we all know the older a building gets the more repairs and updates are needed.

A report on the November 18, 1989 ball stated that it was difficult to get everything going due to not having a ball the year past, but things got done and the ball was held again at the Elks Club with Alpha making over $10,000. Motion made and carried at the board meeting in December that Gene Holmdahl be chair of the benefit ball for 1990.

Members figured that if anyone could get the ball 'rolling' again Gene could.

We can see by the formatting of the minutes that club members are getting more literate with electric typewriters even some personal computers. It's now possible to use a personal computer to do budget reports.

The January 1, 1990 Tournament of Roses Parade included a California Federation of Women's Clubs grand piano float to celebrate the centennial of GFWC. Alpha Club was working hard on all the extra things to do for the year. That didn't mean that the usual things weren't going to get done as well.

We notice now that little by little the bank balance is creeping up from earlier days. It appears that Alpha has decided not to give almost every penny away and is keeping some for rainy days, (clubhouse repairs.) In 1990, the bank balances are running about the same as they are now in 2011!

It was announced at the March board meeting that even though Louisa Van Ausdal was no longer a member, she would continue to do her workshops for children. Louisa was never more than a phone call away and was always willing to give classes for children's groups, sometimes even a grandchild or two of the members.

The "Century of Fashions," Fashion show planned by Alpha was held at the Elks on March 31 and featured Alpha women modeling outfits from each decade going back to the beginning of the GFWC's in the 1890s. Tickets were $15 apiece and the event was a success making over $2,500 for Alpha. This was great fun for all and the front runner of an eventual annual event that became very popular over the last 14 years, making money for one or more charities which Alpha members pick each year and keeping part of the proceeds for the clubhouse fund. It's still held at the Elks, who furnish a delicious luncheon with desserts made by Alpha members. The cost now is $30 each and we usually have a great turnout.

About this time Gene Holmdahl was appointed Trustee for the Lompoc Hospital to promote the newly organized Hospital Foundation. Gene was 77 years old by then but still going full steam ahead.

Mission fiestas were still being held at our La Purisima Mission and Alpha was still fixing and serving food for the event every year in May. However there were still no garden tours during this time. Maybe they ran out of gardens!

As chair of the flower show again in 1990, Marge Scott and her committee made special plans with a theme honoring the General Federation of Women's Clubs by bringing to life the memories of past shows in its table titles: "The Pacific Coast" (1920); "Festival of Flowers" (1954); "Happiness Is" (1975); And Just Imagine" (1967). Esther Baker again won best of show while Marilyn Mitty and Betty Coleman won the sweepstakes in specimens and arrangements respectively.

In September 1990, Alpha held a Rummage Sale, which had been one of our fundraisers for several years. Unfortunately, proceeds usually only amounted to under $500 and unlike the early days of the club, members weren't willing to put in a lot of time if it didn't pay well. Not surprisingly this was the last rummage sale for a while. Now in 2011, we plan to hold one in late summer and newer members are hopeful we can make several thousand! We'll see.

The junior club had a membership ice cream social on Sunday, September 23. They were trying hard to stay afloat and needed more members badly. At the first Alpha luncheon/meeting of the new club year, 1990–91, there were 71 members and 6 guests present. Members were asked for donations of sandwich spreads for the blood bank coming up that Friday.

The benefit ball of 1990 was changed from November to October with the name changed as well to the annual dinner dance and auction. It was a fitting ending to a year of celebration of the centennial. "The decorations were the talk of the town. Gene and her committee women worked long hours to make everything fit the theme "Starlight Terrace." The colors were black and silver. Unfortunately, Gene did get slowed down quite a bit when she fell and broke several ribs (ouch) a month before the event. She continued to supervise however and was able to answer questions over the phone. She even made it to the gala affair with some help from pain pills and a pillow. The proceeds went to the hospital for the emergency room, to Martha Negus Orthopedic School for a 'wheel chair swing,' and to the new Life Line Unit System in Lompoc for 17 units. A total of $12, 773.09 was donated to worthy causes.

In March 1991 the guest speaker, Dr. Barbara Nelson, Lompoc Superintendent of Schools, spoke about concerns regarding state budget problems during the current budget crisis and the difficulty in planning for increased enrollments. Twenty years later those concerns look mild compared to our current situation of big budget cuts for schools.

Esther Baker would again demonstrate flower arrangements in April at the clubhouse focusing on categories of the coming flower show schedule.

At the June 12, 1991 meeting, there were 85 in attendance, 70 members and 15 guests including the students who were awarded scholarships. Plans for the July 10 potluck picnic at Spaceport Park were announced.

"Let's Have a Party" was the theme for the 1991 flower show. Chair, Sue Moore, urged more Valley gardeners to participate, especially men, whose entries had been declining for several years. That year the weather was not cooperative as can sometimes happen in Lompoc. Winds were brisk, temperatures were cool and the sky was overcast.

Betty Coleman won the sweepstakes. Gene and Walter Holmdahl were selected to be parade marshals for the festival parade. This year, 2011 we had a cool rainy spring and everything bloomed late, roses were poor at the time of the show. Even so, we had many lovely specimens and arrangements; it's always a pleasant surprise.

At the September 1991 luncheon, the board recommended that the cost of luncheons should be raised to $4.50. A discussion was held and a member moved that the cost of the luncheons be raised to $5 but the motion failed and so the price was set at only $4.50. Plans were also discussed to install new linoleum as soon as it was paid for on September 22. It was scheduled to take three days to get the job done. Juniors were still hanging on or 'in' as they say, planning a barbecue in October.

In November 1991, the guest speaker was the president of the CFWC. Guests were the president of TAD and other TAD officials. November was usually Reciprocity Month in which Tierra Adorada district and state federation officials visit Lompoc. That time they came from all over the central coast. We sometimes think we get such a good turnout for that luncheon because the visitors love getting out of their larger cities to drive up or down the coast and into Lompoc.

It was reported that the 9th annual dinner dance (benefit ball) had been successful and although exact figures weren't available yet, $1,000 would be given to the Lompoc Women's Shelter for playground equipment, $1,000 to Martha Negus School for another platform swing, with the balance almost paying for the $11,700 fetal monitor for Lompoc Hospital District. At that time the club also had a Treasure Chest project that collected new donated toys and distributed them to children aged one to ten when they entered the hospital.

After a few problems with the installation of the linoleum and having the toilets left in the main room for several days, while things were on hold the installers agreed to come back and reinstall the facilities. Never a dull moment at Alpha!

At the February 1992 meeting, former presidents put on the program. Each past president had to relay or have read a humorous incident that happened during their term/s. Other members provided additional entertainment that included songs and small skits. All past presidents received red roses in a vase. The president of the juniors asked that all members support their bridge tournament fundraiser on the first Saturday in March.

The board recommended that Alpha conduct a home tour on April 11 as a fundraiser and the motion carried. It was announced by the home and garden section that they would not have a program for March, and that in April, May and June their programs would concentrate on flower arranging in preparation for the flower show.

At the March club meeting, they had a small fashion show with Marge Scott and two others modeling clothes from Poppy Hill. Following the fashion show, an Easter hat parade was presented by members with categories: prettiest, original and funniest. Club members were still finding it hard to break away from hats altogether, although very few women wore them by 1992.

That spring, Barbara Cooperider, a long time club member, died from cancer. She was only in her mid-sixties which wasn't considered old in the 90s. She had been a friend to Gene Holmdahl and had served in a number of capacities for Alpha. She had been president, flower show chair, served on many committees and also held office with TAD. Her son asked members who were close to her to write something about Barbara or about a special moment with her that he could put in a box of memories for her small granddaughters who would never have the opportunity to know her otherwise.

Gene had a number of stories about her experiences with Barbara. They had attended TAD and state conferences together. Barbara used to tell people such as the Newspaper staff, when they didn't appear very anxious to put a story in about Alpha, that she would sic Gene Holmdahl on them. Barbara and Gene both were hard workers, but they enjoyed a little fun and humor along the way. Gene loved being a member of Alpha, but she always dreaded this part. When you put everything into your membership and friendships with members it was very difficult to say good-by. Gene would miss Barbara's good humor and their friendship. Early club members and friends Emily, Appie, and Anna, and later, Marguerite, Hattie, Ida and Toot's all suffered the loss of good friends. Clubwomen often bond like sisters.

One way to help get through these losses is to dive back into projects that keep one's mind busy. That was never hard for Gene to do. At this time, she was appointed to the county fair board on July 15, 1992 and welcomed the opportunity. At age 79, Gene was still going strong, after her ribs healed, that is.

Esther Baker was flower show chair in 1992 and Marge Scott was her co-chair. Both women were very experienced in putting on the show as well as winning awards for their entries. The theme was "Pacific Paradise" and members were asked to wear Muumuus or white slacks with a flowered shirt. The show was tropical and beautiful, and Esther won the sweepstakes. It was amazing when we think back at how hard those women worked. We just finished taking down our 89th flower show and many of us didn't even attempt to enter a specimen let alone an arrangement ourselves; we say we're too busy putting on the show. But, then we wonder how did they do it back in the past? To be chair of such an event and all that entails, and in addition, win the sweepstakes. Wow!

At the November 18, 1992 general meeting, a skit was presented "The Club Women." The first skit in awhile put on by the club but it was very humorous and members were pleased they still had it in them and said they should do it more often. President Sandy Morgan also thanked Renee Bristol and her committee for a successful benefit ball.

Although is appears the junior club disbanded at this time due to such a small membership, the club was again considering starting up an evening section of Alpha Club and sent out notices to possible interested parties. At the December meeting, the name "The Pace Setters," was set for the evening section and it was decided they would be excused from the monthly luncheon as set forth in standing Rule #3. (If the club was going to set up an evening section for those who worked why would there be any question of attendance at the monthly luncheon let alone serving on a luncheon committee?) Eight women were present at the first meeting and a chairwoman was elected. The group decided to meet on the third Wednesdays at 5:30 p.m. in a restaurant, except in January. Alpha was trying hard to accommodate the changing woman, against all odds.

Things had changed drastically since those Charter members first met on Saturday afternoons. None of those women worked outside their homes back then, with the exception of Anna Moore, most of them did, however, work at keeping their homes and ranches going, not easy in the early 1900s. Their children were in school during the school year, usually walking to school, no matter the distance. Children were most likely able to run free with their friends all summer, as we all were. There were no organized activities for most children until much later and certainly not the fear of harm to unsupervised children that exists today.

We remember when the first soccer games started up in Lompoc in the autumn of 1974. There was already a Pee Wee Football League and, of course, baseball for little boys which had been organized since the nineteen hundreds. However after the 1950s adults became more involved in their children's sports. When the Education Amendment, Title IX was passed in 1972 and girls were let into organized sports all kinds of youth activity began to accelerate to the point that most children today don't have much free time.

By 1992, the effects of this phenomenon had slowly crept up on younger women with children at home. Not only did most of them work outside the home, but also when they were home they didn't always get a lot of help with cooking and housework. In addition, mothers seemed to be the parent most likely to be the chauffeur for the children and all their activities. It no longer seemed safe to let your child get her/himself back and forth to ball practice or anywhere else for that matter. Needless to say, not many women joined the evening section anymore then they had the junior women's group.

The benefit ball did well again in 1992, and pictures were posted on the bulletin board for those who wanted them with some to be put in the club scrapbook.

At the February 1993 meeting, 17 of the club's past presidents were honored and thanked for their service. Plans were made to hold the benefit ball on November 13 at the Officer's Club at Vandenberg AFB. Plans were also made to select the recipients earlier so they could be listed for members and the public. There were 78 members present and 21 guests altogether for lunch.

The club held a special meeting in March to propose changing the club year, from July 1 through June 30 to January 1 through December 31 (a calendar year). They also decided to recommend to the general membership that a committee be formed to determine the future of the clubhouse. The Pace Setters were planning a fashion show for May 22 at the clubhouse.

At the general meeting on April 21, the recommendation that the club change to using the calendar year effective January 1994 failed! A home tour would be held on April 24. Not a garden tour apparently, but a home tour again.

The June club meeting's special guest was the town Mayor, Joyce Howerton, who was presented with an Alpha Cookbook and Certificate of Appreciation for the excellent cooperation Alpha had experienced from the city that year. The board recommended that the club form an Alpha Club Centennial Committee to function through 1998, motion carried.

"A Day to Remember" was the theme of the 1993 flower show. Betty Coleman was the chair. A new category was used, a "Garden Party Hat," using a straw or party hat with dry flowers or foliage. We did that again in 2002, it was a lot of fun to see what people did with those hats. Categories included; "Over the Hill

Birthday," "Silver Wedding Anniversary," and "Moon Landing." Esther Baker again won the sweepstakes.

The 1993 benefit ball's net profit was $7, 878.47 with $5,000 going to the Lompoc Hospital, $1,300 going toward the Life Line service and $1,575 going into Alpha's charitable fund. Tickets for the event were $27.50 that year.

We noticed that there had not been any potlucks, spaghetti dinners or any sort of fun get-togethers for the whole club in the last few years, but a gourmet section started up in September to meet in members' homes on the fourth Tuesdays and that December, 1993, there was a tree trimming and potluck.

At the February 1994 board meeting, it was announced by the senior director (in charge of clubhouse exterior) that she had two bids from firms for the extension and repair of the driveway. A discussion was held about the amount of work that should or could be done; to just repair the driveway, or widen the sidewalk, or include removing the trees and widening the approach from the street, also what kind of permits were needed. At the same time they were also getting bids for painting and/or pressure washing the exterior. A decision was made to table the painting and consider the drive problem at that time. The club would also donate $30 to the GFWC "Have a Heart" campaign for the Second Century Endowment Fund to ensure the growth and future development of GFWC.

A benefit ball committee meeting was held in March to evaluate, research, and find some alternative to the ball. A few members thought the ball should be "done away with and the focus should be on the flower show only." The majority wanted to continue with the ball. Remember way back in the early 1940s when "it was suggested that the then existing 'Ways and Means' committee prepare one large affair early enough as to not interfere with the annual flower show and that this be sufficient for funds for the year?" Members get tired, burned out, and retire because the amount of work required to run a clubhouse and put on four or five events a year is tremendous. There is an alternative, but like everything it is a trade off. We'll discuss this possibility in the last chapter. In any case back to the benefit ball, since the committee could not come up with any alternative that would make as much money to allow the club to "be as philanthropic as we are now." Therefore, the decision to have the ball and support it was left entirely to the board and members.[1]

In March 1994 the bid was accepted for $3,440 to remove the trees on the east side of the drive, widen the drive on the east and west sides and repair the existing drive. The work was completed and paid for. In 2010 another pavement job was done that included a new entryway with a ramp and more paving in the east part of the front along the entry for two parking spaces as well as widening the entrance to the street, all for another $9,000. The sidewalk and steps, entry and ramp are now safe and the extra wide drive entrance and parking spaces are much appreciated.

April's board meeting included a report from Mildred Joy, who in 1987 had started the Alpha Remembrance Fund to be used toward writing the history of Alpha Club. Her committee was Marge Scott, Betty Coleman, Gladys Williams, Lois Miller and Anita Batty. Mildred reported that by July 8, 1993, $5,819.78 had been withdrawn for the Alpha Cookbook and only $1,615 had been replaced, leaving a balance that date of $4,024.31. After attempts at recording the history on tape, the decision had then been made to type it in book form. Although great effort was put into trying to write the book on the history of Alpha it was not possible. We are grateful to those women for some of the groundwork they have laid, but we are even more grateful for the modern computer that has allowed us to take up this task again. This time, hopefully, we will finish it.

At the same March board meeting in 1994, the issue was brought up again by a letter to the board from Marge Scott asking for more discussion on holding another benefit ball. Other fund raising ideas, such as a fashion show in the spring were discussed.

At the June 1994 board meeting, the issue of the remembrance fund was again brought up. It was announced that the "centennial committee had recommended to Alpha Club that the seed money, not to exceed $1,500 for the centennial come from the remembrance fund."

In response it was suggested there had been work on a club history for several years and the remembrance fund would be needed to publish this history book for the centennial. Sadly we know this didn't happen. Not only did a book not come forth, but also the remembrance fund has almost completely disappeared.

"Barnyard Follies" was the theme for the 1994 flower show. Irma Gadway chaired the show assisted by Harriet Goodland and Marge Scott. The table titles were clever and fun. We remember bringing a five-year-old granddaughter up from the Los Angeles area for her five-year-old trip with grandparents. In our opinion, the show couldn't have been more fitting and when we were sitting in the tea room after talking with several old Alpha friends, we made the decision to move back to Lompoc in the next year or two. We had been gone almost twenty years, but felt we could just pick up where we had left off in 1975.

In October 1994, the club's crafts bazaar was held for two consecutive days with lunch served both days. An ad in the Lompoc Record invited everyone to come to the bazaar. A write up with a picture of various craft items was also included. A week later there was another ad in the Lompoc Record inviting all to come to a membership tea that included some Alpha Club history. The club also continued to contribute to "Penny Pines" and received a commendation from the US Forest Service and the Los Padres National Forest for the 23rd and 24th donations to the future of national forests in California.

A board recommendation at the meeting held on October 20, 1994 states that "a Western-style barbecue and dance be held in the spring replacing the annual benefit ball." The motion carried. Gene Holmdahl spoke to the question, noting the benefit ball had become a fundraiser involving a lot of hard work. The western dance and barbecue would have less effort in planning and decorations for the event.

Everyone was relieved that Gene felt this way. Even though the ball had been her "baby" she too was weary and ready to give it up. The committee immediately began looking for a venue for the barbecue and dance. Also at this meeting it was recommended by the board that approval be given the centennial committee to proceed with a centennial cookbook. The motion carried. (Well, a cookbook is better than no book at all!)

By March 1995, there was no flower show chair, but a chair for the barbecue planned for March 25. The barbecue and dance looked like a lot of fun with lots of western wear and dancing but only $1,200 was raised from the event. A far cry from the big money the benefit ball had made, but better than nothing!

At the June 1995 meeting, a recommendation was approved and passed for "painting and patch work to be done on the Alpha Club kitchen ceiling, install new kitchen hoods with fans, and for new carpeting in the Fireside room for a total expenditure of $3,565."[2]

The gourmet section had taken on some of what made the Roadrunners popular. They would travel to great places for lunch such as Cold Springs Tavern in the San Marcos Pass.

The flower show plans got off to a slow start, as no one wanted to take on the role of chair but Norma Paulson came forward in March and a new member, Pat Bailin was her co-chair. The theme was "By The Sea, By The Sea." Ideas for arrangements came from the neighboring Pacific, murals, and the Cabrillo High School aquarium. Betty Coleman won the sweepstakes and Marge Scott was best of show in arrangements.

In September 1995, the guest speaker for the Alpha meeting was Richard Jacoby, who was on the board of trustees for Allan Hancock College in Santa Maria. There was a lot of talk about

Lompoc getting a campus in the near future and he came to let the Alpha members know that the rumors were true and the hopes were that the center would be open by the end of the decade. As is often the case when a speaker comes to Alpha Club, Mr. Jacoby had an ulterior motive. He was on a fund raising mission. It takes a lot of money to build a college campus, even a satellite.

It had been disappointing that the barbecue and dance was not as successful as it needed to be and so no big event other than the flower show was planned for 1995–96. The Alpha budget must have been tight that year.

In January 1996, Mary Lou Parks moved back to Lompoc. One of the first things she did was call a few old friends and ask them to sponsor her return to Alpha Club. Returning to Alpha Club for that February meeting, which of course was Presidents Day, felt like coming home after an extended trip. There were some new faces, but over half of the members and past presidents there were old friends. "Where in the world can one go away for 20 plus years, and on return, find it's as though you had never left?" she thought to herself as she happily greeted club members. She attended sporadically as a guest for a time while she tried to catch up, but was still working and had serious health issues the first two years back so it wasn't possible to get fully involved.

In May 1996, an article in the Lompoc Record announced that Louisa Van Ausdal and Marilyn Mitty would give workshops for the flower show. Louisa's workshop would be for the children and Marilyn as an expert in specimens.

The flower show theme for 1996 was "Hometown Pride." New to the show was Chaotic Exotics, a local orchid nursery. Visitors and Alpha members were concerned about the condition of the Veterans Memorial Building, which was in need of paint and new draperies to say the least. Alpha had contacted officials earlier to see what could be done but this was an issue between the county and the city and neither wanted to spend the money. Louisa took best of show for an arrangement.

One of the best things about living in Lompoc was the beautiful flower fields. People had been coming to see them since Robert Rennie first started to grow sweet peas in 1908. We especially used to love to take a drive or two down the valley toward Surf and see the multicolored sweet peas, dahlias, larkspur and delphiniums everywhere we looked. Some years there were multi-shades of red poppies waving in the Lompoc breeze. It was just so beautiful. That first year back, Mary Lou took such a drive and stopped along the road every so often to capture some of these beauties on film. She remembers kneeling down in a field of dahlias for a close-up picture of them and thinking that living here in this valley was as close to paradise as one could get in this life. Sadly most of our flower fields are gone now.

There are no big flower seed companies here to grow them anymore. A few still contract with local growers though, and this year, 2011, we saw just a scattering of flower fields blooming. We drove around in early June to look and saw, sweet peas, marigolds, larkspur, dahlias and a beautiful field of stock up by River Bend Park.

At the September 1996 board meeting, the chair of the benefit ball talked some about plans and decorations for a ball to be held in November that would use a holiday theme. Gene Holmdahl offered to help with live auction items.

Plans for the regular September meeting were to have a Hawaiian holiday theme and the wearing of muumuus. A report was given on the purchase of a new refrigerator. (Didn't they just get one? Oh, that was at least 20 years ago.) Just like home, there always seems to be something that needs fixing or replacing. The old one was given to the Salvation Army.

By October, the chair of the benefit ball reported to the board that the ball would have to be postponed as she and Gene had been having trouble securing donations from merchants and the mailing list had been lost. They considered holding the ball the following February but there were conflicts, so final decisions were left unfinished. You have to give Alpha credit when it comes to trying to keep an event going, but maybe the old saying "you can't beat a dead horse" applies here.

It wasn't until the November board meeting that the Junior Alpha Club's balance of their closed account in the amount of $478.81 was deposited into the club's general fund. At this meeting Mary Lou Parks was accepted formally as a member. We had also heard and begun to notice ourselves that Gene had her hands full caring for Walter. He was said to have Alzheimer's and wandered, so she couldn't let him out of her sight. Her son helped when he could, but Gene had little time to spend at Alpha those days.

The craft bazaar went well that November making $4,019 and spending only $609.75. The benefit ball would be postponed until April 12, 1997.

The club has started having spaghetti dinners again, charging members for them, but making only a small profit. We remember attending a few of those, enjoying the tasty home cooked spaghetti and good conversation. They were cheaper than going to a restaurant and most of us didn't have to cook, some did, of course. There was talk at the December meeting of putting on a fashion show. We noticed the club books at this time have members names listed as follows: Last name, first name and sometimes in parenthesis husband's first name, but not everyone with a husband has his name in. Many are by now widows so have no husband's name next to theirs, but even some of us who are married have no husband's name listed. We don't recall being asked which way we preferred to have it. There really seemed to be a problem listing our members without attachments.

At the January, 1997 board meeting, the committee reported on Dott Brackin's proposal to hold a fashion show with the following recommendations to the board: The Alpha Club Fashion Show would be held on March first at the Elk's from 11:30 to 3:00 p.m. There would be a chicken oriental salad, coffee, tea and dessert and the cost would be $15 a person. The recommendation was passed at the general membership meeting. The committee was large and the show was very well done. We had a great turnout and made a profit of $900. We know this wasn't much, but we didn't charge much either. We liked the idea of this fashion show every year. It worked better for the club now that so many were widows. A benefit ball didn't fit well anymore. Mary Lou Parks attended the show not realizing this was the first one of its kind. It was done so well it seemed like old hat to the club. Alpha had found a niche. Women love fashion and we have done better every year.

At that same meeting in February 1997, there was more discussion about getting a book on the history of Alpha Club written. Marge Scott had looked into the cost to have a professional writer do it. Undecided, the board went ahead toward the publication of a flower show history booklet that Marge was writing so that it might be ready by 1998. A cap of $1,500 from the remembrance fund was allowed for this booklet, which was written by Marge and Cathy Velardi in 1997 and sold for proceeds to pay back the fund.

In May 1997, member Betty Coleman gave a workshop for miniature flower arrangements and David Lemon (a local flower seed grower) gave one on specimens for the flower show coming up.

The flower show in June 1997, was the diamond jubilee and is the last one that was included in Marge Scott's booklet: "Alpha Club Flower Show, 1922 to 1997." Marge was again the chair of the show "Jewels of the Valley" and won for her sweet pea arrangement. She wrote in her booklet: "For 75 years the strong women of the Alpha Club have relied upon each other and their special talents to make their community a better—and more beautiful—place." There's a lovely little pamphlet put out that year by the flower festival association that shows a diamond shape sketch with a picture of Marguerite Hall in the center, listing her as the first chair of the flower show in 1922.

Dott Brackin was president for club year, 1997–98. Special sections were crafts, home and garden, gourmet and literary. At this time there was still a rentals chair whose responsibility was to secure renters and collect rental deposits, keep a schedule of when the clubhouse has been rented and inform the Intermediate Director of such schedule so that the clubhouse could be set up and cleaned up accordingly.

At the November board meeting it was reported that the craft bazaar made $2,001.70; the country kitchen, $217.90; the salad luncheon, $377.75; and the Alpha entries in the Soroptimists bazaar made $408.00. The total was $3,300.59 with work done by mostly six members. The crafts section had been busy for years, and for a long time the membership was such that the work could get done by many. At this time, in the late 90s the membership has begun to drop considerably. The craft section had been one of the most consistent money makers for the club, bringing several thousand into the treasury every year.

Members planned to hold a spaghetti dinner on December 5 for $5 a plate—a very reasonable price and another nice evening. The board also passed a motion to hold a dinner dance at the Elks Lodge on March 7 as a kickoff for the centennial and the tree trimming party was held in December with home and garden committee and craft committee doing the work and the eating.

In early February 1998 Lompoc had a fierce storm. Some of us were out in it and hurried home before we blew away. The rain came down in sheets and a wind of over 70 miles an hour blew all night. We remember waking early to silence after the damage was done. We went out to look and saw the Santa Ynez River as it must have looked back before the dam was built. It was large, fast and furious and had overflowed all over the south valley washing crops away. It was beginning to look like Alpha's story with all those memories might not get written. The board was getting anxious and so at their meeting the next week it was decided to invite Marge Scott to come to the next board meeting and give them an update on the book she was writing as the Alpha centennial celebration was coming up in the fall. Unfortunately, Marge told the board that she couldn't possibly finish the book in time for the centennial.

At the same meeting, the board passed a motion to give $15 out of the general fund to the remembrance fund in honor of Walter Holmdahl, Gene's husband.

We notice that the treasurer no longer reads off all individual bills and asks approval to pay them. It was moved and seconded that the treasurer's report of transactions be accepted as read! Only expenditures over $500 need general membership approval now.

At the May 1998 board meeting, Norma Harrison reported for Gene, chair of Alpha's centennial committee that she recommends we combine our membership tea and anniversary party making it a birthday party for the centennial anniversary on Saturday, October 24, 1998.

The 76th flower show in 1998 was all about getting somewhere. The Theme was "Transportation: Past, Present, and Future." co-chairs were Freddie Weyl and Jinx Foster. Marge may have finished writing the history of the flower shows but she wasn't finished with them personally, winning best of show and tying with Esther Baker for sweepstakes.

A nice article in the October 11, 1998 Lompoc Record announced that Alpha would celebrate its 100th Birthday from 2–4 p.m. at the clubhouse. The public was invited. The following is a list of accomplishments of the GFWC:

- Formed 75 percent of the nation's libraries
- Were originators of the Pure Food and Drug Act
- Created model Juvenile Court Law
- Supported raised reflective highway markers

- Supported education and literacy for 100 years
- Helped support restoration of the Statue of Liberty
- Restored Independence Hall in Philadelphia
- Helped create county extension programs
- Installation of call boxes along the highways
- Instigated inoculations for children beginning school

Add that to all that Alpha Club did for our local community over those one hundred years and we have to wonder how our town or any town would have turned out otherwise.

That October, Alyce Martin remembers the club putting on a skit called: "The Sitting" in honor of the club's 100th Birthday. The group, which included Alyce, who played the president, had also given the skit at district federation and won a prize. Alyce remembered that she was at the hotel for Federation on her way downstairs for the performance, all dressed in black for her role and a man on the elevator asked her if she were a judge. We remember the skit well and thoroughly enjoyed it. The script may have been adapted from that "playlet" originally put on by those Camp Fire Girls back in March 1959.

At the November board meeting, it was announced that money from the March fashion show would go to Lifeline Medic Alert and the senior center. The crafts section had been in need of a chair for some time. That section was always a lot of fun and had made a lot of money for the club, but interests do ebb and flow over time. At that time, members were still handling the rentals for the clubhouse.

At the December 16, 1998 general meeting, President Dott Brackin and Laurel Beaudry presented a check in the amount of $6,500 to Ann Foxworthy of Allan Hancock College for a glass display case and books for the soon to be completed new campus library in Lompoc. (There goes that Alpha history book money!)

At the January 1999 general meeting, Second Vice President Erna Brown indicated we needed new members. At that time we had 105 active members. Alpha may not have been ready to admit that all the changes in women's life styles were really starting to affect the membership. The club's approach has always been "Onward Ever!" It was announced that there would be a flower arranging demonstration scheduled for every month until the flower show in June.

President Dott Brackin announced that she, along with another member, would chair the flower show. Because Dott understood the importance of crafts to Alpha's yearly budget and was inclined to take on at least as much as Gene Holmdahl would have, she also volunteered to chair the crafts committee.

The club had started holding an annual Bunco party in February, which even though it always seemed to conflict with some other organization's event, was an inexpensive, easy and enjoyable way to spend a Saturday afternoon and make a little money for the Museum.

At the March board meeting, it was moved that a chair and committee be established representing a broad cross section of opinion to investigate and recommend either re-commitment to Federation goals or resign from the federation. (Here we go again!) After much discussion and planning, the board agreed to bring the recommendation to the general membership at the March meeting. That spring, Alyce Martin's husband, Perry, died and 17 members attended the service.

At the May meeting, Elizabeth O'Connell, the chair, reported on the success of the fashion show and checks were presented to representative from Lifeline, B. J. Betts and Mary Lou Parks as representative for the newly planned senior center. Mary Lou had recovered from her health issues and was chair of the senior commission in Lompoc as well as working as a care manager and private conservator in northern Santa Barbara County. Lompoc had committed to building a senior center and plans were under way. With support from those in the community like Alpha, the seniors would soon have their center. Working mostly full time kept Mary Lou from getting as involved as she would like with Alpha Club, but she managed to attend meetings and help with some events.

Alpha's 77th flower show's theme was "Lompoc's Golden Valley." co-chairs were Dott Brackin and Jinx Foster, who reminded everyone at the June meeting to come to the memorial building for set up on Wednesday and be sure that all members make six dozen cookies for the tea room. The show was a success, making $4,000 that year.

That summer, Marge Scott lost her husband, Bill.

At the September board meeting, it was announced that the committee to study whether we should stay in Federation was unable to meet. It was suggested the president of Federation could speak on this at our reciprocity meeting in November. Other suggestions were to call a special meeting or give 3 to 5 minutes to the federation secretary at each general meeting.

What is it that is said? "S/he who does not know history is doomed to repeat it." We can look back to January 1981 when these same issues came up with some of the club members. Our hope now is that this book will make it easier for Alpha members and other interested parties to understand how important being a part of such a large and involved federation has been. The GFWC's has provided Alpha the information and support needed on our journey toward full status as 21st Century women. We have not finished this journey yet and if we are to carry out the mission of our foremothers, Alpha's founding members, we will need to continue with the support of Federation.

At the October 1999, meeting the Intermediate Director reported that she had the carpets cleaned and because of too much pressure the water heater had started to leak. (A new one had just been purchased the past summer!) A plumber inspected and said the pipes in the clubhouse were old and needed to be replaced. The Alpha Board asked her to get 3 bids so that this could be taken to the general membership for approval due to total cost.

By November's board meeting, the Intermediate Director reported that the new pipes and water heater were installed at a cost of $2,890. A video of the condition of the sewer lines was to be done the following week. The board decided to sponsor a girl's basketball team for the year and would donate $200 to Parks and Recreation for the sponsorship.

At the November general meeting, the guest speaker was from the state federation and spoke on the "Federation and what it can do for you." CFWC would celebrate their centennial on January 18, 2000 in Sacramento. "Women have strength through unity and by working together."[3] It doesn't hurt to be reminded once in a while.

Women's clubs were about to enter their third millennium. The new century was exciting, yet a little scary. The word was circulating that we should expect problems with our computers that they might even crash. All kinds of predictions were floating around. People fear the unknown and a new century can seem ominous.

CHAPTER 15

The Future is Now

January 2000 arrived. Computers didn't crash and the world didn't end as some had predicted. Alpha members did what all people do even when a significant event like a new Millennium arrives. They took one day at a time and dealt with daily concerns. One of which was the need for a craft section and chair. Dott Brackin had gotten way too busy to keep on as chair and the entire section had closed up shop and sold off the last of their items at the Soroptimists bazaar in October. Plans began again for the 2000 flower show with Glenn Ball agreeing to be chair.

The club was still holding Bunco parties every March. Profit from these events was given to a charity of choice, it wasn't much but every little bit helps.

During the late 90s, member's husbands were dying at the rate of almost one every three or four months. There was also a wave of serious illness among members. Time was catching up to many of us and yet we kept things going, doing our share.

One of Alpha's members, Ethel Roberts, wrote an excellent article for the Lompoc Record about Alpha Club and the federation but the withdrawal issue would not be settled until a vote was taken by the membership.

The members spent some time discussing getting a commercial dishwasher at the February board meeting. This is not the first time we had wanted one and it seemed it was not going to happen yet again because the Intermediate Director informed the club that her husband found evidence of termites in the clubhouse. Of course, the dishwasher was put on hold until we could find out how much a termite treatment would cost. At the April board meeting, it was recommended that the Intermediate Director have a termite inspection every year. By the May meeting, it was announced that the termite extermination would be done July 10–14. We can't help but note that it seemed to take almost as long to get the termite problem taken care of as it did to build the clubhouse back in the summer of 1933!

In May, a concern was brought up at the general meeting by Mary Lou Parks that there was no one to give flower arranging work-shops for children at that time, but apparently this issue was solved quickly by Louisa Van Ausdal who agreed she would start holding them again at her home. Mary Lou suggested that we invite the mothers of these children to the membership tea.

The flower show theme in 2000 was, "Mardi Gras into the Millennium" with Glenn Ball as chair and Jinx Foster as her co-chair. It was a rather up-beat time and the show was very festive. Mary Lou Parks remembers helping in the junior arrangement room. Louisa offered her storage shed which was filled with all sorts of goodies from her many years of entering the flower show. She had Mardi Gras masks galore and we hung them everywhere. "The children's room was a delight of color with all those masks and arrangements in categories such as, Carnival on Parade, Shrimp Boat, Fire Works, Masked Mardi Gras Ball and All That Jazz."[1]

As a new club year began in September 2000, we finally had a crafts chair, JoAnne Jones, yea! In October 2000 Mayor Dick DeWees came as a guest speaker and gave members an update on the opening of the community/senior center. Alice Milligan from the hospital board of directors also spoke about "Reciprocity." We wonder now what she was referring to. Surely, after all Alpha Club had given the hospital over the years, she must have realized our hospital fund had nearly run dry.

Norma Harrison was president again, a re-run for her. At the club's Christmas meeting, a few members of the newly formed Lompoc "Pops" Orchestra played Christmas music and Paul May, the first president of the group, spoke to Alpha members about their plans.

The fashion show and luncheon was held on March 3, 2001, and was again a big success netting $1,101.96 in spite of expenditures for unique decorations, which put everyone in the mood for spring.

The theme for Alpha's 2001 flower show was "A New Beginning." We couldn't have known the tragedy that would befall our nation in late summer as we kicked off it's beginning just as we had for 79 years with a beautiful flower show. Table titles were all about first's such as, "Pioneers," "New Moon," "Sunrise," "First Job," "Spring," and "Woman's Suffrage." (Seems like woman's suffrage as a category shows up every once in a while.)

We'd have to say that September 11, 2001 was at least as shocking as December 7, 1941 had been, probably more so. We really had no idea on 9/11! One could say that as a country we may have become complacent and self involved.

Rachel Valencia was president for the new club year and she wrote in the October Alpha Gram about our national tragedy saying how stressful and shocking it all was and how helpful it had been to have Humorist Doris O'Brien as our guest speaker for the September meeting. Rachel wrote that members left the meeting happier after Doris gave them a lot of laughs. She also added a thought for the day from Andy Rooney "I've learned … that being kind is more important than being right!" Staying true to that thought would be difficult, almost impossible over the next decade as our country became more and more divided.

Mary Lou Parks was about to find out how much work goes into putting on the flower show as she had agreed to be co-chair with Dott Brackin for the 2002 show.

There was still talk of leaving the federation and a vote by full membership was taken at the February 2002 meeting, passing with a wide margin to remain in Federation. We then informed our Tierra Adorada District that Alpha would hold a meeting in 2002.

The fashion show was held March 16 at the Elks and was enjoyed by all, including a number of non-Alpha's who enjoyed coming every year.

What a busy year it was for Mary Lou Parks who was on the nomination committee, the health committee and co-chair of the flower show as well as really busy with her work that required that she travel all over Santa Barbara and San Luis Obispo Counties, checking on clients and their caregivers, keep complete records on them, attend their physician appointments and numerous court hearings concerning conservatorships for them.

On top of all that, she had to have her gall bladder out 3 weeks before the flower show, but unlike Gene Holmdahl and her broken ribs, Mary Lou had microscopic surgery, healed quickly and was back on her feet within a week with no problems. It was a good thing because she needed all her energy to get through the flower show weekend.

The 80th flower show was titled, "A Rainbow of Flowers & Memories." Several different categories were part of this show, hats decorated with dried material, nosegays and topiaries. These gave us the fun of a little creative challenge mixed in with all the hard work.

Mary Lou wished that the chair and co-chair of the flower show could set up cots and just stay at the Veterans Memorial Building from Thursday morning when the show gets set up until Monday at noon when members finish taking the show down and storing all equipment back in the Alpha garage. In recent years, as members have grown older and those husbands still around have became unable to help, Alpha members have been forced to hire younger people to help move all the equipment over to the Vet's building and back to our garage storage.

Planning for the flower show usually starts right after the holidays, so that everything gets done in a timely way. There are committees for everything; public relations, securing and working with judges, setting up the show, running the show, soliciting sponsors and patrons, buying the awards and presenting them, working shifts at the door, the tea room and in the two show rooms, tallying up the winners and arranging for them to come for the award ceremony and finally taking the show down. The event itself takes five days of from 3 to 8 hours each day and a lot of teamwork! This is the part of club work that facilitates bonding between clubwomen; you can't get down in the trenches and work this hard without getting to really know each other!

Some members have been doing their part for many years but all in all it is a huge undertaking. This year in 2011, we had wonderful help from some high school boys who moved everything for us for monetary reimbursement and 36 high school cheer leaders who worked in shifts throughout the 5 days for Community Service hours as reimbursement. We certainly appreciate the energy of these young people.

By club year 2002–03, we are again missing a craft section and a home and garden chair as well as a flower show chair. Alyce Martin was chair of the gourmet section and Dott Brackin was president again. It seems like club members had lost some of their enthusiasm. There was even talk at the board meeting of *hiring* someone to chair the flower show. The horticultural group had said they would help. We think this may have been the first time it became really clear that we were in trouble because so few younger women were joining the club. Dott was president for the second time and had been chair of the flower show twice already. Other members had also served in these positions more than once but now there were only a few newer members coming forward. The board talked of replacing the carpet and linoleum but we needed members who were able to put on fundraisers in order to do any of those things.

The Lompoc Civic Theatre gave a presentation for Alpha at the clubhouse on October 13, which made the club only $105, but was a lot of fun. At the general meeting, Glen Newcomb played a flute solo accompanied by Alpha's long standing music chair and pianist, Gwennie Howard. Mayor Dick DeWees spoke about all the activities and accomplishments around town.

Esther Baker was still active and had agreed to be the chair for the 2003 flower show. She was also planning a Christmas open house on December 14 at the clubhouse. People could set a place setting on a card table with their Christmas china. She hoped to have 24 tables decorated and people who attended would pay $10 each. Although there still wasn't a chair for the home and garden section, the group was meeting monthly at the clubhouse and planned an hor d'oeuvres luncheon at their November meeting.

At the general November meeting, it was announced that Norma Harrison would be chair and Esther Baker would co-chair the flower show. Esther was also planning on hosting a Card party in May. The clubhouse was painted and, after some problems that had to be re-done, the clubhouse looked sparkling clean.

A rummage sale was planned for February 2003 at the clubhouse and the fashion show would again be held in April. The club was still holding a prayer breakfast every May. The home and garden section began making preparations for the flower show.

It was announced at the March meeting that Tower Property Management would be taking over rentals for the clubhouse, a job no club member really wanted.

Each May members are still asked to wear hats to the general meeting although the club has dropped many other old activities over the years, this one still seems to be a hit. Very few women actually wear hats now, but we still like to dress up in them at least once a year. This time we had prizes for the "Goofiest," Prettiest and Most Unusual. At the end of club year 2002–03 there were 80 paid members.

At the September board meeting, in club year 2003–04 a proposal was made by Dott Brackin coming from Gene Holmdahl that Alpha Club have a mural painted of the club and its history. Murals had become a big thing in Lompoc. The art association had formed a mural committee and had painted and commissioned other artists to paint a number of lovely murals around town. Most depicted a piece of history of Lompoc and were being painted once or twice a year on various buildings mostly in 'Old Town.' Gene Holmdahl and several other members, Sandy Morgan and Alyce Martin to name a few, had been thinking about a Mural for Alpha for some time and Gene decided to take on this project even though she was 90 years old by that time. Gene pledged $5,000 to the Mural fund to get it started and the understanding was that the club would raise a greater share. Alpha formed a mural committee consisting of Dott Brackin, Gene Holmdahl, Alyce Martin, Myra Walton and Vicki Andersen. They planned for fundraisers and personal contributions. The committee set a budget of $12,000 to $18,000. For the next two to three years they met trying to decide what the Mural should look like, where it should be placed, how to raise the funds needed and many other details.

In November 2003, Alpha members saw an obituary in the Lompoc Record that Harriet Hall Adam McCollum had passed away in Castro Valley at age 85. It was reported that Harriet had Alzheimer's disease.

There were no chairs for the craft or the home and garden sections during that club year either but the home and garden section continued to meet monthly at the clubhouse without a chair until February when they began holding a flower show workshop every month until June.

Members were asked to vote on continuing the prayer breakfast, due to lack of participation. We didn't see the results of the vote, but there were no more prayer breakfasts starting in 2005. Members did vote to have lunches catered for $8.00 each. However, luncheon committees continued to set tables, decorate and make coffee and desserts.

The theme for the 2004 flower show was "International Celebration" and Gloria Heitman was chair. Even though Gloria had never been involved with the show before, she did a fabulous job and Marge Scott was very pleased.

In club year 2004–05 Dott Brackin was president again with Ann Ruhge as first vice president. Some substantial donations were coming in for the Mural fund, including $500 from Stella Reed, but it was time again to prep and paint the entire exterior of the clubhouse at the cost of $2,200.

Esther Baker was still full of ideas to help raise the money needed for Alpha's charities. For the second time she held a "Holiday Open House" featuring 20 or more Christmas Place Settings" on December 11, 2004. A donation of $10 was asked with wine and finger food, desserts and coffee being served. We were unable to attend but heard it was lovely with demonstrations of many creative ways to set a table. We're sure we would have learned something.

A picture in the Lompoc Record dated January 18, 2005 shows Lompoc Mayor Dick De Wees standing with some chamber and Alpha members and Dott Brackin is cutting the ribbon.

Apparently the chamber membership had been dropped along the way and was being taken up again. Alyce Martin is standing in the front.

Alpha Club decided to sponsor a flower festival queen candidate for 2005, which can end up costing more than the club makes. Enough said!

The mural fund was up to $8,100 in collections and pledges by 2005. Club members were also in the process of getting bids to finish the work on the exterior of the clubhouse. While being painted, it was noticed that the eaves had a lot of dry rot and needed replacing. Work also needed to be done on the windows, shutters, screens and railings. After much discussion at the February board meeting, it was decided to get the eaves replaced first. The bid for the rest of the work was accepted by motion and voted on in March.

The Alpha Literary and Improvement Club's 82nd flower show was entitled, "Family Traditions." There were fun table titles such as: "Tea Time," "Party Time," "Sunday Worship," "Caroling," and "May Baskets." The chair was Dott Brackin, again! Dott seemed to be holding the club together that year!

Ann Ruhge was president in club year 2005–06 and she took her job seriously. The condition of the clubhouse bothered her and she wanted to be the one to get it completely fixed up. Her friend, Helen Free, served as third vice president and donated to the mural fund. As president, Ann was concerned that members on the mural committee had put the "cart before the horse" as they say. She could not understand why this group had gotten so excited about a mural when our clubhouse was falling apart. The kitchen was too small and in need of updating, the carpet was worn and old, the electricity might need replacing, a new roof was needed, the list was endless. It was Ann's opinion that Alpha should mend their clubhouse before any other projects were taken on.

At the September board Meeting, 2005 Ann read a letter from Gene Holmdahl stating that she was withdrawing her pledge for $5,000 for the Alpha mural. Her reason for withdrawal was that Alpha members weren't acting fast enough with their contributions. Gene said that two and one half years was long enough for Alpha to accumulate their money to match hers. Helen Free offered to talk to Vicki Andersen, chair of the Lompoc Mural Society to ask her to speak about what our club needed to do to sponsor a mural.

The mural committee dug in, the funds that had been donated were specifically for the mural fund. Alyce Martin held firm on this; it would be unethical to use the funds for any other purpose. Alyce had joined senior Alpha the same year as Gene, 1963, and had been in Junior Alphas before that, she understood the importance of the image of Alpha. Some of the long time members sensed the subtle loss of momentum of the club. Members were getting old, not so many new women were joining. Those who were, didn't always grasp the significance of the club, what "Alpha had accomplished, what it had meant to so many women before them and to the town. The mural committee wanted to capture that sentiment." This was the opportunity, the time was right![2]

At the October board meeting, some unfinished business appeared on the Agenda, "mural versus building repairs." Ann wanted to settle this issue. She wanted to use what was actually in the mural fund (not pledges) to pay for some of the needed building repairs. To her way of thinking, it was unsound to take money from people for a project that the club could not afford. What good would a mural be if the clubhouse was crumbling? Some agreed with President Ann, it certainly made sense, but the mural committee fought her on it. They felt that a mural would help the club tremendously. It would boost membership and the status of Alpha in town. We see this a lot in our own lives, as well as society as a whole. Instead of doing the practical thing, we spend our money on something we want, something that makes us feel good about ourselves and life around us. It's the human way. Helen Free, out of loyalty to Ann, moved her donation to the club building fund.

An old friend returned to Alpha Club in 2005–06, Louisa Van Ausdal. We were all glad to see her back. Of course, she had continued to teach children how to do flower arrangements almost every year as well as enter some of her own, but we had missed her happy smile at club events.

The mural committee persisted and at the December board meeting Dott Brackin reported that Gene Holmdahl was going to donate the $5,000 that she withdrew. At that point all kinds of small fundraisers were taking place, tamale sales, card parties, even plans to write a grant to finance the clubhouse improvements.

Even with all the fund raising efforts, it was reported at the March 8, 2006 board meeting that we would need $17,000 in our mural fund before we could go to the Mural Society with a request. But, we only had $6,800 in the fund and $12,800 counting pledges, which included that $5,000 from Gene. "At this point there were 12 members on the mural committee. Lia Schade, a new Alpha member, was a businesswoman whose job on the committee was to study contracts from the artists. After consideration of the Mural Society's contract, she determined that it was too costly and that by signing it Alpha would give up ownership of the mural. It would be painted on a movable board which would belong to the Mural Society and could be taken down and stored in the Mural Society's building at any time. Lia suggested that Alpha consider having the mural painted on the clubhouse building itself. At that time, another artist recommended that the job could be done for $15,000."[3]

The flower show theme was "Back to the 60s" and again Dott Brackin was the chair.

Table titles were in keeping with those years, "Blowing in the Wind," "Where Have All the Flowers Gone?" "I Have A Dream," and "Beginning of Women's Movement, 1966." We know that the Women's Movement actually began at least one hundred years before that with the Suffragettes, Jane Croly and her General Federation of Women's Groups. The movement seems to come in waves depending on how women feel about their status in the world.

By August 2006 the mural committee had determined the mural site would be the west side of the clubhouse. At the board meeting, there was discussion about moving forward, and picking the artists. Local artists were invited to come to a mural meeting where they were asked to provide sketches for the committee with cost estimates. Insurance was to be included in the cost. Martha Galisky, who was Alpha's chair of the home and garden section, explained what was needed to be done outside the clubhouse before the mural could be painted. All of the old bushes and shrubs would need to be removed for one thing.

Work for the club and clubhouse never stops so at the September meeting, Dott volunteered to clean and paint the kitchen cupboards, Ann Ruhge and Irma Gadway volunteered to be co-chairs of the 2007 flower show but a fashion show chair was still needed. Ann Ruhge, president again, was running for city council and had been called to serve Jury Duty, in autumn 2006. It never rains but it pours for some people. "In November of 2006, Ann was elected to the Lompoc City Council, the first Alpha Club member to serve on the council!"[4]

We note that in club year 2006–07 husband's names have been dropped completely from the membership list. Members stand alone, identified only by their first and last legal name. There may be several reasons. One is certainly that many husbands are no longer with us, but another may be that as women in the 21st Century we are individuals no longer identified by the many roles we play in life.

Only three artists submitted sketches. Leo Nunez submitted a pencil sketch and a team of two artists (women) submitted their sketch in water painting. The committee voted for Leo's work and he began planning his actual sketch on the clubhouse. He found it difficult to fit his work in with the existing doors, windows and fireplace chimney structure to say nothing of the tree that got in the way. Members of the committee began making suggestions as to how to fit the mural design on the wall. Apparently there were some suggested changes that Mr. Nunez eventually decided he couldn't do and he gave up the work.[5]

After a board recommendation was passed by membership to use the women's art team, Nancy Phelps and Sue Trushaft in January 2007, their sketches were presented to members at the club meeting so they could make a choice. The mural committee wanted the option to make changes to the mural as they saw fit. Marge Scott felt the committee should request more sketches of every detail of the mural before moving forward with anyone else. Possibly she wanted to avoid the disagreements that had been so problematic. Some felt that Marge who agreed with President Ann about getting the clubhouse fixed, was just delaying so the mural committee would give in. Finally in frustration over all of the contentiousness, Marge proposed that Alpha should go ahead with the mural but that the artists should be the ones to make all decisions on the mural painting. She brought the matter to a vote, which was approved. Some on the committee were disappointed that they would have nothing more to say.

Lompoc's head librarian, Molly Gerald asked if Alpha Club would assist in presenting an author's brunch to be held at the clubhouse on a Saturday in April and a motion was passed that we would be honored to do so.

The club learned in February that the county had raised the rental fee for the Veterans Memorial Building to $870 a day! Talk about inflated costs; Alpha had always paid a token rental charge of $100 for all five days of use for the flower show. Where would we find $4,350? How could we do that? President Ann wrote a letter to our county supervisor requesting a lower rental fee and it was granted. The club would pay only $250 for all five days. The county absorbed the balance of $4,100.

Gene Holmdahl was at the February (Past President's Day) luncheon as were Alyce Martin and Marge Scott. There were 12 past presidents all together. Jeanne McBratney, a new member, reported on the fashion show coming up in March, which she agreed to chair.

At the March general meeting it was announced that the mural committee asked the home and garden section to revise their landscaping plan. "Since most of the things we were so proud of planting on the west side of the building in the fall were frozen to death in January (hard freeze) this would not be a problem to us" was the response.[6]

The 2007 flower show was "American History on Parade." Categories were Presidents, Explorers, Discovery of Gold, Civil War, Louisiana Purchase and Women's Right to Vote, to name a few. There's a front page picture in the Lifestyles section of the Lompoc Record titled "Alpha ladies, beginning in Harmony, presided over the Flowering of Lompoc" Nine members of the flower show committee are standing with a picture of the clubhouse in the background. Ann and Irma the co-chairs of course, Marge Scott and it was especially good to see Louisa Van Ausdal with her happy smile among them.

In our opinion this was another fun year to enter the show especially if you like history. Mary Lou Parks entered two categories, didn't win much but it always got her creative juices going. Marge Scott purchased the Crystal Awards and Mary Lou worked on the awards committee. We were still charging only $3.50 for pre-sale of tickets, $4.00 at the door. A bargain price for sure.

By August 2007, the $15,000 had been paid to the mural artists and we had a beautiful mural depicting the story of Alpha in as complete a way possible on the side of our building.

Not one member has ever complained. In the end it was a good thing to do.

In early September the club held a garden and wine tasting party in the garden of Alpha member, JoAnne Jones. It was lovely, delicious with all food prepared by JoAnne and her crew of Alpha members, including Alyce Martin. Wine was donated and served by Dewayne Holmdahl. The event made $730 for the building fund. We were sure this would become an annual affair.

At the September general meeting, the board recommended that pledge cards be used to donate funds toward the building fund. They would be tax deductible of course. The deadline was set at December 31, 2007.

At the November meeting, Martha Galisky, home and garden chair announced that they had finished planting the gold and violet pansies, which would be part of the mural design as requested by the artists. It was announced that there was now $2,250 in the building fund available for renovations. An enchilada sale was planned for February.

Work was being done in the kitchen, new paint put on handles and hinges and the kitchen cabinets. It was hoped that new floors and counter tops would be installed soon, as well. Members were urged to complete their pledges. Cookie Lee Consultants held a fundraiser and donated the $300 to the building fund. Members decided to pay $5 each at the Christmas luncheon (instead of it being free) and donate that to the building fund.

By January it was imperative that Alpha Club replace a broken heater. The painter needed to have some uninterrupted days to finish painting the kitchen and then they would deal with new kitchen counters. In the meantime, a leak was discovered in the roof in February and rain was leaking onto the kitchen cabinets. There were also reports of damage done to the clubhouse from renters. Members made $575 from another enchilada sale. No one could say that club members weren't doing their best to raise money but where were those pledges? Unlike the past, it seems that more money was going out than could possibly be brought in!

Louisa was third vice president that spring and we had some very informative programs: the medical director of Lompoc Hospital Emergency Services, the staff from Valley Haven—the senior day care program that would receive some of the profit from our fashion show, the police chief, the mayor, and the administrator of Valley Medical Group and her team.

2008 was one of those years when it was very difficult to get a flower show chair, but Sandy Morrison, a new younger member who worked as a nurse in Santa Barbara, bravely took on the job. Sandy needed to fasten her seat belt because "she was in for a bumpy ride!" It seems that the board of supervisors couldn't let Alpha Club have the Veterans Building at a discount like they did in 2007. The county (the supervisors) had set new rates per day for any renters and they had to stick to those rates. In 2008 the cost would be $7,800 for the five days. Impossible for Alpha Club!

Everyone panicked and Sandy, being new to this undertaking, tried her best to come up with a different venue. She and her committee had only just discovered in early March what Alpha would have to pay the county. It was already very late to be planning the show let alone finding a new venue. Sandy spent several weeks touring other facilities, filling out applications and worrying about costs. The whole situation was just a mess. Alpha had never made much money putting on the flower show even now in 2011 our profit was less than $3,000. It had never been about the money for us although we use some of it for scholarships and other charities. We always need to make enough to cover our costs with a little more for the charities, but that wouldn't be possible with the new rental price. Things were not looking good!

The flower show committee even went so far as to vote to hold the show at the clubhouse. Some, including Mary Lou Parks, cautioned that there were many reasons why that wouldn't work: very limited space, no parking, insurance issues, the clubhouse sits on a corner facing a highway which could cause major risks—just too many problems. She decided to use her connections as Lompoc senior commissioner and called the director of Lompoc's Parks & Recreation Department. She explained Alpha's dilemma begging for his help and he agreed to rent the entire first floor of the recreation center from Thursday through Monday morning, including custodial help to set up and tear down the show, for $1,200.[7]

The panic subsided, Sandy and the flower show committee got down to the business of planning a show in a different venue as well as everything else left to do in just a short time. The show, "Music, Music, Music" went on with very few problems. It was beautiful with song titles as arrangement titles. A new category "Table Settings" was added and Alyce Martin took charge of it. There was a good response to them. They were fun, setting a table in a theme with a floral arrangement included. We were all very happy with the show and the venue. Mary Lou Parks won crystal for best sweet pea arrangement, yea! Sandy had reason to be very proud. She deserved to go off on her boat for a vacation when the whole affair was over. She felt so good about her accomplishment against all those odds that she continued to be flower show chair for two more years!

Susan Lindman was president for club year, 2008–09. Susan's theme was "Reevaluate and Reinvent Ourselves." She was interested in finding new ways to fulfill our mission. The clubhouse needed continued repair and upkeep and we needed new members. Committees were: blood bank, charities, scholarships, flower show, music, lady of cheer, telephone, fashion show, spring garden tour, membership brunch, duplicate bridge, hospitality and remembrance. Many of those committees, with the exception of the flower show, fashion show, and spring garden tour required only a limited amount of work and didn't bring in any money. We still did not have an arts and crafts committee at that time.

Another wine tasting party was planned for October 4, 2008 at the clubhouse by the home and garden section. Cost would be $25 per person. Later it was reported that the event made $350. We attended and thought it was lovely in spite of the fact there was a poor attendance. Competition for that type of fundraiser was growing, Lompoc was becoming a place to buy and drink wine, it seems everyone was using wine tasting for fundraisers.

A Cookbook was planned with some of the recipes that were used for the recent garden parties. An announcement was made that Alpha Club won an award in August from Lompoc's "America in Bloom" contest.

At the October 2008 meeting, President Susan announced that she would write a grant for Santa Barbara Foundation funding. Alpha would be eligible in September 2009. It was also reported that bids were being taken for badly needed roof patch repair. That grant couldn't come any too soon!

By November, the estimate for the roof repair had come in, but it was recommended that the club replace the entire roof with one that is supposed to last 50 years at a cost of $6,375. The motion was made and carried, we couldn't wait for the grant and it's a good thing, as we didn't get one.

In December the board came up with a partial solution for the new roof. Alpha should use three-fourths of the fashion show proceeds to pay for some of it. The recommendation was approved.

At the February meeting, Susan introduced the past presidents who were attending, Evelyn Thompson, Laurel Beaudry, Marge Scott, Alyce Martin, Norma Harrison, Edna Wright, Norma Chierichetti, Peggy Edge, Rachel Valencia, Ann Ruhge, and Judy Harrison. Gene Holmdahl was getting very frail and was not able to attend. Laurel Beaudry seemed to be shrinking away in front of our eyes, but even though it was a struggle for her, she continued to attend meetings.

The guest speaker was Jim Raggio, CEO of Lompoc Valley Medical Center, to talk about the new hospital, which he said was on schedule to open in 2010. A $75 million-bond issue passed with an 87 percent approval. He announced there would be an open house in November.

It was announced to the club members that the mural would need to be repaired by the original artists for $600 after the new roof was put on. Motion carried. The work would be done in April.

The fashion show was late that year, being held on April 20, 2009. The garden tour was held on May 30 and the flower show was the last weekend in June. Seems like everything got put off until the very end of the club year!

In May, 2009 Louisa lost her husband Max. He died just a month short of their 70th wedding anniversary. Another big funeral. Louisa and Max had been so active and supportive of everything in Lompoc.

At the June club meeting, the decorations included long time member Stella Reed's exquisite wedding gown made from her husband's parachute in 1946. Stella later used her gown as part of the décor in her place setting arrangement of roses for the category "My Wedding Day." The flower show's theme was, "Childhood Fantasies." Marge Scott won first place for her table setting and Mary Lou Parks won second. Everything went off like a charm at the Anderson Recreation building again that year.

Susan Lindman was president for the second time in club year, 2009–10. She picked as her goal for the year that: "the club have more fun" as well as all the responsibilities the president of Alpha takes on. At the September meeting, club members were entertained by Loren Cox, member Dawn Cox's daughter. She has studied music and gave an outstanding performance.

In October a recommendation by the board was read to the general meeting: "that repaving of the driveway, paving a small lawn area, replacing steps and adding new handicap ramps be approved, pending receipt of funding." A detailed explanation of the project was given by Martha Galisky, garden chair. It seems the driveway was sloping, causing rain to run under our building and under the neighbor's garage on the east. Alpha's main entrance was crumbling and unsafe and the back kitchen entrance also. We needed space for handicapped parking and to provide for a turnaround area so members and renters would no longer need to back out onto highway traffic. The motion was discussed and passed.

It was also reported at the October meeting that the fashion show would be held in November of 2010, instead of in the spring. The committee realized they might do better holding the show in autumn as there was now a big fashion show being held in spring to support the Relay for Life effort.

On November 9, 2009 Gene Holmdahl died at the age of 96. Members supplied food for the reception after the funeral at the Presbyterian Church. It was a huge event. Gene had been an outstanding Alpha member, as well as her involvement in so many groups and affairs in Lompoc. In those last few years we would see her occasionally at Alpha Club, she usually came for the Christmas luncheon and Presidents Day. Gene still loved to shop and look at merchandise. She could be seen from time to time shopping at Wal-Mart, one of the very few mercantile businesses left in Lompoc, with her son, Dwayne. Gene was always friendly and happy to see another Alpha member.

At the November meeting, there was a discussion about the membership tea and President Susan brought up the idea of having "Friends of Alpha." The by-laws committee was assigned to work on this. Cathy Pepe gave an "informative and lovely program on holiday table settings and wine." Cathy and her husband, Steve, have local vineyards along Highway 246 east of Lompoc. It was also announced that Santa Barbara Foundation had denied our grant! Now what? For one thing, Alyce Martin generously donated $1,000 toward the outside concrete work, a great start but where were those pledges?

The December Christmas luncheon looked especially grand with the donation of wine colored fabric chairs from the Village Country Club. The Holmdahl family donated Gene's collection of Alpha history to the club. We certainly put all of it to good use in this book! The Christmas program was presented by the Cabrillo High School Madrigal Singers as they frequently have done.

It is no big surprise that President Susan announced at the January meeting that the club would be looking for ways to raise money that spring. She would like to see an arts and crafts committee start up again to make and sell things. Martha Galisky reported that the cement work contractor agreed to $5,000 down and payments of $500 a month. Work would start in February, and that it did. If one was a bridge player, it was annoying but necessary to have the noise of the backhoe and trucks to say nothing of the dirt and dust blowing. Everyone was patient however; as they knew the work was very necessary.

At the April 2010 meeting, Anna Dinter, a new member who had been working on the bylaws as chair of that committee, asked if there was any further discussion on the revision and being none they were approved as revised. Marge Scott had been ill but returned for this meeting, thanking everyone for their well wishes. By this time it had become customary for members to donate their winnings from the meeting's opportunity drawing back to the club's building fund.

The garden tour was a great success and netted over $1,000, so the committee went ahead with plans for a tea and wine tasting party on August 21 at member Marilyn Mitty's home. Marilyn had frequently opened her lovely home and gardens for these occasions. This time they would hold the tea from 2 to 4 p.m. and the wine tasting party from 5:00 to 7:00 p.m. A bit much for one day but we needed money!

At the June meeting, two local authors, Mary Lou Parks (Taking the E Ride Through the Golden Years) and Tonya Schultz (You Can Balance Your Life) gave a presentation sharing tips on writing and publishing along with excerpts from their books.

For several months the treasurer, Dawn Cox, had been absent from meetings. The word was she was now employed at an agency she had been a volunteer for. The nominating committee, which included Mary Lou Parks as chair had not received any notice from her as to her ability to serve again, so her name was on the full slate that was presented to the club. As things happened, it became impossible for Dawn to continue so she finished out the club year and resigned at the end of June. Alpha had no treasurer.

The flower show returned to the Veterans Building for its 2010 show, "Carousel of Summer" and it was delightful. It was Sandy Morrison's third time as flower show chair with Susan Lindman as co-chair. The board of supervisors had changed their minds and offered the building to Alpha for only $750 for all five days. A reasonable sum.

The Anderson Recreation Center was forced to accommodate the senior programs in late 2009 so the building they had occupied just since 2000 could be torn down to make way for the new hospital. Even though the staff at the Anderson Center tried to fit everything in, it would not have been possible to hold the show there so we gladly accepted the offer to return to our old home at the Vet's building. Alyce Martin with all her love and knowledge of flowers had never entered the show but she did that year and won first place for her orchids in the category "Tilt-A-Whirl." Mary Lou Parks entered several categories and won a ribbon or two. Marge Scott won a crystal award.

It was while they were working at the flower show that Marge asked Mary Lou if she would be interested in writing the story of Alpha Club. She explained how there had been a committee that started the book back in the 80s but never finished.

Mary Lou wasn't sure she could take on such a project as Anna Dinter (the new president) had already asked her to step in to become treasurer in the absence of one.

Mary Lou had also been initiated as first vice president at the June meeting. She wasn't working much anymore but still was helping a few clients and doing some screenings for a home health agency. After several discussions about taking over as treasurer, Mary Lou agreed but it wasn't until late summer that she decided to go ahead with the book project. As she learned more about it she felt the story had to be written.

At the September 2010 meeting, Alyce Martin announced that she would be chairing the arts and crafts committee. Mary Lou gave her first treasurer's report and there was more money in the scholarship fund than in the operating fund. Martha Galisky reported that the garden tea and wine tasting parties in August were successful. We felt that even though it was lovely and enjoyable for those who came, it was a lot of work to net less than $400.

At the October board meeting, JoAnne Jones stepped into the first vice president position that was vacated when Mary Lou Parks became treasurer and it was approved that Mary Lou should move $3,000 from the scholarship fund to pay off the balance on the concrete work. The plan was to pay back the scholarship fund with money raised during the club year. The total bill of $9,210 for a new driveway, front and kitchen entrance was fully paid by November 1, 2010.

At the December 2010 Christmas luncheon, a musical program was presented by the Lompoc Concert Choir. Some of us couldn't help but wonder where those beautiful caroler's outfits were but it seems the Choir came straight from finals and didn't have time to change. Somehow it didn't seem Christmassy with Carolers in jeans. A bake sale was held again at the luncheon. It would be used to make new tablecloths. We were holding a number of bake sales trying to add money to our building fund, but some of us were buying back the items we baked. Wouldn't it be easier to just donate to the fund? We still wonder what happened to the plan to sign pledges back in 2007?

The fashion show held in November, netted $3,054 and one-third was donated to the Valley Haven Adult Day Program. Holding the show in the fall gave us a much better turnout and so we have already booked the Elks Lodge for the November 2011 show. The literary group held a potluck on December 20 at Ruth Johnson's home, which was a big success with great homemade soup, a delicious casserole and many other goodies along with great conversation. What a warm way to spend a rainy day! The craft committee had started selling items, not a lot, but a start.

In January 2011 plans were underway for the garden tour in May and of course, the flower show at the end of June. As though she doesn't do enough as recording secretary and chair of our fashion show, Jeanne McBratney came forward offering to chair the flower show with a new member, Bobbi Woods as her co-chair. The literary group would meet at Valeria Capell's home and were reading an Agatha Christie novel. Most of the time the group read a book that fit into a certain theme picked by the hostess for that month, every now and then the hostess would request that they all read the same book and do a critique on it. It was always fun to talk about a book that one had read, but it seemed more interesting, competitive maybe when we all read the same book.

At the February meeting, the 2010–11 budget was finally presented by President Anna Dinter and Treasurer Mary Lou Parks. Better late than never is all we can say about switching over programs from one computer to another that couldn't accommodate the past treasurer's program. After much time and effort, we finally got everything to fit and reconcile except that the new treasurer didn't have a planning component in her program. The budget finally had to be put in manually on Excel. We who use them know how wonderful computers can be and/or how frustrating they are when things don't work right!

In March the club had some very cute furry guests from the Santa Maria Kennel Club who sponsor the "Furry Friends Pet Therapy." There was also a discussion about the door on the south side of the building that had literally blown off, disintegrating into scrap during a storm several days before and would need to be replaced quickly. A short board meeting was held after the regular meeting and members approved the purchase and installation of a new door. Flower arrangement classes were continued throughout the spring.

At the May meeting, we had a flower arrangement demonstration given by Michelle Horenberger and the Lompoc librarian, Molly Gerald, spoke briefly about the Children's library, "Charlotte's Web" answering any questions as the club was in the process of deciding where our proceeds for the autumn fashion show would be donated.

It was announced at the June meeting, that the garden tour had netted just over $1,000, which will give us enough to do a door threshold repair and maybe get started on the bathroom work.

The club also voted to help send one of Alpha's HOBY scholarship students who had been chosen to attend the HOBY National Conference in Chicago in July in the amount of $825.

Jeanne, Bobbi and their committee did a splendid job on the flower show, which was entitled, "Surf, Sand & Beach" this year. Several of our newer members entered for their first try. President Anna Dinter won a second place for her arrangement, Kathy Pepe who is a "Friend of Alpha" won for her adorable sweet pea table arrangement "Picnic on the Beach" and Mary Lou Parks won crystal for the best rose arrangement, "Beach Treasures" and second place for her sweet pea arrangement. There were many specimens as usual and although the cool spring didn't give Mary Lou many dahlia blooms in time for the show the one she entered won a third place. Alyce Martin was on a trip with her children this time or we know she would have entered something again and Marge Scott was recovering from a broken hip. She was just happy to be able to come see the show. Louisa is not able to take part in the flower show now. She is mostly at home with her full-time caregivers.

It's hard to see the whole picture sometimes when you're in the middle of everything trying to keep going forward, but now that we have written it all down we can see how very much has been done in spite of some very major problems. We have managed to maintain our clubhouse, weather depressions, recessions and this country's many wars.

We survived the cancellation of the space shuttle program, and 9/11 (the verdict isn't in on that yet.) We were there when women won the vote and later when they gained the right to make their own decisions. We watched as our younger women graduated from college and were proud as they marched off to work. We sometimes have disagreements, even some major ones, but we work them out by allowing everyone in the club to have their say. We continue to recite the "Collect for Clubwomen" at every meeting to remind ourselves to respect our sister club members and do our best as we work to improve ourselves and our communities.

CHAPTER 16

Can Alpha Club and GFWC Survive?

For 113 years the Harmony/Alpha Literary and Improvement Club has been holding meetings, raising money by putting on programs, dinners, dances, fashion shows, luncheons, teas, plays, craft shows, rummage sales and last, but certainly not least, our flower show, so that our club might provide scholarships to local students, support charities and causes in Lompoc, California and even nationally.

Alpha Club was responsible for establishing the first public library in town and then we organized a committee, helped purchase land and secure the Carnegie grant in order to build a permanent library. Alpha Club has supported the Lompoc hospital with rooms and equipment, and donated to many other groups. We have learned from each other and other club groups around the state and country. Alpha has always understood the importance of belonging to the General Federation of Women's Clubs so that we could be connected to a strong support system. The number of things accomplished through GFWC is endless. The list of things accomplished by Alpha Club partly because of that connection is also endless.

The big question now for Alpha and other women's clubs appears to be, can we survive? Can we keep on doing what we have done so well for so long? How relevant are the General Federation of Women's Clubs in 2011? How can clubs like Alpha adapt so that they will continue to survive and remain vital to modern women and their communities in the present and into the future?

An online survey was done at GFWC during the fall of 2009 to gather as much information as possible about all the federated women's clubs. Out of the 100,000 member clubs in GFWC, over 1,000 clubs responded. A 2010–14 strategic plan was then drawn up and accepted by the board of directors in June 2010.

The following is the valuable information gleaned from that survey which gives a profile of women's clubs today:

A. Who Belongs to Women's Clubs Today?

According to a pie chart in a feature titled You spoke, We listened, p. 13–18, in GFWC Clubwoman, May – June, 2011 issue, the following are the results of their survey:

1) 74 percent of women in all Federated Women's Clubs are 55 plus. Ages 55–64 make up 35 percent and those 65–74 are 31 percent while those 75 and over equal 8 percent. Women 25–54 years old make up only 26 percent.

2) As for ethnic diversity there is no way to get that information, as it is not required. There is no discrimination allowed in the GFWC. The only way we were able to identify women of color in Alpha Club was by asking older members and we found there had not been many. There is a huge organization in this country for Black women, The National Association

of Colored Women's Clubs, but many small towns like Lompoc have nothing like that. There have only been a few Hispanic or Asian women in Alpha Club. There are some men in the GFWC but men have never asked to join Alpha Club.

B. How Women's Clubs Work?

1) Alpha Club has a president and board of directors who are nominated and elected by the members annually. Our bylaws state that a member may serve for one year or until their successors are elected. There is always an appointed federation secretary for TAD, our federation district. Other positions are section chairmen, nominating committee, standing committee chairs and a telephone committee chair. Every club has its own unique set-up.

As we have seen with Alpha, clubs can meet as it suits them. Meetings can last as long as each club desires. Each club usually has a program chair as well as fundraising chairs. Each club is autonomous as to structure and what type of meetings they wish to hold. The individual clubs decide which charities they wish to support. GFWC does have a list of programs in which various clubs participate.

C. Who Do Women's Clubs Serve?

1) These are GFWC priority projects compared to those of the Alpha Club

GFWC	Number of clubs participating	ALPHA CLUB
Financial Literacy	191	Seminar on Estate Planning
Juniors' Special Project	234	No current activity

Women's History and Resource Center	279	Disseminated materials for Celebration of Right to Vote, writing HerStory of Alpha Club
Community Safety	418	Donation to Police Activities League (PAL)
International Outreach	505	No current activity
Literacy	523	Support Children's Library
Beautification	615	Won award from "America in Bloom." Annual Garden Tour
Conservation	623	Recycle at clubhouse, Annual Flower Show, Conservation Program, Urban Forestry Program, Garden in Schools Project
Health	623	Support Senior Day Program, Women's Health Topics
Signature Project (Domestic Violence)	712	No current activity
Education	712	Scholarships, Literary Section
Arts	811	Mural on clubhouse, Craft Committee, Flower arranging classes. Fashion Show.

2) The GFWC Mission states:

"The General Federation of Women's Clubs is an international women's organization dedicated to community improvement by enhancing the lives of others through volunteer service." [1]

The Harmony Club's stated mission in 1898 was:

> the mutual improvement of its members in literature and the vital interests of the day.

Down through the years the statement evolved to:

> the mutual improvement of the members in literature and the fine arts, and the development of the interest in civic, social welfare and economic conditions.[2]

Over all the years, Alpha Club and other GFWC clubs have always known what the need is and how to serve our communities. Those needs in our communities have been vast, everything from health, and social issues to civic and legal issues in our local communities states and country. But we think it's equally important to say that we need to serve our membership as well, especially in looking at the needs of younger members.

D. Why Do Women Serve?

1) The survey in the GFWC's "Clubwoman" includes information on why members said that they joined a GFWC Club:

   - 52 percent wanted community service and volunteer opportunities.
   - 27 percent wanted friendship and social activities.
   - 9 percent had other reasons.
   - 5 percent joined for personal growth and development (not as important now that we go to college and have professional lives.)
   - 5 percent for that club's reputation
   - 2 percent joined for the reputation of GFWC.

2) Some women asked the GFWC to create online resources for them. At this time we find some of those

other than the GFWC, already online for busy women. We found many women's groups online. Some are for social networking and some support causes:

- Women's health issues
- Childcare issues
- Women's rights
- Women's support groups

You can go online and find almost any kind of group you want, even women's clubs. These seem to be set up for the younger women, those under 55. Those women who use up all their energy at work and raising their children. Busy women executives who are in middle age may have no way to have friendships even at work. In small towns like Lompoc, women who have busy lives with work and family must sometimes commute to a larger city. Do they find time to go online and use these groups? Is it enough?

3) In another part of the survey the top three service organizations that women said they were familiar with were:

- Lions Club
- Rotary International
- Kiwanis

Needless to say GFWC was encouraged to increase their social media presence. We have noticed that is a problem in general with women's clubs. Some may have a web page and GFWC has a very extensive one, but it's not really out there for the public to see. Many clubs don't have any social media exposure at all.

The 2010–2014 GFWC Strategic Plan.

The plan identified six areas that needed improvement:

1. Leadership:

a) The objective would be to increase educational opportunities and leadership training for potential GFWC leaders by allowing states to pay for a second member to attend the LEADS training by FY 2014.

b) Provide continuing education and resources to current GFWC leaders by giving club leaders comprehensive materials, training, and resources.

c) Empower members personally and professionally by providing tools and training.

2. Membership:

a) Instill a sense of pride and purpose in all GRWC Members by expanding awareness and acknowledgement.

b) Strengthen existing GFWC clubs, try to retain 85 percent of existing clubs by 2014.

c) Establish new GFWC clubs by achieving a net gain of 100 new clubs by 2014.

d) Maximize retention of current members by retaining 80 percent of GFWC's number with a gain of 15 percent...

3. Programs, Projects, & Activities:

a) Develop exclusive and valued GFWC programs and projects by securing at least one corporate or volunteer partner in GFWC's Signature Project: Domestic Violence Awareness.

4. Public Awareness:

a) GFWC will build a brand identity through all organizational entities that is consistent with its mission. The official name of the 25 state federations will be GFWC (state) by 2014. 50 percent of clubs will also have GFWC (club name).

b) Develop a consistent GFWC brand identity. The board will work on this.

c) Become a recognized source of info and resource on women's issues related to volunteers, volunteer management and women's clubs.

d) Enable state federations and their clubs to effectively promote their accomplishments and much more.

5 & 6. Financial Stability, Governance & Management, the last two concerned making GFWC more stable financially with more programs and grants and maintaining a high-functioning board and professional staff at the GFWC headquarters.

The GFWC has some difficult goals to meet in this four-year plan. Numbers two, membership, and four, public awareness, are of particular interest to us at Alpha.

We are planning to use part of the GFWC's Membership Advancement Guide this next club year for a presentation at our membership tea. There are numerous ideas in this guide on subjects like: engaging members, encouraging input, orientation of new members, mentoring new members and getting their feedback to name just a few. The idea of a strategic plan interests us. We have never done that. As we have gone through all the written materials we noticed there were job descriptions and some written procedures especially for large events like our flower show but never a plan to direct us.

Another great idea we at Alpha have been discussing is to set up a Web site and get connected to the virtual world where so many younger people get most of their information. Put Alpha out there. Every club needs to keep up with the 21st Century. We can see that GFWC has moved forward into these areas and we hope to follow but we don't want to lose our uniqueness. We need to keep what works in Alpha Club and expand on it.

Can We Offer More Ways To Serve?

Younger women today are extremely busy, most have jobs outside their home, are raising children, which in today's world seems to require chauffeuring them all over town, trying to keep their husbands happy if they have one and or make a go of it alone. They don't have time to read newspapers, watch TV news or pay much attention to the outside world. Some have become isolated from the bigger picture. Many keep in touch on Facebook and meet occasionally for a night out when it's possible but they are lonely. They don't have much time for girl friends. They long for a time when they won't be so busy so they can enjoy life more.

A few months ago we attended a Networking meeting for providers of Aging Services in and around Lompoc. At the end of the meeting a few of the busier women who had attended were talking about the "Women's Fund." They explained to those who asked that the fund was a group of professional women in our county who don't have time to belong to groups like Alpha Club but want to be involved in their communities helping fill the need. They join the fund, paying a certain amount into it, and are invited to vote on their choice for a project for the year. At the end of each year there is a banquet and a rather large check is presented to the chosen charity. When these women were telling us about it their eyes lit up with pride. They were clearly thrilled to be a part of that group.

These are women who are now employed working in health care and social services in our area. They know the need but don't have time to belong to a group that has meetings and does fund-raising to contribute. So they give some of their paycheck.

It occurred to us that this might be part of a new way to make Alpha Club work in 2011–12 and onward. After all Alpha Club is much more than just a fund. Alpha Club has a long-standing prominence in our town. It has always been a privilege and a pleasure to be a part of Alpha Club. Many women have been proud to belong and have remained members for years. Some have left and returned because they missed the group. The club has already established the "Friends of Alpha" for women who want to be a part of the club but can't be a full member until they retire. They can, however, help with an event, attend a meeting when possible and receive our newsletter to keep informed about current issues. For example, our local district federation, TAD, has a legislative piece in their most recent newsletter about the Equal Rights Amendment (ERA) which is again being advanced with new bills in congress. We have a lot to offer these "Friends."

Why not offer our "Friends of Alpha" a chance to contribute to an Alpha charity fund as well—especially those who don't live in the area but might later? A charity fund would certainly assist Alpha with our many causes and free up some of our fundraising for clubhouse expenses and repairs. Becoming a "Friend of Alpha" offers a connection, a chance to develop friendships and have a social life, which will grow into the opportunity to become a full member when the "Friend" retires from work life. She will be able to walk right into a great new life.

If our "Friends of Alpha" help with projects and donate money to our fund, then Alpha will continue to welcome new members and we can keep doing what we do best, probably even better.

Part of what has kept the Alpha Club going all these years has been our friendships. We all have a need to interact with people, not virtually, but to have real contact. We need to see, hear, and even touch people so we know we are real. Alpha pulls us together in many ways: to work on our causes, to gather for meetings and share lunch together. We celebrate big accomplishments like our annual flower show, and smaller ones like giving out scholarships. We enjoy taking trips around the central coast to attend meetings. We enjoy each other's company while we work on crafts together. We stay with the club because we know that together we can help more people, and especially, because we have all grown to know and care about each other and our community.

We're flesh and blood, younger and older women who share a part of our lives with each other. Not on the internet, e-mailing, Facebooking, or texting back and forth, we don't need to do that because we are able to meet, play and work face to face year after year. We have real conversations that the rest of the world can't hear, we see on someone's face when they're in trouble, we reach out to help when we can.

We can't know what's going to happen in the future, but we can plan and hope that women will hold on to groups like Alpha Club and GFWC so they can continue to move forward in strength, while supporting each other.

The Alpha Club women have always been hard working, strong and caring women and we, who have written this story, **HerStory,** are proud to be part of it.

NOTES

Introduction

1. Jarrad Harrison, "After Suffrage," *The California Federation and the 1913 State Legislation.*

Chapter 1: The Settlers

1. Mrs. James (Ida) Sloan, "Chumash Indians," *Lompoc Record*, June, 1923.
2. Marge Scott, "Alpha Story Notes," 1988.
3. Mira Manfrina, "Early Settlers History," (Lompoc Historical Society).
4. Marguerite Hall, "History of Lompoc," (Lompoc Historical Society).
5. Ibid.
6. Ibid.
7. *Santa Barbara News Press*, 1933.

Chapter 2: The Harmony Club 1898

1. "Rudolph Family," (Lompoc Historical Society).

Chapter 3: Club Meetings: Getting Started

1. "Bylaws," *Alpha Club Minutes*, 1900.
2. "Club Affiliation With GFWC," *Alpha Club Minutes*, May 7, 1904.
3. "Consider Change of Meeting Time," *Alpha Club Minutes*, January, 1905.
4. "The James Sloan—The American Dream," (Lompoc Historical Society).
5. "The Effect of Funny Papers On Children," *Alpha Club Minutes*, 1905.

Chapter 4: The Library and the Vote

1. Edger Clark-Lyman, "Thank You Alpha Club," *Library Foundation Happenings*, vol. 10 no. 1, Spring 2008.
2. John McReynolds, "Lompoc's First Free Library," *Lompoc Record*, December 27, 2006.
3. "Naming Streets," *Alpha Club Minutes*, January 16, 1909.
4. "Choosing the Library Property." *Alpha Club Minutes*, January, 1910.
5. Carolyn Huyck-Strobel, "Carnegie Building Turns 100 Years Old, Chronology of Acquisition." *Lompoc Legacy*, (Lompoc Historical Society, Summer 2011).
6. "Hall/Rennie Bibliography" (Lompoc Historical Society, 1910).
7. Carolyn Huyck-Strobel, "Carnegie Building Turns 100 Years Old, Chronology of Acquisition." *Lompoc Legacy*, (Lompoc Historical Society, Summer 2011).

Chapter 5: The Next Generation, Moving Forward

1. "Emily's death," *Alpha Club Minutes*, January 1914.
2. Ibid.
3. *Alpha Club Minutes*, January 23, 1915.
4. Margaret Heiges, "Club Project," *Alpha Club Minutes*, September, 1921.

Chapter 6: The Flower Show

1. "Dahlias," *Alpha Club Minutes*, February 1922.
2. *Lompoc Record*, 1960.
3. Marge Scott, *Alpha Club Flower Show History, 1922-1997.*
4. http://www.carlisehistory.dickenson.edu, page 278.

Chapter 7: The Clubhouse

1. "Purchase of clubhouse," *Alpha Club Minutes*, April 29, 1933.
2. " Junior Alphas," *Alpha Club Minutes*, 1933.
3. "Kitchen," *Alpha Club Minutes*, 1933.
4. "Margaret's death," *Alpha Club Minutes*, 1034.
5. "Loan," *Alpha Club Minutes*, May, 1936.
6. Marge Scott, *Alpha Club Flower Show History, 1922-1997.*
7. "Dorothy Rudolph," as told by Cathy Rudolph.

Chapter 8: Our Civic Duty, WWII

1. "Alpha Tea," *Lompoc Record*, March 20, 1940
2. Marge Scott, *Alpha Club Flower Show History, 1922-1997.*
3. Ibid.
4. "Meetings," *Alpha Club Minutes*, January 1943.
5. "Alyce," as told by Alyce Martin, 2011.

Chapter 9: Boom Town

1. "Bill Boards," *Alpha Club Minutes*, January 1952.
2. "Goals," *Alpha Club Minutes*, October 15, 1952.
3. "Meeting with Chamber," *Alpha Club Minutes*, January 1954.
4. "Tea Room," *Alpha Club Minutes*, May 1954.
5. "Go Ahead," *Alpha Club Minutes*, January 19, 1955.
6. Marge Scott, *Alpha Club Flower Show History, 1922-1997.*
7. "Flower Arranging," *Alpha Club Minutes*, March 1957.
8. "Dorothy Rudolph" as told by Cathy Rudolph.

9. "S. A. C.," *Alpha Club Minutes*, September 1958.
10. "T.V. Stations," *Alpha Club Minutes*, November 1958.

Chapter 10: Decade of Change: The Sixties

1. "The Path of the Women's Rights Movement," (March, 1998): http://www.ibiblio.org.
2. "Hospital," *Alpha Club Minutes*, January 1962.
3. "Sell-Sell," *Alpha Club Minutes*, January 1963.
4. "Louisa," as told by Louisa Van Ausdal.
5. "Gene," from Gene Holmdahl's Alpha Club History Collection.
6. "Hats," *Santa Barbara News Press*, October 20, 1963.
7. "Gadgets," from Gene Holmdahl's Alpha Club History Collection.
8. "Inflation," *Alpha Club Minutes*, February 1967.
9. "Fall Out," *Los Angeles Times*, June 8, 1967.
10. "Backlash," *San Francisco Chronicle*, June 9, 1967.
11. "Poronography," *Lompoc Record*, January 3, 1968.

Chapter 11: The New and the Old

1. Mildred Joy, *Alpha Club President Report*, 1970.
2. "Mary Lou," as told by Mary Lou Parks.
3. "Lochinvar" *Lompoc Record*, January, 1972.
4. "Luau," *Lompoc Record*, May 29, 1972.
5. "Good Will," *Lompoc Record*, December 27, 1972.
6. "Harriet's Wedding," *Lompoc Record*, June 16, 1973.
7. "Marge," as told by Marge Scott.
8. Marge Scott, *Alpha Club Flower Show History, 1922-1997.*
9. "Lets Go Hollywood," *Lompoc Record*, 1979.

Chapter 12: The Communication Era

1. "Smoking Ban," *Alpha Club Minutes*, March 1988.
2. "Mrs. Reagan's Invitation," *Alpha Club Minutes*, April 1988.
3. "Ball Problems," *Alpha Club Minutes*, October 1988.
4. "GFWC Survey," *The GFWC Clubwoman*, 1988.

Chapter 13: The Color Question

1. "Color," *Alpha Club Minutes*, February 15, 1989.
2. "Wilkins, Hicks et al.," *Alpha Club Minutes*, February 1989.
3. "Color Question," *The Club Woman*, (GFWC magazine) 1901.
4. "Bylaws," *GFWC Constitution and ByLaws*, 1904.

Chapter 14: The GFWC Centennial

1. "Benefit Ball," *Alpha Club Minutes*, 1993
2. "Clubhouse Work," *Alpha Club Minutes*, 1995
3. "CFWC Speaker," *Alpha Club Minutes*, 1999.

Chapter 15: The Future is Now

1. "Flower Show, 2000" as told by Mary Lou Parks.
2. "Mural Committee, 2005 " as told by Alyce Martin.
3. "Mural Committee, 2005" as told by Martha Galisky.
4. "Mural Committee, 2005" as told by Ann Ruhge.
5. "Mural, 2006," *Alpha Club Minutes*.
6. "Mural, 2007" as told by Martha Galisky.
7. "Flower Show Location, 2008" as told by Mary Lou Parks.

Chapter 16: Can Alpha Club and GFWC Survive?

1. "Mission Statement, 2010–2014 Strategic Plan," GFWC.
2. "Mission Statement, The Object, 2011–12," *Alpha Club Book*.

BIBLIOGRAPHY

Alpha Literary and Improvement Club. *Club Books*. 1898-2011

———. *Minutes*. 1903-2011.

———. *Scrapbooks & Picture Albums*.

Carnegie Libraries of California. "The Lompoc Museum." http://www.carnegie-libraries.org/california/lompoc.html.

Carver, Ashley (associate director General Federation of Women's Clubs). *Woman's Forum*. (Washington, DC 1988)

———. *GFWC Constitution Bylaws*. (Washington, DC 2011.)

Foley-Chellis, Mary Lou (Legislation and Public Policy Chair, Tierra Adorada District, CFWC). "The Equal Rights Amendment (ERA)." *TADTidings*. September–October 2011.

General Federation of Women's Clubs. "History and Mission of the General Federation of Women's Clubs." http://www.gfwc.org/gfwc/history.

———. "You Spoke, We Listened." *The Clubwoman*. May/June 2011.

———. "Agenda for Women in the 21st Century." *The Clubwoman*. August–September 1988.

Guensler, Tammy. Centennial Chair- 1900-2000. *CFWC Centennial Celebration, Resolution to Salute "A Century of Service."*

Hall, Marguerite. *Lompoc History*. Lompoc Historical Society.

Harrison, Jairod. *After Suffarage*. http://www.sfsu.edu/epf/1997.

Holmdahl, Gene. *Benefit Ball Reports.* Gene Holmdahl Files and Alpha Club Minutes. 1985–1995.

Huyck-Strobel, Carolyn. "Carnegie Building Turns 100 Years Old, Chronology of Acquisition." *Lompoc Legacy.* Lompoc Historical Society. Summer 2011.

King Elliott, Elizabeth. "The Race problems in the General Federation." *The Club Woman*, July, 1900.

The Lompoc Centennial Committee. "Lompoc, The First 100 Years." 1974.

Lompoc Library Staff. "Thank You Alpha Club." *Library Happenings* 10, no. 1 (Spring, 2007).

Lompoc Record. Editorial, "A Moral Decision." Sunday, January 22, 1989.

———. "Annual Yuletide Festivities Enjoyed by Alpha Clubwomen." December 27, 1972.

———. "Creative Writing Contest Outlined by Alpha Section." October 21, 1972.

———. "Harking Back to School Days." June 30, 1975.

———. "Lochinvar is Fun Presentation." January, 1972

———. "Temperance." April 22, 1974

———. "Temperance picture of Max Van Ausdal, Mary Lou Parks and Mrs. Anderson." April 22, 1974.

Lopez, Carol A. (president, California Federation of Women's Clubs) "Why Every Club Should Belong to Federation," a letter to Dott Brackin (federation secretary for TAD) June 8, 2001.

Manfrina, Myra. "Early Settlers History." Lompoc Historical Society Files.

Oswald, Julie (GFWD Women's History and Resource Center Associate). "Strategic Plan." (Washington, DC: General Federation of Women's Clubs, 2009).

Pho, Kevin M.D. "Female Physicians Make Less Money than Male Doctors." Medpage Today's Kevin M.D.com. http://www.kevinmd .com/blog/2011/02/female-physicians-money-male-doctors.html.

Rankin, Ellie. "The California Federation of Women's Clubs Grove." *California Clubwoman* 86, no. 2 (Summer 2011): 13.

Reyes, Donna. "Elks Vote Again on Blacks Application." *Santa Barbara News Press.* January 21, 1989.

Rudolph, Belle. "Belle's Diary 1892-93." Lompoc Historical Society.

Scott, Marge. "Written Excerpts from Pro/Con Presentation: Relinquishing Membership in GFWC/CFWC" (2001).

Scott, Marge and Committee. "Notes from Early Alpha Club Minutes." From Marge Scott's Alpha Club History Collection.

Scott, Marge, and Cathy Velardi. "Alpha Club Flower Show History 1922–1997."

Scully, Joanne. "Challenger Tragedy." *Lompoc Record*, January 27, 2011

"She's Connected." Social Networking Site for Busy Women. http://www.shesconnected.com

Utah International, Vandenberg Village. *History of the Utah Construction Co.* Lompoc, California, 1965–1970.

Zachman, Mrs. Robert (chair of the Terra Adarada District). "Mini course on Alcohol." A letter to Marge Scott about program on alcohol abuse for schools sponsored by Automobile Club, 1978.

Zaretsky, Staci. "Woman Lawyers and Gender Bias: The Mommy Track Can Kill Your Salary." (March 25, 2011) http://lawyerist.com/women-lawyers-and-gender-bias-the-mommy-track-can-kill-your-salary/

Harmony/Alpha Literary and Improvement Club, Lompoc California Membership Tree

Margaret McCabe
b. 1852 Ohio
d. 1934 Lompoc

|

Olivia McCabe
b. 1882 Lompoc
moved away

|

Hazel McCabe
b. 1896 Santa Barbara
d. 1980 Lompoc

|

Betty McCabe
b. 1924 Lompoc
d. 1980 Lompoc

Idella Rudolph Webb
b. 1870 Ferndale CA
d. 1933 Riverside CA

|

Elizabeth Rudolph
b. 1844
d. 1910

|

Gertrude Rudolph
b. 1878 England
d. 1955 Lompoc

|

Helen Rudolph
b. 1894
d. 1978 Lomita CA

|

Dorothy Rudolph
b. 1911 Missouri
d. 1963 Lompoc

Nina Rudolph
b. 1874
d. 1916 Alameda CA

Emily Bissenger
b. 1861 Michigan
d. 1914 Lompoc

|

Idella Bissinger
b. 1886 Lompoc
d. ?

Cevilla Sloan
b. 1860 Iowa
d. 1902 Gilroy CA

|

Ida Sloan
b. 1859
d. 1953 Santa Barbara

|

Stella Sloan
b. ?
d. 1909

|

Irene Mae Sloan
b. 1886 Iowa
d. 1921 Santa Barbara

|

Clara Pauline "Toots" Sloan
b. 1892 Iowa
d. 1983 Apple Valley CA

Anna Moore
b. 1868 Santa Barbara
d. 1952 Fair Oaks

|

Bertha Moore
b. 1896
d. 1978

|

Donalda Moore
b. 1893 Lompoc
d. 1962

"Appie" Rennie
b. 1862 Iowa
d. 1910 Los Angeles

|

Marguerite Hall
b. 1887 Lompoc
d. 1977 Lompoc

|

Harriet Adam
b. 1918 Lompoc
d. 2003

Later Arrivals in the 1960s and 70s

Alyce Martin
b. 1927 Tenn.

|

Julie Casarez
F.O.A.
b. 1957 Lompoc

|

Emily Cisneros
b. 1991 Lompoc

Gene Holmdahl
b. 1913 Iowa
d. 2009 Lompoc

Louisa Van Ausdal
b. 1918 CA

Mary Lou Parks
b. 1934 South Dakota

|

Mary Beth Parks F.O.A.
b. 1957 Omaha NE

|

Katie Kidney F.O.A
b. 1995 Santa Clarita CA

Marge Scott
B. 1925 Nevada

*F.O.A. denotes
Friend of Alpha